PATRIOT ACTS

PATRIOT ACTS
NARRATIVES OF POST–9/11 INJUSTICE

EDITED BY

ALIA MALEK

WITH A FOREWORD BY

KAREN KOREMATSU

Associate editors
DALIA HASHAD, VALARIE KAUR,
SHIRLEY VELASQUEZ, BRUCE WALLACE

Research editor
ALEX CARP

Assistant research editor
DAHLIA PETRUS

Additional assistance
JILL HABERKERN, SANA MALIK,
MIKE VALENTE, VALERIE WOOLARD

VOICE OF WITNESS

VOICE OF WITNESS

M^CSWEENEY'S BOOKS
SAN FRANCISCO

For more information about McSweeney's, see *mcsweeneys.net*
For more information about Voice of Witness, see *voiceofwitness.org*

Illustrations by Julien Lallemand

Front cover photo courtesy of Getty Images
Back cover photo courtesy of Reuters

ISBN (Hardcover): 978-1-936365-37-1
ISBN (Paperback): 978-1-936365-38-8

VOICE OF WITNESS

The books in the Voice of Witness series seek to illuminate human rights crises by humanizing those most closely affected. Using oral history as a foundation, the series explores social justice issues through the stories of the men and women who experience them. These books are designed for readers of all levels—from high school and college students to policymakers—interested in a reality-based understanding of ongoing injustices in the United States and around the world. Visit *voiceofwitness.org* for more information.

VOICE OF WITNESS BOARD OF DIRECTORS

CONTENTS

FOREWORD 9

INTRODUCTION 15

ADAMA BAH 23

TALAT HAMDANI 49

RIMA QAMRI 69

GURWINDER SINGH 95

KHALED EL-MASRI 109

AMIR SULAIMAN 131

RANA SODHI 149

HANI KHAN 165

ZAK MUHAMMAD REED 171

GHASSAN ELASHI 187

SARA JAYYOUSI 207

UZMA NAHEED ABBASI & ANSER MEHMOOD 213

YASIR ALADDIN AFIFI 233

FAHEEM MUHAMMAD 249

FARID RODRIGUEZ 253

SHAHEENA PARVEEN 271

RAED JARRAR 295

NICK GEORGE 319

APPENDICES 329

ONE STORY CAN MAKE A DIFFERENCE

by Karen Korematsu, co-founder of the Fred Korematsu Institute

Almost a year after 9/11, an article appeared in the *Los Angeles Times* by Jonathan Turley about Attorney General John Ashcroft's plan to establish camps for U.S. citizens deemed to be "enemy combatants." Turley, a professor of Constitutional Law at Georgetown University, wrote, "Attorney General Ashcroft's plan...would allow him to order the indefinite incarceration of U.S. citizens and summarily strip them of their constitutional rights and access to the courts by declaring them enemy combatants."

I remember standing in my parents' kitchen at the time, talking to my father about this. I asked him, "Daddy, how do you feel about this latest news?" and he replied, "Why did I bother to reopen my case if the U.S. government is going to do this again?"

For those of you who do not know the story, my father was Fred T. Korematsu, a second-generation Japanese American who defied U.S. military orders to be incarcerated along with 120,000 people of Japanese ancestry living on the west coast. On February 19, 1942, after the bombing of Pearl Harbor, President Franklin D. Roosevelt issued Executive Order 9066. This order gave the military authority to send Japanese Americans to ten concentration camps throughout the U.S. during World War II. At that time, my father was twenty-three years old. He had tried to enlist in the U.S. National Guard and the U.S. Coast Guard, but was turned away by military officers who discriminated against him due to his Japanese ancestry. However, he still wanted to contribute to the defense effort, so he worked as a welder in the Oakland shipyards.

My father knew what his rights were as an American, and believed that the mass forced removal was unconstitutional. The incarcerated Japanese Americans were never charged with any crimes, had no public hearings, and were deprived of due process of the law. For those reasons and more, my father refused to obey the exclusion orders that led to his arrest on May 30, 1942.

He was convicted in federal court, and his case was appealed all the way to the U.S. Supreme Court. In 1944, the Supreme Court ruled against him, arguing that the incarceration was justified due to military necessity. My father carried the burden of that loss for almost forty years, not only for himself but also for all those others who were incarcerated, including his family.

Then, in 1982, Professor Peter Irons and Aiko Herzig-Yoshinaga, two seminal figures in the Japanese-American community's fight for redress and reparation, uncovered key documents that government intelligence agencies had hidden from the Supreme Court in 1944. These documents proved there was no military necessity for anyone of Japanese descent on the west coast to be forced into concentration camps in 1942. On that basis of government misconduct, my father's case was reopened in 1983 by a courageous group of young attorneys who worked for him pro bono. On November 10 of that year, my father's federal conviction was overturned in court. It was a pivotal moment in civil rights history. Judge Marilyn Hall Patel's comments that day about the lessons of *Korematsu v. U.S.* resonate to this day:

It stands as a caution that, in times of distress, the shield of military necessity and national security must not be used to protect governmental actions from close scrutiny and accountability. It stands as a caution that, in times of international hostility and antagonisms, our institutions, legislative, executive and judicial must be prepared to exercise their authority to protect all citizens from the petty fears and prejudices that are so easily aroused.

My father was right to stand up and fight. Certainly, he wanted to vindicate himself and other Japanese Americans, but he also hoped that this type of racial discrimination would not happen to any other ethnic groups in America. After his conviction was overturned, my father's focus and mission was advocacy and education. He traveled throughout the U.S. with my mother and members of his legal team to speak to universities, law schools and organizations to tell his story and convey the lessons of civil rights history.

On January 15, 1998, my father was awarded the Presidential Medal of Freedom, this nation's highest civilian honor, from President Clinton. Over the years, my father, a humble and quiet man, was continually honored and recognized for his achievements—his courageous stand during World War II, his work for the 1988 Redress and Reparations movement, and his dedication to civil rights education—but he always accepted those awards on behalf of all Japanese Americans who had been placed in U.S. concentration camps.

After 9/11, my father and the Japanese-American community were quick to speak out against the dangers of racial profiling and scapegoating that targeted Arab, Middle-Eastern, Muslim and South Asian (AMEMSA) communities. They witnessed the backlash that was building against these communities, and could see all too well the parallels between the Pearl Harbor bombings and the terrorist attacks of 9/11.

The narratives in *Patriot Acts* are compelling and diverse examples of the human and civil rights violations that the AMEMSA community has suffered in the wake of 9/11. Prejudice stems from ignorance, and the most effective nonviolent response we have is education; this is why these stories need to be read and shared.

One of the narratives in this collection that struck a personal chord is that of Rana Sodhi, whose brother Balbir was shot to death outside the gas station where he worked, simply because he wore a turban and "looked like the enemy." His death was the first reported hate murder in the immediate aftermath of the 9/11 attacks. Then, in August 2002, his brother Sukhpal, a cab driver in San Francisco, was shot and killed in his taxi. In his narrative, Rana recalls meeting a Japanese-American man who told him stories of living in a concentration camp during World War II. This prompts Rana to reflect, "This is what happens in time of crisis." Later in the narrative, Rana responds to the passing of the Arizona law S.B. 1070—a law which gives police the power to stop and detain anyone they suspect of being in the country illegally—by raising the question, "How many times can a person be stopped before they feel like they are not seen as American? What does an American look like?" This sentiment is echoed throughout the book by other narrators, and it reminds me of what my father had felt all those years before reopening his case: Am I an American or am I not?

Rana honored the loss of his brothers by becoming a community leader and educator, and his message is clear: "If no one stands up, then it will happen again and again."

I believe that stories like these are the best form of education. It took almost forty years before the Japanese-American community started telling theirs, and only in recent years have their oral histories been recorded. My father's experience is a reminder of the impact one story can make, and an example of how one person standing up for what is right can make a difference for all people. He passed away in 2005, and remains an inspiration to me.

In April of 2009, I co-founded the Fred T. Korematsu Institute for Civil Rights and Education, a non-profit program of the Asian Law Caucus in San Francisco. Our mission advances pan-ethnic civil and human rights through education, activism, and leadership development.

In September 2010, California Governor Schwarzenegger signed Assembly Bill 1775 to establish Fred Korematsu Day of Civil Liberties and the Constitution, making my father the first Asian American in U.S. history to be recognized statewide. January 30, my father's birthday, will now mark Fred Korematsu Day, and will be celebrated on this date in perpetuity. The significance of this special day is education about my father's story, the Japanese-American internment, and the implications and relevancy of the discussions of our civil liberties and the U.S. Constitution today. To this end, a key focus of the Korematsu Institute has been to develop K-12 curriculum for teachers throughout California, and to make these resources available to teachers in other states. We look forward to working with Voice of Witness on creating curriculum elements that illuminate parallels between post-9/11 discrimination and the Japanese-American internment.

Since the announcement of Osama Bin Laden's death on May 1, 2011, we have all been warned that the War on Terror is not over, and that we must be prepared for any fallout. In my mind, we must remain vigilant in speaking out against any injustices that we witness, and, in remembrance of my father's words, "Protest, but not with violence, otherwise they won't listen to you. Don't be afraid to speak up!" I'm glad to see that, in the face of the ten-year anniversary of 9/11, the stories in Patriot Acts are coming to light. I hope they will serve as examples of courage in the face of adversity, and encourage others to tell their own stories, so that the lessons of civil liberties will continue.

Karen Korematsu is the co-founder of the Fred T. Korematsu Institute for Civil Rights and Education and a National Advisory board member of the Fred T. Korematsu Center for Law and Equality at the Seattle School of Law. She also serves on the boards of the Asian Law Caucus of San Francisco, the Institute's parent organization, and the Asian American Justice Center.

IN THE DECADE OF A SEPTEMBER MORNING

by Alia Malek

On the morning of September 11, 2001, walking to work in Washington, D.C., I passed by the World Bank and the IMF—which were bracing themselves for that weekend's anti-globalization protests—and couldn't help but note how remarkably exposed those buildings were. But what was there really to fear? The sort of insecurity and uncertainty that plagues many of the world's other countries—something I had felt living in the Middle East and in Europe—was something that we had been spared here in the United States, and a fact that we had long taken for granted.

By the time I arrived for work at the Department of Justice, my co-workers and I realized that the first plane that had flown into the World Trade Center was not a small one as initially reported, but rather a commercial jet. Soon after, we were gathered together around a television, watching the second plane hit the South Tower. We all knew then that the country was under attack. I quickly recited the very Arab American prayer (which now has a Muslim American version as well) that we say in moments like these, moments when anything goes *boom* and all of a sudden an entire people are called to task for the acts of individuals: "Lord, please don't let it be Arabs."

Then we heard about the Pentagon, much closer to us than New York City. At the same time, there were also (false) reports of bombs at the White House and on government property throughout Washington, D.C. My co-workers and I were quickly told to go home.

My mind went to two places at once: the first, to making sure everyone I knew in D.C. and New York City was alive and safe, and letting everyone know I was okay as well. The second, since it was already clear that the attack was being attributed to Arabs/Muslims (as if ethnicities and religions were interchangeable), was to making sure everyone I knew who was Arab or Muslim, or who might pass for one, remained alive and safe. After all, our communities had experienced backlash before in relation to news of terrorist attacks or wars, when the magnitude of the destruction and casualties was nothing like what had just happenened.

D.C. buildings had begun to empty rivers of scared and confused folks onto streets already flooded with people. We'd been told that the D.C. Metro had stopped running, so I walked toward my home with a close friend who was, like me, a DOJ Civil Rights trial attorney. She grew up in Savannah, Georgia, and is neither Arab nor Muslim. She is, though, of Indian descent—close enough, I feared, for the purposes of those looking for a scapegoat. Ironically, I, as a fair-skinned Arab, look the part much less, given how Arabs and Muslims are visualized in the American imagination. As we walked the streets, I could feel suspicious looks cast toward her instead of me. This made me feel oddly guilty. I decided that, in a worst-case scenario, I would persuade any potential assailants to let her go, that I was the one they wanted, as absurd as that was—but such is the capriciousness of race. Needless to say, the confusion, fear, and anger of that day made the absurd somehow rational.

Many of the dynamics we saw emerge after the 9/11 attacks have remained in this country to this day: notions of collective guilt; confusion over what differentiates an Arab from a Muslim from a South Asian from a Middle Easterner from a Sikh, and so forth; uncertainty as to how to fit these groups into a limited American racial paradigm that never imagined their presence to begin with; the racializing of Islam itself, i.e., giving

Muslims one phenotype, despite the fact that they come from all ethnicities; the struggle to determine who can be a "real" American and what can be a "real" American religion; and, of course, the rise of fear and suspicion. The relative *lack* of fear that characterized us prior to 9/11—evident in the unguarded nature of the buildings I walked past on the morning it all changed—has never fully returned since it evaporated in seconds on that same September day, when we realized that something this unpredictable and awful *could* happen here, at any time.

Additionally, for specific subgroups of Americans, regardless of their citizenship or of having lived here for generations, there is now the concurrent anxiety of being perceived as foreign and suspicious—and thus condemned to being perpetually judged as part of a monolithic group, rather than as individuals. Thus for many Americans, individuality went from being a right to being a privilege. While this is not entirely a post-9/11 phenomenon for some, there were many who only after 9/11 felt so stripped of their sense of belonging. Suddenly they were being forced to account for the origins of their names or the details of their religious beliefs, rituals, or clothing. Some, after years of thinking that racial categorization in this country did not really implicate them, who had concluded that they were "white" since they weren't perceived as "black," have described the sense of suddenly and permanently being disavowed of that notion after 9/11.

This anxiety of being viewed through the lens of suspicion, fear, and generally negative perception is shaped by two mutually re-enforcing causes. The first is the post-9/11 backlash that we saw in the immediate years after the tragedy, a backlash that has blossomed into today's Islamophobia—which, it should be noted, does not victimize only people who are actually Muslim. Their expressions have been varied. Individuals have carried out hate crimes ranging from vandalism to murder. Employers have discriminated against their employees, school districts against their students, landlords against their tenants, and lenders against potential borrowers. Schoolchildren have bullied their classmates. Places of worship have been vandalized and placed under surveillance. The construction of mosques, such as the one at Park51, have tested our founding principal of freedom of religion. Congressmen have held hearings that perpetuated suspicion and fear toward the Muslim-American community. There was little space in the public imagination for the concept of Muslim-American heroes such as Salman Hamdani, a first responder who died on 9/11, and whose reputation was smeared by media portrayals of him as a possible terrorist. His mother Talat is one of the narrators readers will meet in this book.

The second is the darker side of the War on Terror, which the United States declared after the attacks of September 11. Within weeks after the attacks, some 1,200 Muslim and Arab non-citizens were arrested and detained, though eventually none were found to have any direct links with the 9/11 terrorists or their actions. In addition, the Department of Justice summoned for voluntary interviews 5,000 non-citizen men in the U.S. who were on non-immigrant visas from Arab and Muslim countries suspected of harboring terrorists. Of the 5,000, only five people declined to be interviewed, and 104 letters sent by the DOJ were returned because of incorrect addresses. Although the interviews yielded no information relating to the terrorist attacks, the DOJ indicated soon afterwards that it would be contacting another 3,000 young Arab men for more voluntary interviews. Major Arab and Muslim organizations, initially supportive of the government's efforts to combat terrorism, widely condemned the continued singling-out of their communities, and indicated they were no longer willing to cooperate with such tactics.

As part of the War on Terror, agent provocateurs and informants have been sent into the ranks of those gathered in prayer. The government has spied on, detained, deported, and rendered individuals under policies that have been widely criticized by civil rights and liberties watchdogs. The Transportation Security Administration has perceived threats in the Arabic language, whether spoken or written on T-shirts and flashcards, illustrated in the narratives of Raed Jarrar and Nick George.

In the meantime, the mainstream media and pundits ensured that the national dialogue surrounding Muslims, Muslim Americans, and Islam was often loud, heated, and as sensationalistic as possible.

While the injustices, counted individually, can sometimes seem minor, in the aggregate, they suggest that some religions and ethnicities (the lines of which are often blurred and difficult to define) inherently cannot be American. Dehumanizing, or in this case, de-Americanizing, individuals is often the first step toward justifying policies, laws, and treatment that would otherwise offend our sensibilities.

Yet even though myriad actors from across American society have participated in this process, the personal stories and lived experiences of these realities remain excluded from the general understanding of the American experience, as well as the mainstream narrative about 9/11 and the War on Terror.

Thus, as we now approach the ten-year anniversary of 9/11, we hope with this book to give voice to some of the people who have had their human rights or dignity violated here in the United States by post-9/11 policies and actions, whether by state or private actors. Because of the diverse nature of the backlash, the War on Terror, and the fact that we are examining a ten-year era of actions and policies that have been visited upon an equally diverse (though identifiable) group of people, the narratives found in this collection are similarly quite varied. They include those of Adama Bah, a sixteen-year old Muslim girl detained on suspicion of being a suicide bomber; Rana Sodhi, a Sikh man who lost two brothers to hate crimes simply because, as Sikhs, they wore turbans; Rima Qamri, whose family was torn apart by bullying and discrimination; and Hani Khan, who was fired from her job for refusing to remove her hijab.

They also include the stories of people who either have been adjudicated in our courts of law of grave crimes, or are the family members of those convicted. Their inclusion is nonetheless important because the law enforcement tactics used, or the basis of those convictions, have been called into question not only by civil/human rights and liberties groups, but also by the communities themselves who bear the impact of these methods and prosecutions. Thus readers will also meet Ghassan Elashi, convicted of material support of terrorism and incarcerated in a Communications Management Unit (the highly secretive, almost exclusively Arab/Muslim prisons in the US); Sara Jayyousi, the daughter of a man also convicted under material support and incarcerated in a CMU; and Shaheena Parveen, the mother of a young man convicted of the Herald Square bomb plot, a plot conceived of and planned by an FBI informant. Together, these stories weave a portrait of how the fabric of everyday life has irrevocably changed for so many in this country. With this book, we want to make sure their experiences are included in the national dialogue as the country collectively pauses to reflect on what this decade has meant for all of us.

On the night of September 11, after making it back to our homes, afew of us from the Department of Justice—people from Arab, Middle Eastern, Muslim, and South Asian backgrounds—discussed how the Civil Rights Division could help people as the backlash we anticipated came to fruition.

We set up a special initiative at the DOJ to ensure that people knew how to report civil rights infractions and hate crimes, and to help those complaints reach the relevant federal agencies. I would eventually leave the DOJ on the eve of the invasion of Iraq,unable to reconcile the values of civil rights with the policies the U.S. government was enacting both domestically and internationally. Eventually, I would transition away from working as a lawyer and toward a career in journalism. What I saw happen in this country after 9/11, initially from my perch as a lawyer, made quite clear for me that our ignorance of the American lives and experiences of certain groups had facilitated a backlash and a slide into xenophobic and nativist behavior that betrayed the very values I had joined the DOJ to protect.

With this in mind, I wrote my first book, *A Country Called Amreeka: US History Retold Through Arab American Lives*. I felt that the invisibility and absence of Arab Americans from historical and contemporary narratives about the United States had been damaging not only to them but also to the country as a whole. Despite having arrived here in numbers in the late nineteenth century at the same time as many other groups, including Italians and Greeks, Arab Americans were not seen as part of the mosaic of American people. This invisibility has not only robbed them of being seen as truly American, but has also given us all a false idea of what our history is and who our fellow Americans are.

Filling in some of the missing tiles from the American mosaic is what I seek to do in my work and with this book. I am grateful to Voice of Witness for inviting me to participate in amplifying the unheard voices in this volume, in the hopes that what emerges is a clearer, more humanized picture of the historical and current moment that we all share.

ADAMA BAH

AGE: *23*

OCCUPATION: *student*

INTERVIEWED IN: *East Harlem, New York City*

On March 24, 2005, Adama Bah, a sixteen-year-old Muslim girl, awoke at dawn to discover nearly a dozen armed FBI agents inside her family's apartment in East Harlem. They arrested her and her father, Mamadou Bah, and transported them to separate detention facilities. A government document leaked to the press claimed that Adama was a potential suicide bomber but failed to provide any evidence to support this claim. Released after six weeks in detention, Adama was forced to live under partial house arrest with an ankle bracelet, a government-enforced curfew, and a court-issued gag order that prohibited her from speaking about her case. In August of 2006, Adama's father was deported back to Guinea, Africa. Adama, who had traveled to the United States with her parents from Guinea as a child, also found herself facing deportation. She would spend the next few years fighting for asylum and struggling to support her family in the United States and Guinea.

I didn't know I wasn't an American until I was sixteen and in handcuffs.

My mother came to the United States with me in 1990, the year I turned two. We originally came from Koubia in Guinea, West Africa. My dad was here already, living in Brooklyn and working as a cab driver. He went on to open his own business later.

Then came my brother, who is now nineteen, my sister, who is seventeen, and two more brothers who are thirteen and five. I'm twenty-three. We moved to this apartment in Manhattan, and we have been living here for thirteen years.

I think a lot of people in Africa and third-world countries hear about the riches in America. It's the land of opportunity. So my dad came here for that. From the stories that my mom tells me, their lives back in Koubia were farming and that's it.

Growing up in New York, I remember having many "cousins" around. They're all Guinean. They weren't real family, but whatever community members we had here, I considered them family. I remember having them come over, I remember us running around and messing up things.

My friends were Latino and African American. At that time, I fit in with them. I was going through the same issues as them, like boys, going through puberty, he said/she said kinds of things. Those were the kinds of problems that I wish I had now.

WE ALL DID IT?

I went to public school until seventh grade. My dad wanted me to learn about my religion, so he sent me to an Islamic boarding school in Buffalo, New York. What's weird now that I look back is that my parents aren't really religious, we didn't really go to mosque. But my dad heard about the school from somebody who recommended it.

I was thirteen when 9/11 happened. Every teacher came in late, and they sat us in a humongous circle. My teacher said, "I have to talk to you guys. For those of you who are from New York, I want you to brace yourselves. I have some bad news. Sometimes things happen in life that we don't understand." She started telling us about God and how to be patient and steadfast. And then she said, "The Twin Towers were hit today."

I remember freaking out, panicking, trying to reach my family.

When she called us back for a second meeting, that's when she announced that a Muslim might have done it, and that there might be hatred against Muslims. When I heard that, I was like, "Wait, what do you mean? We all did it? We didn't plot it. I don't have nothing to do with it. Why are we all getting the blame for it?" So many thoughts went through my head that time: *Who is this Osama bin Laden guy? What is he up to? Why would he do this? This is against Islam.* None of us knew who bin Laden was. We were making jokes about the guy. My friends said, "Your name is very close to his name: Adama, Osama."

When I finally reached my family the next day, they told me they were fine, and my dad said, "*Shh*, don't talk about it. Be quiet, bye." He would not talk about anything over the phone.

THE WAY I LEFT NEW YORK CITY WAS NOT THE WAY IT WAS WHEN I CAME BACK

I felt 9/11 when I came back to New York for Ramadan[1] break. There were six of us classmates who had to get on a plane to come back to New York. At that time, we covered our faces. I remember coming to the airport dressed all in pitch black with our faces covered. We were even wearing gloves; all you could see were our eyes, that's it.

I couldn't believe the looks on the everyone's faces. Everybody was scared, pointing. You saw people turn red. We were whispering to each other, "What's going on?" Honestly, I was scared. I thought those people were going to beat me.

We didn't know what was going on around the country. We didn't know about the hate crimes—we didn't know anything, though the day after 9/11 someone threw a rock through the window of the school.

That day at the airport, we got extra screenings, our bags were checked, we got pulled to the side. The guards were so nasty to us, the people were so nasty to us, the airline was so nasty to us. I remember us boarding the plane and the captain looked at us and shook his head.

---

[1] A holy month of the Islamic calendar that Muslims observe by fasting during daytime hours.

It made me feel like crap because I was being singled out. I'm thirteen, I've never been through something like this. I've never had racism directed toward me before. I've been sheltered from things like that. So, that was my first time. People cursed at us, yelled at us, and sucked their teeth, saying, "Go back to your country, you Talibani, go back to Osama bin Laden."

This whole time, I thought I was American. I thought, *You can't touch me, I'm American.*

My parents didn't know I wore any garb until I came home. My mom opened the door, she saw me, and she closed it back. She told my father, "You have to tell her to take this off. I told you not to send her to Buffalo!"

They disapproved of my niqab.[2] They said to me, "Take that off, take that off."

When I originally left New York City for school, it was peaceful and happy and everybody was cheery and saying hello. When I came back after 9/11, everyone was like, "What do you want, where are you from?" There was more fear. The fear was toward me, and I felt the same way. People didn't take the time to talk to me, or ask me why I was wearing a niqab. Walking down the street, people would curse at me, they would even throw things. It was just nasty. It actually made me want to wear it more.

OH, YOU'RE NOT UGLY

I came back to New York public school for ninth grade. I left the Islamic school because I didn't like it. I remember telling my dad, "I'm too controlled there." I wore my niqab for a few months with colored contacts to make the niqab look pretty. Might as well make something look pretty— if you can't see my face, look at my nice eyes! But it was actually fun. I didn't have any problems in high school. The other kids always asked me to see my face, though. Like, "I wonder how you look under there? You're probably ugly." We would make jokes about it. I'd say, "Yeah, I look hideous. That's why I wear it, of course!"

---

[2] A type of face veil.

Then, after a while, I thought, *This is not a mosque.* So in the middle of ninth grade, I took it off, because you know what? This niqab is not a must. It's really not.

So one day I walked into school, I was still wearing an abaya,[3] but I had my face uncovered. My teacher just looked at me and said, "Adama?" And I remember all the students just coming in to look at me, in the middle of English class, to see what I looked like.

They said things like, "Oh, you're not ugly! You have nice teeth." I replied, "Thank you." I was just smiling.

WHAT DID I DO?

The morning of March 24, 2005, my family and I were in the house sleeping.

Someone knocked on the door, and my mom went and opened it. These men barged in, waking us up. I always sleep with the blanket over my head. They pull the blanket off my head, I look up, I see a man. He said, "You've got to get out!" I'm like, *What the hell, what's going on?*

I saw about ten to fifteen people in our apartment and right outside our door in the hallway. They were mostly men, but there were two women. Some had FBI jackets, and others were from the police department and the DHS.[4] We were all forced out of the bed and told to sit in the living room. They were going through papers, throwing stuff around, yelling and talking to each other, then whispering. I heard them yelling at my mother in the background, and my mom can't speak much English, and they were pulling her into the kitchen, yelling at her, "We're going to deport you and your whole family!"

This whole time, I was thinking, *What's going on? What are they talking about?* I knew my dad had an issue with his papers, but I didn't think

---

[3] A loose robe, usually worn with a hijab (head scarf). For more details, see the glossary entry on veiling.

[4] The Department of Homeland Security.

that my mom did. They kept saying, "We're going to send all of you back to your country."

Then I saw my dad walking in, in handcuffs. They had gone to the mosque to get him. It was the scariest thing you could ever see; I had just never seen my father so powerless. He was always this guy whom you didn't mess with. If he said do it, you did it. He was just someone you didn't cross paths with.

They took him to the kitchen, whispered something to him.

He sat down, looked at us. He said, "Everything's going to be fine, don't worry."

And then I knew nothing was fine, I knew something was wrong. They told him to tell us what was going on. He told us that they were going to arrest him and they were going to take him away.

The FBI agents told me to get up and get my sneakers. I was thinking they wanted to see my sneaker collection. I have all types of colors of sneakers. I went and grabbed them. I said, "I have this one, I have this one, I have this one."

One of the agents said, "Choose one."

My favorite color is blue, so I picked up a blue pair and said, "This one."

He said, "Put them on."

I said, "Okay, but I know they fit me."

He said, "Put them on!" He was very nasty. Then he said, "All those earrings have to go out." I have eight piercings on each side, a nose ring, and a tongue ring. I went to the kitchen to take them off, and they followed me in there.

My breath was stinking. I asked, "Can I at least brush my teeth? My breath stinks really bad. Can I use the bathroom?"

They said, "No. We have to go. You're coming with us."

I said, "Where am I going to go? Am I going with my dad?" I put on my jacket. They let me put my headscarf and abaya on. Then one of the women took out handcuffs. I panicked so badly, I was stuttering, "What did I do? Where are we going?"

First time in my life, I'm sixteen years old, in handcuffs. I looked at my dad, and he said, "Just do what they say."

My mom didn't know I was going. When we got out the door, she said, "Where she go? Where she go?" The agents said, "We're taking her," and they held my mom back. The man who seemed to be in charge put his hands on my mother to stop her.

They took me and my dad and put us in the same car. I was scared. I said to him, "What's going on? What's going to happen?" My dad said, "Don't say anything, we're going to get a lawyer. It's okay, everything is going to be fine."

There were two Escalades driving with us. I was looking around, paying attention. I recognized the Brooklyn Bridge, I recognized a lot of landmarks, but I didn't recognize the building where my father and I were taken. We got out of the car and we walked past a security booth where the cars drive up to, before taking a ramp beneath the building to the parking lot. Once we were inside the building, they put me in my own cell. It was white, with a bench. No bars. No windows. There was a door that had a tiny glass pane, and I could see who was out there. I just saw a bunch of computers and tables, and people walking back and forth and talking. I kept seeing them talk to my dad.

I don't know how long I was in there.

I was nervous, I was panicking, I was crying, I was trying to figure out what was going on. And I was constantly using the bathroom.

The toilet was an open toilet, though. There was a camera on the ceiling in the middle of the room. I was wondering, *Can they see me peeing?* I just wrapped blankets around me as I was peeing.

I'M NOT THIS PERSON

I was taken out of my cell to be interrogated. Nobody told me who they were. It was just me and a man, sitting where all the computers were. Nobody else was around me. There was a guy all the way down at the other end with my dad, but that's about it.

He asked me questions like, "What's your name? What's your age? What's your date of birth? Where were you born?" They knew I was born in Guinea. Then he asked, "What is your citizenship status?"

I said, "American."

He asked me all these questions about my citizenship status. Then after a while, he said, "You know you're not here legally, right? You know why you're here today, right? You weren't born in this country. You know you're not American?"

For a second, I was just so mad at my parents. It was as if one of the biggest secrets in the world had just been revealed to me. I don't know if it was to protect them or if it was to protect me, but that was the biggest secret someone could ever hold.

The guy's attitude didn't change when he realized I didn't know what was going on. He was nasty the whole time. He just sat there explaining the process to me. He asked me if I wanted to see a consular officer.

I asked, "What is a consular officer?"

He said, "You don't know what a consular officer is? Those are people from your country. From Guinea."

I said, "What about them? What do I have to see them for?"

Finally, they called my dad. They gave us a document about how we could see a consular officer. My dad knows how to read English, but he said to me in Pular,[5] "Pretend you're translating to me in my language." Then he said, "Whatever you do, do not say you can go back to your country. They will circumcise you there."[6]

My dad wasn't just coming up with a way to stay. There was a real fear of female genital mutilation in Guinea. It happened to my mom. In order to get married in Guinea, a female would have to be circumcised. My dad's brothers would do it, they would make sure I got circumcised.

---

[5] A language widely spoken in Guinea.

[6] Female genital mutilation is a cultural rather than legal issue in Guinea. In June of 2001, the State Department issued a report that cited 98% of women in Guinea between fifteen and fifty as having been victims of female genital mutilation. Since then, campaigns to eradicate or alter the process have resulted in a significant decrease in recent years.

My parents made a decision when they had girls that they would never do it. That's the main reason why our parents never took us back to Guinea, not even to visit.

The guy told my dad, "Hey, you've got to get up, you've got to leave." To me they said, "We have to fingerprint you." When we were done with the fingerprints, they took a picture of me. I was then sitting on a bench in the main entrance when this young lady walked in. Her name was Tashnuba. I had seen her at the mosque before, but I didn't know her personally. I just recognized her face and knew her name. I said "Hi," but in my heart, I started panicking, thinking, *What the hell is she doing here? Who am I gonna see next?*

Finally I was brought to another room. This room had a table, a chair on one side, and two chairs on the other side. A federal agent walked in. She said, "I need to talk to you about something." The questions she was asking had nothing to do with immigration. They were terrorism questions. She asked me about people from London, about people from all over the world. I thought, *What's going on?*

The male interrogator told me that the religious study group Tashnuba was part of had been started by a guy who was wanted by the FBI. I had no idea if that was true or not.

The study group at the mosque was all women. So it was women learning about religion, women's empowerment, why we cover, how we do the prayer, when to pray, things like that. It was more for converts and new people who had just come into Islam. There was nothing about jihad or anything like that.

I wasn't part of the group, but Tashnuba was. We were the same age, sixteen. So, they asked me about this group and they told me they'd taken my computer and my diary. My diary was a black-and-white notebook. I had phone numbers, I had notes, I had stories in it, I had everything. Basically, they asked me about every contact in there, they asked me about every little thing. But, there's nothing in there about jihad, there's nothing in there about anything that's suspicious. There was nothing in there at all. So I wasn't worried.

They said, "We have your computer, we can find whatever you're hiding."

I said, "Go ahead, look in my computer. I have nothing to hide."

They kept making a scene, like there was something big there. They said, "Don't lie to us. If you lie to us, we'll have proof, we'll catch you in your lie."

I knew there was nothing in my computer, but at the end of the day, I started to doubt myself. I thought, *Okay, what's going on now? Is there something there?* Their technique is to make you doubt yourself. But then I thought, *Wait a minute, I'm not this person. What are they talking about?*

The interrogation lasted a long time. This Secret Service guy came in. He asked me how I felt about Bush. I said, "I don't like him." I was being very honest with them. There was nothing to hide.

The Secret Service guy was just too aggressive. He said, "I don't understand—why do you choose to cover when women choose to wear less and less every day?"

I said, "It's freedom of choice. Some people want to show some stuff, some people want to hide things. Some people want to preserve their bodies, some people don't want to. They want to show it to the whole world."

He said, "I don't understand. You're young, why are you doing this?"

Then they asked me about Tashnuba. They asked me about her name, they asked me about her family, but I told them, "I don't know her."

They said, "Tashnuba wrote you on this list."

I said, "What list?"

They said, "She signed you up to be a suicide bomber."

I said, "Are you serious? Why would she do that? She doesn't seem like that type of person."

They were trying to make me seem like I was wrong about who I knew and who I didn't know.

They took me out of the interrogation room briefly, because my dad wanted to talk to me. They had him sign papers consenting to let them talk to me because I was underage. We didn't know that we were supposed to have lawyers. The FBI never told us that.

My dad said, "Everything is going to be fine. I want you to be brave. I'll see you later."

YOU PUT ME ON A LIST?

Back in the interrogation room, they told me Tashnuba and I were going to leave. I said, "Where's my dad, can I say bye to him?"

They said, "He left already."

I started to cry because I'd had my dad there the whole time. I said, "Where is he going to go? What are you guys going to do?" They said that he was going to see an immigration judge before the day ended.

I asked, "When am I going to see him? Where am I going?"

They told me to stop with the questions. They brought Tashnuba and handcuffed us both, hands behind the back. The cuffs were very tight, and I remember they left marks.

We got back in the Escalade. I'm very traumatized when I see Escalades now. This time, I didn't know where they took me, but it was on Varick Street in Manhattan. When we arrived at our destination, the agent told us to walk in casually because all these people were walking past us on the street. He said, "Act casual and people won't say anything."

Tashnuba and I, all by ourselves, got in this elevator. We went up, and we went into this large room that was divided into smaller holding cells. The cells didn't have bars but were enclosed with glass. They put us into our own cell. From there, we saw a bunch of men in one of the other cells, all yelling and screaming and talking, all in orange jumpsuits. Tashnuba and I just looked at each other.

She said to me, "You put me on a list?"

I said, "No! They said you put *me* on a list." We both realized they had been trying to set us up. So they didn't have anything on us. They'd come for her early in the morning, too. They didn't detain her parents, they just detained her. Later I found out why they'd taken my dad. After I'd been reported as a a suicide bomber, the FBI started investigating my whole family. That's how they found out about my dad being here without papers.

Tashnuba and I were then trying to figure out what was going on, what they were going to do, if they were going to release us.

That's when a lady walked in. She said, "What are you guys in for?"

We said, "We don't know."

"I hear you guys did something."

"What did we do?" We were asking *her* for information.

She said, "We're going to take you to Pennsylvania."

Tashnuba and I looked at each other, like, *Pennsylvania?* I said, "What are we going to do in Pennsylvania?"

She answered, "They didn't tell you? There's a detention center there."

YOU NO LONGER HAVE RIGHTS

The FBI drove us to Pennsylvania, across state lines, without my parent's permission. We got to the juvenile detention center late at night. When the FBI agents dropped us off, I wanted to scream, "Please don't leave us!" I didn't want to be left there. I didn't know where I was. There were too many faces for one night for me.

The female guard told me and Tashnuba we had to get strip-searched. We said that was against our religion.

The guard said, "It's either that or we hold you down."

I said, "Hold me down and do what? I'm not doing a strip-search." I'm stubborn like that, but I was in a situation where I had no choice.

So, she said, "Who wants to go first?"

Tashnuba went first. They searched her hair, checked her body parts; they checked everything. She then had to take a shower and change into a uniform they gave her, and then she had to go. When they took her downstairs, the guard said, "Okay, your turn."

The guard stood there and said, "You're going to have to take off everything. Take off whatever you feel comfortable with first."

I said, "I can't do this. I can't." I was in tears. My own mother doesn't look at me naked. It's my privacy. I said, "It must be against some law for you to do this to me."

She said, "No, it's not. You no longer have rights."

"Why not? What did I do?"

"You're just going to have to take your clothes off."

I was crying, but she just looked at me and said, "Kids here sneak in things and I have to search you."

I had on my abaya, and that was the first thing I took off. Second thing I took off was my head scarf. Third thing I took off was my top. Fourth was my bra. I stopped there for the longest minutes. I put my hands across my chest, just to get that little dignity for myself.

She said, "Come on, I don't have all day."

I said, "I can't do this, I can't, I can't."

"Drop your pants."

So, I took off my pants, I took off my underwear, and I kept my legs closed against each other, trying to cover myself. I was just holding myself with the little bit I could.

She said, "You cannot do that. You have to let loose, or else I'll call another guard and we'll hold you down and search you. This is your last warning. If you want me to call someone in, I'll call them in right now, but it's not gonna be nice. We're going to hold you down and search you."

I said, "Okay." I let go of my arms.

She said, "Lift your breasts."

I lifted my breasts.

She said, "Open your legs more."

I opened my legs.

She said, "Put your hands in there, to see there's nothing."

I said, "There's nothing there!"

She said, "Just do it."

I did it.

She said, "Turn around, put your hands up."

I did that.

Then she said, "All right, now put your fingers to your hair, pull at your ears. Show me your ears, open your mouth."

I showed my mouth.

"Show me your nose."

I put my finger up my nose, put it up so she could see.

Then she gave me a blue uniform: sweat pants, socks, underwear, a bra, and a hair tie, and a little towel and washcloth. She told me to take a shower in five minutes, and then she left.

I knew I only had five minutes, but I just sat at the corner of the shower and held myself and cried. I was thinking, *I cannot believe what I just went through.* I was just crying and crying and crying. I don't know how long, but then I just told myself that I had to get up. I washed myself really quickly. I've never felt like I needed God more than I did on this day. So, I did ghusul, which is like a special shower for prayer. I prayed, "God, you've got to hear me for this one. I've never asked for anything that I desperately needed but this one."

I dried myself and put my clothes on. There was a little mirror there. I looked into it. My eyes were red from crying.

The guard returned and told me I had to take off my head scarf. I said, "It's part of my religion." And I was having a bad hair day, I was not ready to show my hair. She let me keep the scarf, but later the supervisor took it from me once she saw me.

I was then taken to my cell. As we walked, the guard said, "You must keep your hands to your sides at all times." You had to look straight, you couldn't look anywhere else. There were cameras everywhere, but I wasn't listening, I was looking around.

I still didn't know why I was there. I didn't know if it was immigration or if it was for the stuff they were interrogating me about. When I got to the cell, all the lights were out. I could see Tashnuba in the corner, praying. There was one blanket, and it was freezing cold in there.

We stayed up the whole night talking about everything. I found out her mom had just had a baby; my mom had just had a baby too. Tashnuba was the oldest, I was the oldest. I asked her age, she asked my age. I asked what school she went to, what she was studying, what she wanted to do with her life.

We were laughing, like, "Pinch me. This is a prank."

She said, "Maybe it will be all be straightened out by tomorrow."

I don't know how we fell asleep, but I remember at one point we were both crying.

THERE GOES A TERRORIST

I was just so angry, and I was trying to contain all this anger. I was so mad at America as a country. I remember the first morning in detention, we went for breakfast and we were supposed to salute the American flag. I'm like, "Fuck the American flag. I'm not saluting it." I said it. During the pledge I put my hands to my side, and I just looked out the window.

Each morning I did that. I remember one of the guards asking me, "How come you don't pledge allegiance?"

I said, "You guys said it yourself. I am not American."

*

Nobody told me what was going on. I wasn't brought before a judge until probably my fourth week there, and it was via video conference.

An article came out in the *New York Times* about why Tashnuba and I were there, that we were suspected of being suicide bombers. I never saw the article while in prison. I saw it when I came out. After the guards read what happened, things changed. They would whisper, "There goes a terrorist," or "There go those girls."

After the article came out we got extra strip-searches, about three times a day, and the searches got stricter. They would tell us to spread our butt cheeks, and they made nasty, racist comments. I remember the guards laughing and going, "Look at those assholes. Look at them. These are the ones that want to take our country down." Things like that.

If I talked back, they would tackle me down and I would be put into solitary confinement. All I wanted to do was get out. I knew that I was going to have to take shit from everyone, because I did not want to be in solitary.

We also lost a lot of privileges because of the head scarf. We weren't allowed to use the bathroom privately. So when I had to go, I was like, "I hope I stink this place up, I pray that my shit would make this place close down or something. I hope my poop brings toxins."

I remember even having tissue stuck up my butt when somebody did a strip-search once, and I did it on purpose. I was like, "I hope after this, they'll think, *I will never want to strip-search her again*. It didn't work. I still got strip-searched. I even tried leaving caca there. I tried everything.

*

Those first three weeks I was there, my family didn't have any idea where I was. They had to do research to find out, and hire a lawyer. The lawyer, Natasha, came to see me at the detention center. She asked me, "Do you know why you're here?"

I said no.

"There's a rumor going around about you being a suicide bomber."

I laughed so hard.

She said, "That's not funny."

I said, "Are you serious or are you joking? If you knew me, you would laugh and say 'Hell no.'"

I have a family, I am somebody. I wanted to live. I said, "I'm not ready to meet God yet."

She said, "But they're not charging you with anything except over-staying your visa."

My mom came to visit me after my lawyer. She was so skinny. You could tell she wasn't eating. It was the worst visit ever because she didn't want to say anything at all. When I asked about my dad, she just said, "He's fine." She knew that he was being held in New Jersey at the time. I just knew that she was upset. She was so drained.

A WAY TO GET ME OUT

After a while, my lawyer called. She said she had good news. "I have a way to get you out of jail. You're going to have to wear an ankle bracelet."

I said, "I'll wear anything."

The day that I was supposed to be released from the detention center, I said goodbye to Tashnuba in the cafeteria. I wanted to hold her and let her know it was going to be okay. But I couldn't hug her, or it would've been solitary confinement for her. So I looked at her and I said, "May Allah be with you, and be patient." And I walked away.

I haven't spoken to Tashnuba since then. She'd told me that her mother made an agreement with the federal government: if they released her daughter, they would go back to their country, no problems. I think their country was Bangladesh. So as soon as she was released, it was right to the airport.

I stayed there six and a half weeks. By the time I came out, I was seventeen.

Federal agents picked me up. This guard walked past, and he said, "Arrest that fucking nigger terrorist." But I didn't give a damn, I was so excited I was leaving. The whole world could burn down, but as long as I was leaving, I didn't care.

HOME AGAIN

As soon as we got to New York, I was just so excited and happy to be home again that I forgot I had to wear an ankle bracelet. I thought everything was going to go back to normal, but in a way, I knew deep down inside things would never be normal again, because I was so traumatized.

We came back to my house. My mom had to sign papers, and they released me. They put the ankle bracelet on the same day.

Once a week I had to report to Federal Plaza so they could check the bracelet. When I got there, I recognized it was the building where my father and I had been taken to a few months ago. I just looked at it and my heart started beating so fast. It triggered the memory, and I started to cry so badly I just could not control it. It was one of the most traumatizing moments of my life.

I wore the ankle bracket for three years. You can still see my bruises from it. My heel always hurts. This is all black from the ankle bracelet. I had to wear the bracelet and check in every week. I also had to be under curfew, which was 10:00 p.m. and then 11:00 p.m.

Every night our phone would ring, and I would have to press this button and they would have to hear it. I couldn't get any sleep. The man who put the bracelet on me told me, "If you take it off, we're going to put you in jail. If your phone is off, you're going to jail."

That was the best threat you could ever make to me. I did everything possible not to tamper with it, just to keep it on.

They never said how long I would have to wear it. It was pending my immigration case. I was only ever charged with overstaying my visa, that's it. I was never charged with anything related to terrorism. They wanted to deport me.

For days, my mom didn't want to talk because she thought they were recording us with the ankle bracelet. She was always like, "*Shh, shh.*"

I'd say, "They're not listening."

I didn't know if they weren't listening, and I didn't care. I'd get on the phone with Demaris, my friend from high school, and we would say things on purpose, like "Fuck the government!"

I MISS HIM BEING THE ONE WHO TOOK CARE OF EVERYTHING

My dad got deported around 2006. That was the hardest.

I didn't see him for a long time after I got released from juvie. He was in New Jersey. I wasn't allowed to go, because it was outside the distance I could travel with my ankle bracelet. My mom and my siblings were able to visit, but they couldn't go a lot because it was a lot of money to get out there.

They made an exception to let me travel to New Jersey just before he was deported. I couldn't look at him. I was just crying the whole time.

He said, "I hope you take care of the family. It's your job." It's always about, "It's your job, it's your responsibility, you're the next person in line."

I miss a lot about my dad. I miss his company. I even miss him yelling at me. My brothers and sister, we used to walk around saying our dad was a dictator. But we needed him. I just miss him being the one who took care of everything. I didn't have to worry about everything; no bills, no nothing.

WE WERE STARVING

I thought I was going to be able to come back to school, that the government was going to apologize and write me a check, and I would be set for life. But it was the opposite way around. When I came back, I had to drop school to work to support my family. No way my dad can work in Guinea; there are no jobs there. So I support my father, his family, my mom's family, and I support my family here too.

I would work three or four jobs, whatever job I could find—babysitting jobs, cleaning houses. I worked at an interpretive service for a while, until I found out that could get me back in jail, because I had no documentation.

Sometimes we were starving. For days there would be no food in the house. Finally we met a social worker who told us we could get public assistance. Nobody tells you about this stuff.

I started feeling distant from my friends because I was going through something that none of my friends had gone through. I was growing up really quickly, maturing so fast.

Everything that I do in life is to take care of my family. Everything revolves around them. My family here wouldn't be able to stand on their own feet, not without me. I didn't want my brother and my sister to work at all. I didn't want them to miss out on what I missed out on.

But I was drained. When I came back, I was also going through my emotions. I would come home so angry, like, "Leave me alone, don't touch me."

Now that I look back, I wish there was something that could have been done. I wish I would have told my story to a newspaper, but I was always afraid to say something, because they always threatened me with going to jail.

That's why I kept so silent and cried about everything. I feel like it's too late for me now.

I AM NOT AMERICAN NOW. I AM A REFUGEE.

In 2007, Adama was granted asylum on the grounds that she would face forcible circumcision if deported to Guinea. In court, her mother gave testimony on her own harrowing experience of being circumcised.

I had the ankle bracelet up until I got asylum. The day I got it taken off, I had the cheesiest smile. I went to the guy I had to report to every week, and when he took off the ankle bracelet, I said, "My legs! That's what my legs look like!"

But for at least a year, I still had a feeling I had the ankle bracelet on. I felt like it was still there. And sometimes I would be out, and I would think, "Oh my God, my curfew," and I would just start panicking. I had to calm myself down again.

I am not American now. I have asylum. That means I am a refugee.

I AM NOT GOING TO GO THROUGH THIS

In 2009, to celebrate winning her asylum case, Adama arranged to take a vacation in Texas with friends. When she tried to board her flight at LaGuardia Airport, a ticket agent told her she was on the No-Fly List. Federal agents came and handcuffed her and took her to the airport security station, where she was held for almost thirteen hours before being released.

In 2009 I started working for a family as a nanny. I met them through an old friend who was also working for them. They are a very nice family, they spoil me too much, beyond spoil. They pay me on time, they take care of me, they give me Christmas bonuses, they give me vacations, they take me everywhere.

We were supposed to fly to Chicago on March 31, 2010. I went to the airport before them because I just wanted to know if there would be any problems or anything. I was there with my luggage, and I had brought a friend because I was afraid of repeating what had happened before. I don't know why, but I just had a fear that something was going to happen. I even called my lawyers, but they said nothing should happen, that I should be fine. But I got to LaGuardia Airport and a problem did happen.

The same thing happened as before. The airline supervisor called Port Authority police and other government officials. I called my lawyer and he came. They kept asking me questions, like, "What did you do to be on the No-Fly List?"

I wasn't able to get on the plane. I could tell the family were disappointed. They ended up taking the other babysitter. I lost money that day. They were going to pay me for going, and I was counting on that money.

As soon as I got out of that room, something in me just triggered. I told myself, "I'm done. I'm tired. I am not going to go through this again." I told my lawyers, "I want to sue these motherfuckers," and so we filed a lawsuit against Attorney General Eric Holder, FBI Director Robert Mueller, and Director of the Terrorist Screening Center Timothy Healy.

About a month later, we received a letter from James Kennedy of the DHS[7] Traveler Redress Inquiry Program, but it didn't tell me anything. It didn't tell me why I wasn't allowed to board my flight at LaGuardia or what would happen if I tried to fly again.

---

[7] The Department of Homeland Security.

Some months later, my friend gave me a ticket to go to Chicago, on November 12, 2010, as a gift. I didn't know if I could fly, but I didn't know how to find out if I could without trying again. It was LaGuardia again. This time, I walked up to the ticket machine, punched in my name, and it said, "Go see a ticket agent." I said to myself, "I'm not going to be able to fly."

I gave the ticket agent my name and my state ID, and he printed the ticket. I looked at him and said, "You printed it?"

He said, "Yeah."

"And it went through?"

"Yeah."

When he gave me my ticket, I started to cry. He was just looking at me, like, is this girl nuts?

I WANT TO LIVE MY LIFE NOW

I grew up too fast. I experienced some things that a lot of people around me haven't, so it's hard to talk to my peers. I've never gotten to escape. All my friends went to college, and now, four years later, they've all graduated, and I'm just like, "Wow, they're graduating college and I haven't even gotten there yet."

I have a bigger picture of life. But I feel like things are not changing as quickly as I want them to. I want to be done with school already, I want to have my own car, I want to be in my own space. I want to live my life now. I don't mind taking care of my family, but for once, I want to do something for myself: I want to go and do something overseas. I want to be a traveling nurse. I want to help people, I want to educate.

Even though everything is said and done, I still live in constant fear of federal agents taking me or any of my family members. They did it when I was innocent, and they could do it again. I have so much to lose, including my family. I remember the look of helplessness on their faces the day they took me and my father away.

Still, the United States is home. It's the only place I know. I am hopeful for this country, because of people like me and my siblings. We know how it feels to suffer, so we can change things.

Now I study Islam on my own. At the end of the day, I still believe in God, because I feel like things could have been worse; I could have been in Guantánamo Bay. I still have my family, I still have my health. So, in a way, I know there is still God. There has to be something you can believe in at the end of the day.

TALAT HAMDANI

AGE: *60*

OCCUPATION: *former teacher*

INTERVIEWED IN: *Long Island, New York*

Talat Hamdani immigrated to New York City from Pakistan with her husband
Saleem. Salman, their eldest of three sons, disappeared on September 11, 2001.
Salman was an emergency medical technician (EMT) and a New York City police
cadet. In October of 2001, the New York Post *published an article that portrayed*
him as a possible terrorist who may have been involved in the attack. The Post *also*
suggested that he was not missing, as his family believed, but hiding from officials.
Thirteen days after the Post *article ran, Congress passed the USA PATRIOT Act,*
which specifically commended Salman for his bravery and as a hero of Muslim faith.
Salman's body was identified in the rubble of the World Trade Center in March
2002, and Mayor Bloomberg, Congressman Ackerman, and members of the New
York Police Department honored him at his funeral service.

It says in the Qur'an that a time and place is written for us to die. And
even if it doesn't seem possible, you make it there in time.

I don't know for sure what happened to my son. Maybe he is dead,
as they say. I just don't want to accept it. And even if he died trying to
help people, also as they say, how can it be comforting to lose your child?

How do I live without answers? I'm living by just not thinking about the questions. I don't think I'm going to get them. But I sure do want them.

*

I was born in Karachi, Pakistan, in 1951. I am the sixth in a family of eight siblings. My father's dream was that all four daughters would be doctors. My three sisters, they are all medical doctors. So when I didn't make it into medical school—I studied English literature in college—he said, "Oh, you must do your PhD and put 'doctor' in front of your name!"

My husband Saleem was a family friend. He was eighteen and I was fourteen when we started talking to each other. He was very dashing and very handsome. We fell in love a few years later and got married in August 1975. I was twenty-four. We became really good friends. We understood each other.

Salman was born December 28, 1977. He was the first grandson on his father's side of the family. His birth was happiness.

About six months later, my brother told me that American visas were open. I had no desire to ever leave Pakistan, because I was happy. At that time, I was teaching high school in Karachi, I was close to family, and I had a new baby. Like you see me now, I was always content with what I have. But my husband Saleem always wanted to move out of Pakistan. In spite of me being an educator, and he the manager of Three Star Battery (a company like Duracell), we couldn't save money. The income was very nominal, and he wanted to have a nice standard of living.

So he applied for a visa, they called him a week later, and he got it. He came to New York City in July of 1978, and I came in February of 1979 with Salman.

ARE YOU BLACK OR WHITE?

Saleem came here as a photojournalist for a media company, but his contract was only for two years. When those two years were up, he didn't want to go back, so he got a job over here at a junk yard in Mamaroneck.

Saleem had rented an apartment in Greenpoint, Brooklyn. When I arrived, I couldn't believe how cold it was! But I was happy because I was with him again, because we were a family again.

I went looking for jobs the same year that I arrived. I can't sit at home for nothing! I wanted to work as a teacher, but a friend of my husband said I had to be a United States citizen, so I didn't even look into it at the time. Instead, I found a job as a stock girl at a sundry items warehouse. My sons Adnaan and Zeshan were born in '81 and '83.

In 1986, my husband bought a partnership in this convenience store, a bodega, in Greenpoint. After Zeshan was born, it did not pay for me to work and pay the babysitter, so eventually I quit my job and I joined Saleem in his business. I also took classes at Queens College because I had to have some intellectual activity, some stimulation.

*

In 1989 we moved to Bayside, Queens, and I got my teaching license in 1992. I became a full-time teacher at Middle School 72, in an African-American neighborhood in South Jamaica, Queens. On my first day, one question the students asked me was very intriguing.

They said, "So are you black or white, Ms. Hamdani?"

I said, "You tell me. Do you think I'm a black person or a white person?"

They said, "Oh, no, you're a white person."

I replied, "Well, the white people don't think I'm a white person."

So they said, "Well, you're not black."

Then I told them, "I'm brown, you would say, but I do get a lot more respect from black people." That has been my experience in America.

On the streets I dressed as an American, I assimilated very well. I don't think there was anything unique about me. I had Pakistani girl-friends and I had American girlfriends. I get along with everybody very well. But when I was at the warehouse job, there was this resentment from the other workers about me being an immigrant. Similarly in the store, when customers got upset at me and Saleem for the price of something or for whatever reason, they would tell us off, saying, "You guys come here from abroad and make money—go back to where you came from, you Arabs!"

They didn't know we were Pakistani, because most of these convenience stores were owned by Yemenis. We bought our store from a Yemeni also.

I would say to them, "If you guys want to make money, you can too. But we have to work eighteen hours a day, seven days a week. You don't want to do that."

But they were disgruntled people. One thing I did feel was that being an immigrant, we had to work three times as hard to get recognition. People were promoted or put ahead of me, in many situations. So I felt that we had to do a lot more than others to prove that we are really good, and that is not right.

WHAT DIVERSITY IS ALL ABOUT

We spoke Urdu at home and with the kids. When they were young, they would understand it, but they wouldn't respond. Once they became mature, about eighteen, nineteen, they started picking it up and speaking it.

In Greenpoint, they went to a Catholic school. I think they were the only Pakistani kids in the class. There were other immigrant children in the other classes, but there were no other Muslims.

They were fine there, except one day, when Salman was in the fourth grade, he came home and said, "I don't want to go back to school." He was upset because of the resentment he got from his classmates. Everybody went to church for one period a day, but I had told the principal I didn't want my child going to church, so they would send him outside with the principal. Resentment started among the students that he was a teacher's pet, and finally they told him, "You're not a Catholic. You don't belong here."

So I spoke to the principal, Sister Miriam, and she said okay, she would take care of it. A few days later, Salman said, "I need the Qur'an."

I said, "Why?"

He said, "Because the teacher told everyone to bring in their book of faith."

And after that there was no problem. He had a class on different faiths. That's what diversity is all about.

SALMAN

Salman was a regular kid. He was a *Star Wars* fan, and he especially liked Luke Skywalker. Once I asked him, "What is this *Star Wars*?" and he said, "If you don't know the saga of *Star Wars*, then you are not an American, Mama!" He had all the movies and T-shirts, and he read the books; he was an avid reader. When he bought his car in 2001, the license plate read YUNGJEDI.

I still have the license plate. I still have the T-shirts.

Growing up, the boys were into everything—baseball, basketball, swimming, skiing, rollerblading. They played on teams at the Greenpoint Y, and Salman was the coach for the basketball team there the year after he graduated high school. He wanted to do so many things, whatever he came across.

The brothers were very close. Salman was the big brother, and he would take them out to the movies, the batting cage, to archery, all types of sports activities.

The boys had all kinds of friends. It was a mixed group because Greenpoint is a mixed neighborhood. It's a New York thing! I don't think any other state can comprehend it.

I think they went through an identity crisis. Even though we are Pakistani, I remember Salman telling me, "You're Indian," and telling my younger boys, "You are Indian, this is your heritage." The race is Indian, you cannot deny it. And all three worked at Bombay Palace Catering! I don't know if they can cook, but they can serve.

He also helped the DJs at the Desi parties when they needed an extra hand.[1] He could dance Bhangra, all the boys did.[2] Me too. Life was so different before 9/11. I haven't danced since, except at Zeshan's wedding.

Salman wanted to become a doctor. He studied biochemistry at Queens College and graduated in June of 2001 and was living with us in Queens." That summer, he started working as a DNA lab analyst at the Howard Hughes Medical Institute. He was also in his last year of NYPD cadet training. Not only did it help bolster his application for medical school, but it was also something he would have been interested in pursuing if he didn't get accepted into medical schools. After the training, he would have been able to join the NYPD as an officer and go into NYPD forensics.

WE JUST WAITED FOR HIM

The night before 9/11, Salman was going over his application for medical school. That night, my husband Saleem wasn't feeling well. He was all flushed, so he called Salman to take his blood pressure. It was fine, but Salman said, "If you feel bad, if you feel something wrong, just call me again." That was the last time I saw him.

On the morning of 9/11, I was in the classroom from about 8:00 a.m. to 10:20 a.m. When I came out of the classroom, there were teachers huddled up in the hallway outside the assistant principal's room. At first I thought, *Let me go see, maybe the superintendent has come in for an inspection.* But then I could sense that something was wrong.

I heard the teachers saying that the Twin Towers had been hit. I called my husband. He was crying profusely, and he said, "You know, Salman is there!" He knew it. I don't know how, but he knew it.

I was trying to convince him Salman wasn't down there, that he was at work, at the Howard Hughes Medical Institute. That's at 65th

---

[1] Desi refers to the people and cultures of, or originating from, the Indian subcontinent.

[2] Bhangra is a genre of music and dance from the Punjab region that has incorporated elements of contemporary rock and hip hop as the Indian diaspora spread throughout the world.

and York Avenue—far away from the World Trade Center. But Saleem believed our son had gone down there to help because he was trained as a first responder and would have seen the towers burning on his commute to Manhattan. He knew Salman would have gone down there, that's all I can say. I said to him, "Don't worry, he'll call. He'll come home."

At school, we carried on teaching. At one point during the day, I went into the school's media room, where some of the other teachers were watching the news on television. I found a seat up front. Then I saw what was happening on TV. It was so surreal. I just didn't know what to believe or what not to believe. One of the teachers said, "It must be some crazy Muslim, you know." Another teacher who knew I was there nudged her not to say it, and she kept quiet. But then I got up and left.

I got home at around 4:30 p.m. My youngest son, Zeshan, was home. He was trying to reach Salman. We called Salman's office, we called his cell, but nobody was answering. This whole time I was thinking, *Salman is safe.*

Still, I called up the police department and the ambulance company to ask if they'd sent him down there as an EMT. They said, "No, we did not send him." There had been no contact between the NYPD or the EMT company. They had not seen Salman at all that day.

I told Saleem, "Don't worry. He'll be home."

That night, we just waited for him. Nothing. He didn't come home.

When the telephone systems were up and running and a call still hadn't come all night, then we got really worried.

We never discussed the attack. I didn't think it had anything to do with his disappearance. We were definitely just focused on finding Salman.

THAT HE WAS DEAD NEVER CROSSED MY MIND

The next day my husband and I went to Salman's office. The staff there said that he never showed up. The security guard went and got Salman's cell phone for us; Salman had left it there the night before 9/11. We asked the security guard what to do, and he said, "Maybe go down to St. Vincent's hospital. That's where they have the injured."

So we went down to St. Vincent's and there were long lines, and of course we were both crying. We went to see the list of the injured and the dead. Every three or four hours they were generating a list. We spent the whole day looking through the lists, again and again. I felt very hopeful because Salman's name was not on any of them.

Then on the third day, Thursday, we made a flyer for him. It had his picture and it said MISSING. We went to Manhattan again, to the Armory downtown. There were so many people over there. We posted the pictures everywhere, in different places. Everybody else was posting their pictures too.

That Salman was dead never crossed my mind.

On that day, I think he would have gone there to help, definitely. He was that type of a person.

FROM MISSING TO WANTED

We went to Manhattan for twelve days searching for him.

I had no clue. I was just searching. He could have been dead, he could have been injured. We were still hoping to find him on the injured list. They gave out a list of all the hospitals where the patients had been sent. There was something like 170 hospitals between the five boroughs and New Jersey. We went to many of them, and I called many of them. No one had his name.

Soon after, two police officers came to our house, a female and a male from the NYPD Bureau of Criminal Investigation.

I said, "What brings you to my house?"

They both looked at each other, and then they said, "Oh, we're just visiting, just paying a visit to all the victims' families in Queens."

The female officer was looking around the house very intently. She came into the kitchen, where I had a big collage of pictures on the refrigerator. There was a picture of Zeshan's graduation, with Salman, Adnaan, Zeshan, and Zeshan's friend, who was an Afghani. She said, "My husband works at Queens College Housing." The police had a center over there, where Salman worked. "Can I take his picture? Maybe my husband will recognize Salman."

I said, "Yeah, take his picture."

She took the one with the Afghani kid. I never got the picture back, and they never came back.

*

A few days after the cops came to my home, a regular customer, a Pakistani man who worked at the MTA,[3] came to my husband's store and said, "They're asking for your son at the MTA. They're asking for anyone who knows your son to step forward." At that point we'd had the store for fifteen years, so Salman had practically grown up in front of him. Then he said to us, "Your son didn't die, he's being detained. You should write a letter to President Bush."

And so we did write a letter to Bush, and I sent a copy of the letter to everybody, including Senator Charles Schumer.

To keep hope alive, I kept telling myself that Salman did arrive at the WTC after the collapses and that he was being detained by the government, the CIA, FBI, whoever it was.

MISSING OR HIDING?

In October, my family and I decided to go to Mecca just to pray, to get some answers. On October 9, there was an announcement on the television for people to go identify bodies at the medical examiner's office. So I said to my husband, "Before we go to Mecca, let's go and look at all the bodies."

Someone at the Armory had given us a handout with a phone number. So I dialed that number, and I said, "I want to see the dead bodies."

[3] Metropolitan Transportation Authority, the government agency in charge of public transportation in New York.

This man on the other end said, "Who are you? Why are you calling here?"

I explained who I was and why I was calling. I said, "I want to know where we go to look at the bodies."

He gave me an address and said, "Okay, you can go out there."

The next day, we headed to Manhattan. We had Salman's cell phone, which was the only cell phone we had at the time. The man from the medical examiner's office, or whoever he was, was calling every fifteen minutes, asking, "Where are you now? Where are you going?" Finally, when we arrived there, it wasn't the dead bodies; it was the Red Cross center. So there were no bodies to be seen.

It was a big place with cubicles. The staff there told us we were entitled to all the benefits for survivor families, but we had to accept the death certificate. I said, "No, he might not be dead! We don't want any benefits, we just want our son."

We were not ready to accept his death. It was too soon.

*

For the rest of the day we kept receiving phone calls from a man who said he was a detective with the NYPD. He gave a name and a phone number.

He asked, "What was Salman wearing? Who was he going to see? What was he doing that day? Did he have a girlfriend or not? Can we take his computer? Do you know his password?"

I refused to give him Salman's computer. I said, "Why should I give you his computer? It's not needed. First tell me where my son is."

He called again at 11:00 p.m. and finally I yelled at him, "Don't you dare call here again!" After that, he stopped calling.

*

On October 11, the evening that we were leaving for Mecca, that's the day when all the press reporters came back to my house. This *New York Post* guy came in asking questions, like, "What happened? Where would your son be? What are you doing? Isn't your son Adnaan the president of the Muslim Student Association at Binghamton?" That made me think *Oh, so he's done his homework, and that is what he is looking at, the Muslim angle.*

I said, "I don't trust you. I don't want to talk to you." Then the *Newsday* guy came in, and guys from the *New York Times* and the *Daily News.* They told me, "There's a flyer circulating within the NYPD with your son's picture on it. It says WANTED! That's why we've come to your house."

When I heard that, I was shocked. I remember saying, "He's alive and he's being detained, and he will come back." The hope was so intense.

We then went to Mecca. The day after we left, the *New York Post* article hit the stands. The headline was MISSING—OR HIDING? All this insinuation, this is just a garbage paper. But the *Daily News,* the *New York Times,* and *Newsday* all wrote very fair, sympathetic stories.

When we came back, there was a message on the answering machine from Congressman Ackerman's office telling us to contact them, that he had news of my son. When I called him, what he really wanted was to interrogate us. He asked, "What was your son wearing that day? Where was he going? What would he be doing?"

A few days later, I think the third time that we spoke, he said, "I'll be very point-blank. Do you think your son would be involved in any wrongful activity?"

I said, "No! I know my son." And that was the end of it.

Then, one very peculiar thing Ackerman had us do was write a letter to Attorney General John Ashcroft. He said Salman might be with the INS.[4]

I asked why, and he said, "Because he's not born here."

I said, "Even if he's a citizen?"

He said, "The dividing line is whether he was born a citizen or not."

Ackerman led us to believe that Salman was being detained, so we were hopeful again that he was alive. We wrote a letter to Ashcroft asking him to tell us if he had our son.

---

[4] Immigration and Naturalization Services, the government agency responsible for enforcing federal immigration laws.

I have yet to find out why they would begin to suspect him, as opposed to helping us find him. I think maybe it was the fact that he didn't work down there at the WTC, and I called them up the second day asking, "Did you send him down there to help?" Maybe that could be it. There was so much fear and suspicion at that time. And his first name is Mohammad. Maybe that caused the suspicion. Who knows? But it was wrong, very wrong.

A BAG OF DUST

I went back to teaching that November. By this time, there was nothing more my family could do to find Salman. We were just thinking that he was alive and he'd come back home one day.

Every day we would check the *New York Times* because they were disclosing the names of the dead and the injured. His name was never there, and I would tell this to the boys. So we were all still hopeful.

Also we had heard on the television about a big dragnet that had detained many people. There was a senatorial meeting, and Ashcroft was summoned to it and he was asked by the senators, "How many people do you have detained?" So the more I heard about what was going on with the government, the more hope I had that my son was being detained.

Then, on March 20, 2002, we received the first piece of information about his whereabouts. We were going to sleep in the living room. Since 9/11, we had been sleeping there because my husband had said, "Salman will come home one day and he doesn't have a key, so I don't want the house to be locked." So he kept the door unlocked all the time, and he slept in the living room, and of course I had to sleep with him. I couldn't leave him alone. We used to spread a couple of blankets on the carpet and then sleep right there.

That night, at 11:30 p.m., these tall men in overcoats knocked on our door. They said they were from the precinct. They did not show badges but I let them into my house because they said, "We've just identified your son's remains. This is the medical examiner's number. You can call them right now and confirm."

My husband just collapsed to the floor and broke down, poor guy. I told them, "Okay, you've done your job. You guys have got to go now."

I told Saleem, "Listen, nothing's going to change anything. Let's go back to sleep. No need to call anybody. We don't know who these people were." I just wanted to calm him down.

Then the next day we went down to the medical examiner's office at Bellevue Hospital. A man from the office came, and he said, "They found the lower part of his body."

I said, "Okay, prove to me that this is my son. I want to have his DNA tested by my own person."

So he pulled the file toward himself, and he said, "You know, Mrs. Hamdani, go get yourself a lawyer. If someone wants to test it, they have to do it in our presence. Whenever you're ready, we have the remains."

My brother, who lives in New York, handled everything. The remains were sent to the funeral home in Queens. The medical examiner's office said they'd given us his lower body. But I'm sure from that big debris that was there at Ground Zero that they didn't find any bodies; all they gave anybody was a bag of dust. My sister tried to prod the bag for a sign of Salman's body, and she told me there was just dust in that bag, that there were no bones in there.

I don't know what to believe or not to believe, honestly. They gave us a pair of jeans and a belt that were found in the debris. They were Salman's. But the jeans were not burned or anything. They had cut one of the legs to get it off, but there were no bones.

On March 21, we went to California, where my sister lives. I knew there would be a lot of press outside my door in Queens again, and I did not want to talk to them. We came back in April, a day before the funeral.

THAT'S HOW I WANT TO GO

We had the funeral on April 5, 2002. The NYPD arranged it, and Salman got an honorable funeral under the American flag. I think after Congressman Ackerman investigated, the suspicions about Salman were put to rest. At that point, I took it as a redemption of Salman's dignity. The slander that had been done in his name was taken care of.

The funeral was at the big mosque in Manhattan, on 96th Street on the East Side. I'd made a collage of his pictures. The NYPD had the bagpipe player play the bagpipes, they brought the casket in, they laid it upstairs. There were many cadets there. Mayor Bloomberg came, Ackerman came, Commissioner Kelly came.

My family all spoke at the funeral, and the cadets spoke too. That was how Salman had wanted to be sent off. He had expressed it at the funeral of a sergeant who'd died in '99. He'd said then, "Mama, that's honor. That's how I want to go."

You can say it put a closure to all my misgivings, and the cycle of thinking, *Could he have survived? Could he have not survived?* It put everything to rest.

WE STARTED LIVING OUR LIVES

After the funeral, all the guests that had come, my family members from London and Pakistan, everybody left within a week or so. We accepted Salman's death, all of us, and started living our lives. That was it.

The store became a kind of shrine to Salman. My husband had all of Salman's pictures posted over there. Every day someone would come and light a candle for him. It was very sad.

I realized it wasn't good for Saleem's mental health, so I advised him to sell the store. I didn't want him to stay in depression, so he sold it in mid-December of 2002.

Before 9/11, Saleem was a very full of life person, the life of the party, very happy. But he never recovered from our son's death. He became very angry, and angry with his God.

We came back slowly and gradually to life. It didn't come back all at one time.

In February 2003, we went to hajj, and then in July 2003, Adnaan got married in Pakistan. The wedding was good, we enjoyed it. At that time, though, I don't think any of us was really happy again. If you look at the wedding pictures, Saleem wasn't happy. You could see sadness on his face.

*

Saleem became sick in September of 2003. He had become a diabetic earlier that year. Then he had breathing problems, and had a stent put in October. In December he had walking pneumonia. Then, in February, he went into the hospital. The doctors said he had cancer of an unknown origin that had metastasized to the brain and the skin. He died later that year, on July 21, 2004.

After he died, it was a new type of fear: living alone. The boys were not doing good in their education. In December 2003, I had a head-on auto collision that damaged my spine. I couldn't teach after that, because as a teacher you have to read and use your hands, which I wasn't able to do. I worked until spring of 2005 as a mentor-teacher, and then in the fall of 2005, the mentor-teacher program got eliminated.

For me, home is now here on Long Island. Many people say to me, "Oh, you're alone now, downsize, sell the house."

I say, "I live in a resort! I come down, I pull all the windows up and I see the sky."

Sometimes there are moments I get very sad. Especially after my sons come and leave, and I'm all alone again.

I do miss Saleem too. I think of him in the evening. The only time I don't think of Salman is when I'm very busy.

Almost ten years have gone by. Maybe we'll have a grandson in our family and we'll name him Salman.

I GOT TO KNOW THIS COUNTRY MORE

Before 9/11, I wasn't political. I was politically uneducated.

I never had any expectations from Bush, so there was nothing of being disillusioned. But I was angry, and I still am angry because of the path of wars and revenge and division along religious lines.

Because of 9/11 I started to study the history of American policy-making. What do they do when they get attacked by anybody, an outsider? Whenever they get attacked and they pass a law, who are they going to target, hold responsible for this action? It's nothing new. It has happened before; it will happen again. I got to know this country more. It made me a lot wiser about how people react.

I also became more quiet. I gave others a chance to talk as much as they could, to reveal themselves, what they're saying. Initially I was all mouth, I would talk and talk and talk. But after 9/11, going through that traumatic time, I don't trust anybody anymore. I just trust my sons. That's it.

I WANT TO TEACH THE NATION

Every Muslim should be proud to be a Muslim. After 9/11, many people have tried to blame Muslims and put them down, and the majority of the Muslim community is intimidated or does not understand the severity of the situation. I met someone yesterday and he said, "We have to apologize for those people who carried out the 9/11 attacks."

I said, "Why? Why do you want to apologize for them? They are criminals! I'm not going to go apologizing for everything a Muslim does wrong. I'm only responsible for my actions. Why should I be held accountable for the actions of another person? It's as simple as that."

I think it's good that we are having this national debate, because that's the only way we will educate the other side and resolve things. And the only way to do this is by talking about the issues and making them understand that there is no such thing in Islam that tells you to go kill people, that suicide bombing will get you ten thousand wives in heaven. There's no such thing in the Qur'an at all.

How are we going to do that? Interfaith dialogues are happening. I participated in one several weeks ago in Westchester. Once people see the faces of regular Americans who are Muslims, I think their fears are allayed to a certain degree. That's what we need to do.

I'm going to continue voicing my feelings regarding 9/11 and how it is wrong to hold American Muslims responsible for what happened that day, because we also lost, and we are fighting for our rights as Americans. I'm also trying to reach out to Muslim families of 9/11 victims.

American Muslims have a rough time ahead, they really do. But I would still tell Muslim immigrants who are thinking of coming over here that this is the best country to be in. Come over! You have to work very hard in order to make it over here, but you are secure here, in spite of all that's happened.

*

After Salman's funeral, the Shaheed Mohammad Salman Hamdani Memorial Fund was established to send a Pakistani student to medical school. So far, only one student has gone to medical school at Howard Hughes Medical Institute, which financed the scholarship. Last year, the scholarship was transferred to Queens College, because the HH program is very small.

I'm establishing a foundation to raise funds. I think I'll call it the Salman Hamdani Foundation. This foundation is not only to raise funds for the scholarship, but it will also be to generate awareness of interfaith tolerance, cultural tolerance, and diversity.

I remember two years ago, I said, "I'm tired of teaching secondary school. I want to teach the nation now." And I think that's where I'm headed now.

MY REAL LAUGHTER

I'm happy again. It was one day in 2007, something happened, and I was alone, and I just laughed out very loud. And I was shocked. I said, "I'm happy again today!"

Since 9/11, I hadn't laughed, not my real laughter. But I just laughed with the wholehearted laughter that I used to have. I said, "Well, Subhan'allah, God is glorious!" After all this, one can still be happy again.

RIMA QAMRI

AGE: *37*
OCCUPATION: *student teacher*
INTERVIEWED IN: *Brooklyn, New York*

Rima borrowed her eldest daughter's hot-pink Ugg boots to wear with her jeans, sweater, and hijab for our interview. She told us of the happy life she and her husband Ali had built for themselves and their five children in a picturesque beach town in Delaware, and how their lives changed after the 9/11 attacks. Rima's daughters Sana and Layla were subjected to different forms of harassment and bullying in two Delaware school districts by both students and teachers. They were so traumatized by their treatment that, at different points, the children had to receive home instruction and counseling, and the family moved to another district. Rima's husband fell into a severe depression and eventually returned to his native Palestine, leaving Rima to support her family. She found a job as a caregiver for the elderly, and is now studying to be a teacher.

Unable to get any recourse from teachers, principals or school district supervisors, Rima sued one of the school districts in 2005. The case will go to trial this summer.

All identities have been changed to protect the children involved.

I never thought 9/11 would play such a big role in my family's life. Our life is divided in two: pre-9/11 and post-9/11. Before 9/11, life was good. It was stable and happy. But then our whole life as we knew it ended.

Now I feel kind of broken, like our world was turned upside-down and I haven't really found my footing yet. I feel like we are hanging on by the tips of our fingernails.

I feel like a refugee in my own country.

I THOUGHT I BELONGED

I was born in Michigan in 1974. When I was four, my family moved to New York, and I was raised in Brooklyn.

My parents are both immigrants to this country from Palestine, from the outskirts of Jerusalem. They went through a lot of hardships surviving the occupation. My mother came to the United States with her parents when she was young. My father came here to try to make a living and to find the American Dream. After working different blue-collar jobs, he started a small business.

I never had a doubt about my Americanness. I thought I belonged right there in Brooklyn. That's all I knew. That is, until I went to Palestine on a family trip and my world opened up.

A SURVIVOR OF TORTURE

In the summer of 1991, I went to Al-Quds, the Muslim name for Jerusalem. I had just turned seventeen. Experiencing Palestine and what my own people were going through under Israeli occupation made an impact on me.

I met my husband Ali, and we got married that August. It wasn't expected. Ali was twenty-five, and he was from a completely different world from what I knew. He was a warm, humble, sincere man with a terrific sense of humor. And he was cute.

I was prepared to stay in Palestine because I just fell in love with the culture. I wound up getting a high school diploma there. Then I thought that in the future I'd go to college, but life got in the way.

Ali and his brothers built houses, that was their business, and so he built a little house for us outside Al-Quds, toward Ramallah.[1] It was right next to his family's house. I really loved being around the family. He was one of nine brothers and sisters, and they would all come over and have communal dinner together out of one big serving tray. They were very close, very loving, very welcoming.

If we were left alone by the Israeli soldiers, it would have been really nice. But it was always scary because they were everywhere. Ali couldn't travel to central Al-Quds to see relatives, or go to the souk, or the Al-Aq Mosque, because Israel prevents Palestinians with West Bank IDs from entering Jerusalem, even though it is in the West Bank. I could go with my American passport, but it basically meant that we weren't allowed to go out together in Al-Quds.

Then it got terrifying. One afternoon, as I was making tea after he came home from work, my sister-in-law came knocking frantically on the door, saying, "Hide Ali! Hide him!"

I said, "What do you mean 'hide him'?"

She said, "They're here, the soldiers are here!"

So I had to shove Ali into a closet and put big heavy blankets over him and hide him because the soldiers were ransacking my in-laws' house right next door. Ali and his brothers were not involved in political activity, but that's what the Israeli soldiers did to young men.

That really shook me, because being American, you don't have that sense of no recourse, like, who do you call? You can't call the police and tell them somebody's intruding, because the intruders are the army. They didn't find Ali that day, mercifully. But then it got really brutal to be there. One of his brothers was taken by the army and tortured.

Eventually, I found out through his mother that Ali was a survivor of torture. When he was sixteen, like many of the young boys in Palestine, he was kidnapped by Israeli soldiers, imprisoned, and brutally tortured for almost a year. He told me bits, but he didn't discuss it too much. What I admired was that he came out of it very pure-hearted, not bitter.

---

[1] A Palestinian city in the central West Bank.

He was still very strong in his faith.

But what happened with our kids actually brought it all back to him, so eventually, I learned all the ugliness.

A TASTE OF FREEDOM

When my visa expired after we got married, the Israeli government refused to allow me to stay in Palestine with my husband and new extended family. I wanted to bring Ali to America, to give him a taste of freedom and opportunity. To be able to just get in your car and drive wherever you want—he'd never experienced anything like that, and I really wanted to share that with him.

Some Palestinians wanted to leave, but with him it wasn't like that. I had to actually talk him into it. He wasn't really thrilled about the idea of coming to the States, because his whole family was still in Palestine. And that was kind of appealing to me too, to see that love for his family and love for his country, no matter how broken it was.

We came to an agreement that when things settled down there we could go back and forth. We wanted to raise our kids in the best of both worlds.

So in February 1992, we came back to the United States and we started our life here. Ali did very well adjusting, because he had a very positive attitude. What really struck me about him was that every single person he'd see outside he would say hello to, he'd have to greet them, and they'd say hello back.

It was nice being together in the United States. I had my first baby, Sana, in '94. That was the best feeling in the world. I really fell in love with being a mom, and I delighted in staying home with her. We had four more children: two girls, then a boy, then my youngest daughter. The last one was born in 2000.

In 1997, we moved to a beautiful beach town in southern Delaware. My husband started a business and we enjoyed our life at the beach. We were in a small enough community that people got to know us. On Ali's day off, I volunteered in the schools, tutoring kids and helping the teachers. The kids were assimilated, and my friends were of different cultures. Ali loved to cook, and we would often invite our friends and neighbors to our home for fabulous meals.

We were happy. It was the American Dream.

ON SHAKY GROUND

We heard about 9/11 on TV. It was shocking. It was devastating.

Thank God, my family in New York was safe, but we were in shock with the rest of the country. Ali and I were crying, but we tried to hide it from our kids. They were really young, so we didn't watch TV in front of them.

When it became clear that Arabs and Muslims were involved, it was terrifying for us. For the kids' sake, I shielded them from any kind of negative perception about themselves, and so they had really strong self-esteem.

The first couple of weeks after 9/11, I would say people's reactions were "polite hatred." People would see me in my hijab and give me the finger while I was driving. I'd be shopping, pushing the baby in the cart, and then I'd hear somebody loudly make a comment to somebody else about Afghanistan, terrorists, or whatever else.

This was totally new to me, because here we were in a lovely beach town, with our beautiful life, and you don't think that people are suddenly going to look at you like you're the enemy. That's how naïve I was.

I totally didn't anticipate people in our community having ugly reactions. I mainly thought that we had to turn off the TV in front of the kids and things would be fine.

I remember one time around Christmas, I was in a store with my daughter Zena. She was a year old and had beautiful Shirley Temple curls. Some woman was decked out in her Christmas gear, in her sweater and her jingle-jangle earrings, and she said to me, "It's a good thing you don't put a scarf on that baby's head. Don't do to that baby what your mother did to you, because that would be a shame."

She then went on a really illogical tirade about Osama bin Laden and how "you people come to this country and you're taking over."

That's when I knew we were really on shaky ground. Ali was shocked, but still optimistic.

RAMADAN CUPCAKES

Since my eldest, Sana, was in kindergarten, I'd been bringing in treats for her class every year at Ramadan.[2] My daughters would help me put together little treat bags and tie them with ribbon—I was a stay-at-home mom, that's what I did! I had time for that.

In 2001, Sana was in second grade, and that year Ramadan lasted from mid-November to mid-December. Sana's teacher invited me to talk to the kids about our holiday when I brought in treats for them.

I like to treat my kids equally, so if I was going to do this for Sana, I wanted to do it for my other daughter Layla, who was in first grade. Her teacher said it would be okay to just come in, and Layla and I could sing a song for Ramadan and then have cupcakes with all the kids.

So one night before school, in early December, the girls and I were baking our cupcakes. They had M&Ms in them—not exactly traditional Ramadan, but my girls like M&Ms and chocolate frosting. So the girls were putting together their treat bags when I got a phone call from a doctor in the community. His daughter was in the same class as Layla. His tone was very threatening, very ugly. He said, "I heard you're coming in to do some Ramadan presentation. I would advise you not to."

I said, "What are you talking about?"

"You should be aware that I speak not only for myself but for many parents at the school. We're telling you that this is not appropriate, and we don't want you to come in."

I said, "Didn't I just see your wife yesterday come into school for

---

[2] A holy month of the Islamic calendar that Muslims observe by fasting during daytime hours.

the Christmas activities? What are you talking about? What are you so afraid of? Let's talk."

He said, "Just like it would be wrong for a priest to come in and talk about the Bible and that stuff, it's wrong for you."

"You're equating me with a priest? I'm a mom, just like your wife is a mom who came in to do the Christmas activities. And they're doing that all month long! I don't understand why you're doing this."

As we talked more, I found out he was originally from Brooklyn, not from some small-minded community. It hurt, because he was a doctor, he was educated, and he should have known better.

I started crying and said, "Our daughters are six years old, and Layla is so excited about it; we just baked these cupcakes, and we are coming in tomorrow."

He hung up on me. Then he called back about ten minutes later and tried to intimidate me some more. He said, "I want to know what time you're going to come in."

I told him, "Excuse me, but if you speak to me in that tone I'm not going to talk to you anymore. If you'd like to come over, we can discuss this in a civil manner, but don't call me up and threaten me."

Then he said, "Well, there's the timing right now, you know, with 9/11. You should understand that this is a very sensitive issue."

I said, "No, I don't understand. What do my daughters have to do with 9/11?" The rest of the conversation didn't go well, and he didn't back off.

The next morning I got a call from Layla's teacher, asking me if I was still coming in the following day. She told me the doctor was there, and that he was really upset. Then she said, "There are also some other parents who don't want you to come in."

She wanted me to back off, but I told her I wasn't going to let my kids down. And I said, "I'd like to know, first of all, how did they know I was going to come in? What did you tell them to get them all riled up?"

Then I got a phone call from the principal, who said, "I know you're coming in, but I really have to know what you're going to say to the kids."

I said, "Okay, we're going to be singing a song that my mom wrote, and it has no mention of religion. I'm not going to bring up Islam, or the origin of the holiday. It's just, you know, 'this is our holiday and we made some treats.'"

She said, "Well, I just really needed to know, because he [the doctor] came in with a tape recorder, threatening to sue me if we allowed you to come in."

I just laughed and said, "Should I be bringing protection now? I mean, what should I expect?"

She said, "No, it'll be fine, just come in."

The next day, I went in. I did Sana's class first and it went beautifully. We sang the song. It was very sweet. It's just a sing song kind of a thing, like, "Ramadan helps us to think of the needy, so we don't become too greedy."

Then I went to Layla's class. The doctor wasn't there, but his daughter was. I was nervous. The teacher was cold, but she kept her mouth shut and she actually had other adults in there, sitting as an audience.

We just talked very briefly about Layla having a holiday that we wanted to share with everyone. We told the kids to remember that they were very lucky, because some people in the world don't have much of anything.

All I know is Layla's face was lit up, and that's what I tried to focus on. She was very happy, so that meant a lot, that she was able to share that.

The kids were really receptive and lovely. When they're six, they don't care. It's just a time to have cupcakes.

ANNIVERSARIES

On the 2002 anniversary of 9/11, our minivan's windshield was smashed while parked in front of our house. I noticed it when I took the kids to school. The windshield wiper was broken off, and a note was inserted. It said, "Get the fuck out of this country, you sandniggers."

I don't know who did it. I was very shaken, but the kids were oblivious to it. I took them to school that morning and I went straight to the principal. This was a new principal. I showed her the note and asked her to keep an eye on the kids. She said she would, so it was just a short conversation.

My husband at the time was overseas to visit his father, who was sick, but I let him know what happened. We thought maybe it was just some punk, some kid.

I also went to the police, who classified it as a misdemeanor, non-hate crime. I was so shaken that I didn't even bother pursuing it. I just wanted it on record that this happened.

That was an eye-opener. But we got the windshield fixed and the kids were fine, and that's all that mattered.

For Ramadan that year, the girls had really nice teachers and there was no problem with bringing in treats. I splurged and ordered Arabic pastries from New York City. The girls' teachers loved them, but the kids would have probably preferred cupcakes!

That year in school was okay.

OSAMA SANA

It was September 11, 2003. When I picked up the kids from school that afternoon, Sana collapsed in my arms, sobbing and crying. She was so emotional that I had to pull over to the side of the road. She asked me, "What does the Qur'an tell us about Christians, Mama? And why did Muslims do 9/11?"

Ali and I hadn't talked about 9/11 with the kids. They were so young that we'd avoided the topic.

I let her tell me what happened. She said her teacher, Mrs. C., had taught the class about 9/11 that day. She'd taught them that Muslims were bad, and that they were responsible for 9/11. She had described Palestinians as enemies of America. She'd also said that the Qur'an teaches Muslims to hate Christians, and that Muslims bomb Christians any chance they can get. During that class, one of the kids had said, "Well, Sana's mom is one of them" and then the kids had started hissing at her and calling her a terrorist. They'd called her names like "Osama Sana."

I was in disbelief. I had to hear from the principal. I wanted to hear that Sana had misunderstood, that this hadn't really happened. It was so hard to believe. It still is.

When we got home I called the principal about it. She said, "That doesn't sound like our curriculum. Let me talk to the teacher and I'll get back to you." So I asked her to please call me back right away because I needed help understanding what was going on. In the meantime, I comforted Sana the best I could. I told her it was ridiculous what she'd heard from the teacher, and that it wasn't true at all.

I sent Sana to school the next day. I called the principal again in the morning and waited for her to call me back. By 1:30 p.m. she still hadn't called, so I went to the school to see her. The receptionist told me the principal was out, so I said I'd wait. While I was sitting in the office waiting area, I saw Sana's teacher, Mrs. C., coming in to get her mail from the teachers' mailbox. I said to her, "Hey, are you busy? Do you have a free period? Can we talk?"

She said okay, and we went into her classroom to talk. When I asked her if the principal had talked to her, she said no. I said, "Really? Well, Sana came home in tears yesterday. Can you tell me what happened?"

She said, "I don't understand. What could you be talking about?"

I asked her about her class on 9/11 the day before, and she said, "Oh yeah, that's part of our curriculum this year. We have a book that the district ordered." Then she showed me the book. It was called *September 11, 2001*, a little paperback book by a textbook publishing company out of Texas called Steck-Vaughn.

The cover had a picture of the Twin Towers on fire. I thought it was a very traumatic image for fourth-graders; my daughter was only nine at the time. So I flipped through the book briefly and it was appalling. It was an indictment of Muslims and Arabs. But it wasn't just the book that was the problem, it was the teacher's comments that Sana had told me about. I asked her, "Well, did you say those things?"

She shrugged her shoulders. She didn't even deny it. Then, when I told her Sana was really upset, she got very defensive. She said, "Well, today we continued reading it, and your daughter didn't tell me she had a problem with it."

I was taken aback. I said, "So after she's called a terrorist, she's supposed to stand up and say, 'But it's not true'? You know that my daughter is Muslim and you know that this is a very sensitive issue. I'm just shocked."

She just put her palms up and said, "I didn't put the curriculum together. You have to go through the district." The book was actually taught in every fourth-grade classroom in each school in the district, not just ours.

I took the book home and read it. Then I wrote heartfelt letters to the principal, the teacher, and the superintendent, telling them how inaccurate and dangerous this book was.

In the meantime, I told Sana to just plug away, and that I'd take care of it. Some of the school kids continued to call her names, but she still had a good network of friends who were supportive. When you're nine, that's what matters. I thought she was doing fine.

The school district never responded to my letters. The principal never got back to me. Whenever I called her office, her secretary always told me she was out. They knew my voice.

So I let it go. I just got busy looking after my kids.

That year there were no Ramadan cupcakes. We didn't want to bring more attention to ourselves.

WE'RE GOING TO BURN IN HELLFIRE

The first week in December, Sana started getting sick. She was violently throwing up and having nightmares. She asked me if we were going to burn in hellfire. She'd become worried that God wouldn't love her because she's Muslim.

That week, Mrs. C. had taught them about the legend of the candy cane. She'd handed out candy canes and told the kids it was in the shape of a J for Jesus, and that the red stripes symbolized the blood of Jesus.

Then she told them things like, "The blood of Jesus will save us all if you believe."

Sana had started writing on Post-it notes little things that struck her about the candy cane. I have her little nine-year-old handwriting, just scribbling stuff, trying to sort it out for herself. She wasn't even sharing it all with me at first, she was so thoroughly confused and traumatized.

She said she didn't want to be a Muslim anymore; she didn't want to be any religion. And I said, "That's fine, you don't have to be any religion. You can figure that out when you're older. But you're still a child of God no matter what, and God loves you regardless."

By this time her personality had totally changed. She wasn't happy, and she didn't want to go to school anymore. She even wanted us to move away. She said the kids were still making fun of her. But she was still able to do some normal things, like go to the party of one of her best friends. I think it meant a lot to her that at least some of the kids still loved and accepted her.

It hurts as a mom to know that she suffered so much, especially because, oh my God, it was just so needless. That whole period was completely soul-crushing.

By this time, Ali had started to become distraught. He couldn't handle his kid's pain. It's a terrible helplessness, in the face of so much that your kid is going through.

*

After the Christmas break, Sana refused to go back to school. So I reached out to the ACLU[3] and Drew Fennell, the director of the Delaware chapter, drove down to Lewes Beach in January to meet with Sana's principal and Mrs. C. Drew was fantastic. She didn't come in gung-ho as a lawyer; she came in to try and facilitate a discussion. She brought them information on how to handle religion in a classroom and how to be sensitive, and how we can go from here.

---

[3] The American Civil Liberties Union, a civil rights organization that offers legal support.

During the meeting, the principal was pretty quiet, but Mrs. C. got really hostile. She said, "Your daughter should be removed from my classroom, since she obviously has issues."

So Drew asked her, "Well, is this in the curriculum, your Christmas lessons?"

Mrs. C. replied, "I taught them as legends. We discussed legends, just like we discuss Native American legends. The kids enjoy them and your daughter is the only one who takes issue with it."

Drew asked, "Well, how do we go from here though? Something needs to be said to this child who feels like she's gonna burn in Hell. There needs to be some sort of apology, something. You need to talk to her and make her feel valued."

Drew suggested presenting something about other religions to counter the anti-Muslim, the pro-Christian stuff, but Mrs. C. refused. She got very defensive and said, "Well, if you bring up Islam that would open up a can of worms."

She was angry that she'd been called into the meeting and she said, "I wasn't prepared." Then she left abruptly without saying goodbye, nothing. The principal said, "Okay, looks like we need to have some sort of discussion."

I emphasized to her that I didn't want Sana removed from the class. I said, "She did nothing wrong, and someone needs to tell her that, you need to tell her that."

The principal said, "Just send her back to school and I will make sure that Mrs. C. apologizes to her."

So in good faith I sent my daughter to school and I told her it was going to be fine. But the principal clearly did not talk to Mrs. C. Sana came home crying that day. She told me that her teacher had addressed her in front of the whole class and said, "So, your mother tells me that you're not comfortable in my classroom. I think you'd be more comfortable in a different classroom. Why didn't you come to me if you had problems? Why did you have to go and tell your mother?"

She was talking to her as if they had a peer relationship! Then the kids started taunting Sana, saying, "Yeah, loser Muslim! What are you doing here?"

Sana decided to stay because her best friend wrote her a little note, saying, "No, don't go, I'll miss you" with a little sad face and tears. Mrs. C. ignored Sana for the rest of the day.

When you have children, you want the best for them, naturally. You want them to thrive and you want them to be healthy. The worst thing is when nothing you do, nothing you say, no amount of comforting, no amount of hugs that you can give, no amount of your love can help them. You're just powerless. And when you send them to school, you expect these adults to take care of them, and when it doesn't happen, it's just so unbelievably crushing. In retrospect, I feel really guilty because I shouldn't have kept subjecting Sana to it. They gave me the first indication in September of what they were capable of, and I kept sending her back for more.

The next day I went in to see the principal and told her about what happened. I wanted to know why she hadn't followed through on her promise to make Mrs. C. apologize. But she just said, "I'm not going to do that. You got me in hot water. That teacher is upset that you brought in the ACLU, and that she didn't have her representative there."

So the principal twisted around now that she was in trouble.

I said, "Sana is over there in the waiting area, in tears. Do you have anything to say to her?"

She replied, "I have five hundred kids to deal with in this school. I don't have time for this." And she left.

When Sana showed up in class that day, the kids called her "loser Muslim," and followed her around calling her a terrorist. She had about four friends in the class at that point. The teacher totally ignored her, yet she was able to carry on.

A FRESH START

In February 2004, the ACLU contacted a lawyer for us. Her name was Lori. She had a meeting with the school district. She told them that somebody needed to go around to these kids who were verbally abusing Sana and let them know they needed to stop it. These kids needed to get their act together because we had been more than patient with them. The school district then assigned their director of curriculum to do an investigation.

After the meeting with the school district, Lori got very sick. Turns out she had a heart condition. She got pneumonia and was hospitalized. Then the school came back and said that the only thing that they could do was to put Sana in a new classroom and start fresh.

At that point, without Lori, I was just overwhelmed and I gave in. I let them put Sana in a new classroom.

The day she was moved to a new classroom, Sana went at lunch to say hi to her friends from her former classroom. They all started taunting her and making faces at her. All of them turned against her, because the talk in the school was that she was a "loser Muslim" who'd gotten kicked out of class. Even her best friend totally ignored her, turned the other way. One of the girls told Sana that her mom said she couldn't talk to her any more.

I got a phone call from the guidance counselor saying that Sana had broken down in the cafeteria. She said, "She's inconsolable, you should come." When I got there, she was quaking and sobbing really badly. That was probably the worst day that school year, because by then she was completely, totally broken.

I took her home and she went to bed, crying until the little vessels in her face burst. For the next few days, she didn't get out of bed.

At this point, the friends' mothers started ignoring me, as well as people I thought were my friends. I called them, but they didn't return my calls. I didn't have a support network, and it was a very, very lonely time. I was crying every day. I wasn't handling it very well. I felt powerless to help her.

My husband was really affected too. At that point, I started losing him too.

WE WERE SINKING

Ali was shutting down. He wasn't the same person I married. Seeing Sana like this precipitated his breakdown; it brought back the trauma that he'd gone through in Palestine. He was a mess.

What happened to Sana totally altered his whole way of relating to everybody. He told me I was foolish to think that these people would ever accept us.

He was not able to help. He was neglecting a lot of things. He was on the couch mostly, watching mindless TV.

During that time, Sana had a homeschool instructor, but she wasn't really able to do much except the basics. I was just happy she was able to get up and take a shower. That's how bad it was.

I got a letter from the principal saying that I was to have no more communication with anybody from the school except her. The guidance counselor was forbidden from talking to our family. Basically, the kids had nobody to go to. Fortunately, Layla had a good teacher at the time, and that made a difference. But her grades started slipping. When your whole family is affected, you're affected too.

We were sinking. We lost our business eventually because Ali couldn't do the most basic of things, let alone go to work. We couldn't keep it open any more. The day we shut it down, Ali just totally wanted to leave the country. He was adamant that we needed to get out and go back to Palestine.

Six months later, we lost our house too.

In April, our ACLU lawyer Lori got better, and we met for coffee. She was Jewish, and she told me she'd had a similar experience to ours growing up in a small town in Ohio. So what was happening to us meant a lot to her. We really bonded. She said, "We need to get Sana better and bring her over to my house so I can talk to her."

Then a couple of days later she died. She was driving home from getting ice cream and her heart just stopped. She was only forty-seven. Peace be upon her beautiful soul.

Ali said, "If that isn't a sign, I don't know what is."

He was grasping at anything to just leave. But what do you do? My whole sense of belonging anywhere at this point was shot. It was deeply traumatic.

After Lori died, the ACLU told us they couldn't find us another lawyer. I couldn't understand why no lawyers in the entire state of Delaware would take our case. Nobody wanted to help.

I felt really overwhelmed. I was looking for somebody to help us. I was getting all of these letters from the school district and from the principal, saying that my kids were not being bullied, and that any issues we had had nothing to do with the school but with the community. She was shifting the blame. There were also letters attacking me personally, saying that I was a troublemaker.

It was very difficult for me to sit down and type letters back and respond because I was trying to keep my family together.

In the spring of 2004, the Department of Justice (DOJ) became involved in Rima's case after a lawyer in D.C. heard about what was happening and referred the case to the Civil Rights Division, Educational Opportunities Section. They interviewed Rima and then conducted an investigation. The result was a settlement with the school district in 2005, which included sensitivity training and required the district to remove the 9/11 book. Rima was shut out of the negotiations with the district and did not find out about the DOJ settlement until after the fact.

ANOTHER SCHOOL DISTRICT

Ali wasn't able to comfort his kids at all. I struggled to get him into family therapy, but it was a disaster. The one time that he was able to go in and see the therapist was in May 2005, but he was so distant it was like he wasn't even there.

We finished up the school year with Sana still at home.

The money was all gone at this point. We were really struggling. My parents helped us out financially, but we had five kids, and it was really hard.

Even throughout the investigation by the Department of Justice, the school district didn't make one gesture to show that Sana could be safe there, that I could send her back the next school year. The things that they were saying about us and about Sana! They treated me like a criminal. They banned me and my girls from speaking with the guidance counselor at school. They prevented my girls from being able to have any kind of safe person that they could go to.

The lies, the cover-ups—it was disgusting. I decided we needed to go to another school district.

I wished we could move far, far away, but we didn't have resources to pick up and go and be able to provide for five kids. I was really hoping things would get better and we could resume our lives. Most importantly, Sana was in therapy with a very good therapist who was helping her. So we had to be able to stay near.

It was summer already, and I wasn't even thinking long term. The immediate goal was to get Sana healthy enough to be able to walk into a school. Just getting her to be able to do that would be a triumph.

The therapist went to a school with me down in Ocean View. I met with the principal and she seemed pretty receptive to us. She told me that Sana wouldn't have any issues in their school. That was the deciding factor.

So I rented a place there, and with a lot of therapy, Sana was able to go back to school. She still struggled with different things but it was amazing that she was even able to go back. She is remarkable.

Shortly before we moved, I went to the beach one day, really early in the morning. It had been a particularly bad night with Sana and her father: they had both been just awful. Sana was in bed, inconsolable. That day at school a kid had threatened to slit her throat in the school library. At the other end of the house, Ali was lying on the couch, catatonic. I had four other kids who were being ignored but they were at least in school.

So I went to the beach and I just cried my heart out for hours and hours. I don't even know how long I was there. And I asked God for some kind of help from somewhere.

That afternoon I came home and there was a message on my machine from a minister from the Episcopalian church in Lewes. He was a friend of Drew's from the ACLU. He reached out to me and ever since he's been an incredible moral support. I call him "Baba Mark" because he looks like Santa Claus and he's phenomenal with the kids. It's been important for them, to experience this benevolent side of Christians, because they have been on the receiving end of some really ugly, twisted stuff.

At that time I was still hoping and praying that Ali would agree to see a doctor and get better. I guess I was hoping that we could salvage something, but no, he refused. He got worse and worse.

Grudgingly, he physically came with us to Ocean View, but in 2005 he finally left.

I COULDN'T HELP HIM

Ali had moved down to Ocean View with us, so I kept holding out hope. He was kind of there but not there.

He had been saying for the past year that we just needed to leave. He kept equating what was happening to us to what Israelis do to Palestinians. I just thought this was naïve, stupid. I thought with medication, with something, he'd stabilize.

I couldn't help him. I was doing everything I could just to try and keep the kids whole.

He left for Palestine in July 2005. The day he left, things got really ugly. He was yelling and he tore up our wedding picture. I put the kids in the car to try and spare them. I didn't know what he was going to say, and I didn't want to damage them any more.

That day I think it finally sunk in that it was final.

He packed a few things. He didn't care about clothes, but he packed his papers, his passport, his birth certificate. Then he kissed the kids goodbye. They were crying because they understood that he was leaving.

He left us in July 2005. Following Ali to Palestine is impossible for the kids and me. The Israelis would never allow us to stay because we are not Jewish. Either they would turn us away at the border, or they would issue a three-month visa. After the visa expired, we would be considered illegal trespassers and we would be expelled.

The day after he left, I cried for half the day. Finally I said to myself, "Okay, now I need to be practical and find a job," so I started pounding the pavement looking for work. I was getting sick from stress and so I went to my doctor and told her I was feeling on the verge of a breakdown. Then I fell apart in her office, and she offered me a job right there, as a caregiver for geriatrics. It was exactly what I needed at that moment. She was a real caretaker. She gave me hope.

YOUR PROPHET IS A KILLER

Sana completed elementary school and went on to start seventh grade at a magnet art middle school in Selbyville, Delaware. Rima hoped that the focus on the arts meant that the school was "very liberal and open." However, when the school started teaching the Renaissance across all subjects, teachers and students connected the crusades with the Iraq war and non-Christians. As a result, Sana once again suffered from bullying and discrimination. She did not complete her school year at the magnet school, and ended up enrolling in the regular middle school, also in Selbyville.

When Sana started eighth grade, Layla was in seventh grade. Layla's teacher, I don't even know how to describe him. His name is Mr. B., and he's a social studies teacher. I had heard from a Jewish family that I needed to watch out for him, and that he taught a 9/11 lesson every year. So the day before September 11, I called him and asked him if he planned to do anything for 9/11. He said, "Yeah, I'm doing a week-long lesson."

God help us, a week long lesson on 9/11?! So I asked him what he taught the kids for a week, and he said he taught the origin of 9/11 and the ramifications. He said, "It goes back thousands of years to the time of Abraham and Abraham's sons. We talk about the religious wars that go back thousands of years. And they all lead up to 9/11."

I asked him, "Are you aware that Layla is a Muslim?"

He replied, "She can contribute what she wants to the discussion."

It was déjà vu. I said, "She's not going to be subjected to this. Is there any way we can meet about this before you do the lesson?"

"Actually, no," he said. "I've prepared this, and I've been teaching it for six years. The district knows, it's not a secret. If she wants, she can opt out of the lesson."

So I opted Layla out, and she didn't go to school for that week.

In November, I asked a friend, Reverend Kerry, a Presbyterian minister in our town, to accompany me to a meeting with Mr. B. and the principal. I asked Mr. B. to explain exactly what he taught, and where he got his information from.

He said, "Well, it's all over the internet. These are reputable sources on the internet and its common knowledge that the religious hatred goes way back."

Reverend Kerry, thank God, was pretty neat. He said, "Actually that's not my understanding. It's very alarming if this is what you are teaching in the classroom. It's not appropriate."

I said, "Our greeting when we see people is *assalamu alaikum*, 'peace be upon you,' because this is our essence. That's what this child's essence is. So when you're propagandizing, telling this classroom full of impressionable minds that the origin goes back thousands of years, and it's the heathen brother versus the righteous brother, and all that 'sons of Abraham' stuff, it's very dangerous and inaccurate."

Mr. B. said, "Well, you know you could have come in and presented your piece, but you chose not to. My understanding is your prophet is a killer and a marauder."

Reverend Kerry said, "What are you talking about? Where do you get this? And even if that is your personal belief, you have no right saying that to your students and parents! I mean, this is her religion."

What was especially troubling was that Mr. B. also said, "I am very open to hearing what you have to say. If you want to attack Jesus, you can do it right now."

During the meeting, the principal was hands-off. He really didn't say much, even though he knew what Sana had gone through before, what our family had gone through.

So I pulled Sana and Layla out of the middle school for the rest of the school year and I home-schooled them the best I could. But I was working two jobs and going to school myself, so they got cheated out of a decent education.

TRYING TO MOVE ON

Sana is in eleventh grade and Layla's in tenth grade now. Time really flies! They're taller than me now. They are pretty remarkable young ladies. I also have two in middle school, but I put my foot down and told the school that we didn't want that social studies teacher Mr. B. Thank God they accepted that.

To some extent, high school has been better than middle school. Sana has a couple of friends. I wouldn't say she's happy. She's just plugging away.

The fact that the girls are more mature means that they're able to cope better with things that happen. I hate to say it, but they have become accustomed to some of those things, like being portrayed in a negative light because of the wars in Iraq and Afghanistan. In our area particularly, there are a lot of families and teachers who have a loved one deployed or know someone who has gone to Iraq or Afghanistan, and so that's their frame of reference. For a while the kids asked why this was happening to us. And that's the hardest thing, not knowing what to tell them or how to help them.

I guess maybe the girls kind of expect it now; they're no longer caught by surprise, but it still hurts.

Unfortunately, I have heard it said that people feel that, as Americans, we are at war with Arabs and Muslims. There are people who genuinely feel like we are the enemy.

I don't know where to place that fault. I don't want to get swallowed up into the bitterness and the blaming. I just think, things happened, and I'm trying my best for the kids' sake to be positive and to move on. I hope the kids are able to be happy one day and, you know, just be like everybody else and not have to worry all the time about how they are perceived.

I am increasingly tired of labels. I'm tired of divisions. I'm tired of the "us and them."

I don't even know that I would call myself religious now. I know I have deep faith in God and I identify as Muslim, but the only label I'd put on myself is "human being." That's what I wrote on the census form under "race." I refuse to be boxed in anywhere.

GURWINDER SINGH

AGE: *18*
OCCUPATION: *college student*
INTERVIEWED IN: *Queens, New York*

An integral part of the Sikh religion involves never cutting one's hair and wearing a turban. For Sikh children in school, this exterior appearance of their religion, along with their ethnicity, makes them targets for bullying. After 9/11, harassment towards Sikh students has additionally reflected the misidentification of Sikhs as terrorists, and has been manifested through physical abuse, verbal threats of violence, and derogatory name-calling such as "terrorist" and "Bin Laden." In 2006, the Sikh Coalition conducted a survey that involved 439 Sikh students under eighteen years old in New York City. Over half of NYC students said they had been bullied. For every three out of five students who wear a turban, harassment occurs daily. Additional surveys conducted by the Sikh Coalition in New York (2006) and the Bay Area (2010) have reflected a lack of response from teachers and school administration regarding these incidents. In New York in 2008, a policy called Respect for All *was implemented in an attempt to address the school system's inadequate handling of bias-based bullying. A 2009/10 report compiled by the New York Civil Liberties Union, the Asian American Legal Defense and Education Fund and the Sikh Coalition showed that only 14.3% of teachers surveyed believed the* Respect for All *program was effective, with others citing a lack of information about the program and no training or resources at their disposal.*

Gurwinder has experienced bias-based bullying first-hand. In February 2011, he met with us at his family home in Queens. He spoke slowly and thoughtfully, mining his memory of his encounters with harassment and bullying during his childhood. Our interview was the first time Gurwinder had spoken about many of these experiences. A few weeks after our meeting, he spoke at the White House Conference on Bullying Prevention.

I haven't told anyone some of these stories until now. I feel relieved, because I think it's good to share what I've kept in the dark. People should know how Sikh kids are bullied. I went through a lot, and now I want my life to be peaceful.

THEY CALLED ME "TERRORIST"

I was born on October 21, 1992. When I was two, my parents moved from Hoshiarpur in Punjab, India to New York. I grew up in Richmond Hill in Queens, and I have lived in New York my whole life.

Ever since I can remember, I've gone through so much. It started when I was really young. It wasn't exactly bullying—that started in elementary school. But the other kids didn't like me very much. I couldn't get along with them, because my joora[1] made me look different. They used to walk away from me, or if I said something to them, they wouldn't reply.

When I got to elementary school, other students would call me Egg Head. Or they would ask me stupid questions, like, "What's inside there? Is it a potato?" I was really slow in the way I spoke, and I'm still kind of slow, so they would make fun of me when I tried to say something back. This would happen in class, but the teachers wouldn't do much.

Sometimes my mom would come to school to defend me, but she had trouble helping me because she couldn't speak English properly. I

---

[1] The name for the bun of hair tied at the top of a male Sikh's head, often covered with a turban.

felt really lonely, but it just became part of my life.

*

When 9/11 happened, I was eight years old. I was in the cafeteria, and I saw the mother of a student run in, looking really frightened. She said, "Come with me! We have to get out of this place!" I said, "What is going on?"

I was confused. I just stood there. A few minutes later, the teachers and school security guards escorted all the kids out of the cafeteria and told us to go home.

When I got home, I saw a plane going through buildings on TV, and then I saw them collapsing. I thought, *What's going to happen?* I was scared that they would bomb again, or attack my area. They were showing pictures of bin Laden, which made me even more scared. I thought he was a monster.

After 9/11, things got worse. Kids called me names, and they would ask me questions like, "Are you related to Osama bin Laden?" "Is Osama bin Laden your uncle?"

They called me a terrorist, or a terrorist's son. The kids on the bus looked at me with fear, so I tried to avoid looking at them as much as I could. I would just hide myself.

One time on the bus ride home, an African-American kid pulled my patka[2] off my hair. I couldn't do anything; I was helpless. No one was there to stand up for me. I didn't know how to stand up for myself either. I had to walk home with my patka off, and my joora open, and it was very embarrassing. I was crying, wondering what I could do. My mom used to be the one who did my joora, so I didn't know how to do it myself.

Every time I got on the bus after that, I wondered, *Will it happen again?* Anytime I saw someone who might pick a fight, I got anxious. I wouldn't look at them at all. I just tried to disappear.

---

[2] A small head covering wrapped around a young Sikh's joora, or bun.

EVERY DAY WOULD BE THE SAME DAY FOR ME

My school was very diverse. There were Latino, African American, Asian American and South Asian American kids. It was also pretty dangerous. There were gangs, and I saw cops in our neighborhood a lot.

Sometimes I saw other Sikh kids getting picked on at school. I felt really bad, because I wanted to help them, but usually I didn't do anything. I had to look after myself. Whenever I could help, the kids I helped would avoid me. They would tell me, "Just stay away." I think it's probably because they were going through problems too. All of us were going through it.

Another time, a kid in class came up from behind me and started hitting me. I fell down and I was surrounded. There were six other kids with him, and they got me on the floor and started stomping on my arms and my back. They hit me in the head too. It really hurt. I wasn't able to defend myself, because there were so many of them. The whole time they were cursing at me, using vulgar language.

I never told my parents any of this. My dad drives a taxi, and my mom is a housewife. They weren't educated much. My dad went up to fourth grade, and my mom went up to tenth grade in India, and that's all.

I don't know why I didn't tell them anything. I wanted to keep it to myself. I just thought, *Tomorrow will be a new day*. But every day would be the same day for me.

Half the time, they picked on me for the way I looked. The rest of the time, they picked on me because of my religion. It really hurt. When I was attacked, I was angry. But when they called me names, I felt lonely. They would just get away with things, and I felt so helpless. They were very clever. I wasn't.

A TREE WITHOUT LEAVES

In 2003, in the summer before middle school, I came home one day and told my dad, "I want to cut my hair." I was ten years old.

My dad kept asking, "Are you sure? It's very bad to cut it because of our religion."

I told him again, "I want to cut my hair." I had made my decision. I didn't want to look different from everyone else.

Finally, my dad took me to the barber shop, and they cut my hair. I couldn't look at myself in the mirror. I just saw hair falling off. I thought of leaves falling from a tree, and a tree doesn't look good without leaves. The leaves make it look more beautiful.

My mom was the one who used to comb my hair every morning, wash my hair, put oil on my hair, and braid my hair. She was shocked and sad to see how different I looked. She said, "I worked so hard to grow your hair, and you just cut it off."

When I had my hair cut, I didn't feel as bad about it as I did later, when I was exposed to Sikhism more and I learned that cutting your hair is disrespecting your religion. When you're baptized, the Five Beloved Ones[3] tell you that you are not supposed to cut your hair. That's part of your five Kakkars, your five sacred symbols.[4] Now I know it was the wrong decision, but at the time I was forced by the way people treated me.

After I cut my hair, I started acting differently. All the bullying had changed me, and I guess I started acting like the kids who bullied me. I turned into one of them. I was rude and mean to other people. I was becoming a bad person.

I started hanging around with bad kids. They would ask me, "Do you want to smoke?" I would tell them no, but sometimes I wondered, *Should I be in a gang? Should I join them?*

I came close, but thank God, I didn't join a gang or ever take drugs. I think I didn't do it because I asked myself, *How will this impact my par-*

---

[3] A group of five people, representative of the Five Beloved Ones of Sikh history, who administer Sikh baptism rites.

[4] One of the five articles of faith, Kesh, is uncut hair, usually tied and wrapped in the Sikh turban.

ents? I knew it was bad. Still, all of this started affecting my schoolwork. I no longer had any interest at all in reading, writing, or studying.

The fights didn't stop after I cut my hair. One time in seventh grade, I had to squeeze in the cafeteria lunch line, because the whole line was smooshed. Someone pushed me from behind. It was a Punjabi Sikh kid who used to hang around with the bad kids. The kid had a joora. He got really mad at me for having cut my hair, and he started striking and punching my face. I thought, *He's a Punjabi kid and now he's treating me like this?* I started bleeding from my nose, and then everything went blurry and I fainted.

The next thing I knew, the deans came and took both of us inside their office. The deans didn't listen to me at all when I told them I hadn't done anything. They said, "It takes two people to fight," and they suspended both of us.

THIS TIME I HAD STRENGTH

My life was so boring in middle school. I didn't do anything except go to school, get yelled at by someone, get bullied, go home, and go to sleep. I was really lonely.

Then in eighth grade, when I was thirteen, I met a friend at school called Nishaan. He told me about music classes taught by Bhai Surjeet Singh, a great musician at the gurdwara.[5] I went to the gurdwara and saw the whole group singing and playing on different instruments. I thought, *I should get involved too!*

So I started going to the gurdwara after school to learn to play the tabla.[6] At first, I still behaved the same way as before. The bad things that had happened in my past were still part of my life. I tried to forget them, but I couldn't. But slowly, as more time passed, I started

---

[5] A Sikh house of worship, which often also acts as a community center.

[6] A small drum, or percussion instrument, often used in Sikh prayer services.

changing. I felt really energetic when I played the tabla, and I liked the beats. So I started going to the gurdwara a lot more. I became very interested in everything there, and began to talk with people, and it made me feel better.

I went to the gurdwara in the morning to do paath[7] and help with prakash.[8] I also got my parents involved in the gurdwara. My mom became a vegetarian and started doing paath too.

I also learned more about our religion, *Sikhi*, and how much our gurus had to sacrifice for our religion to live on. Sikh martyrs were killed brutally for their beliefs, and they would not let anyone touch their hair. They would say, "You can cut my skin off. You can cut my head off. But not my hair."

I became really calm, and started respecting myself as a Sikh. Eventually I decided to take amrit.[9] I thought, *If I take amrit, God will help me. Maybe there will be a change in my life. Maybe I will be free.*

So I started growing my hair again. This time, I had strength, so I could put up with the bullying.

*

In my last year of middle school, my hair was growing back, and I started to look different again. I used to be friends with this one Hispanic kid. We used to meet each other in the cafeteria. But after I started growing my hair back, he started looking at me differently, and he would avoid me. I would ask him, "What's up?" and he would say, "I don't know you."

One day, he got into a fight with me in class. The teacher went out for a moment, and he threw something at me, maybe a pencil. I got up and turned around and asked him, "Why did you throw this at me?" He

---

[7] The daily prayer or reading of Sikh religious texts.

[8] A daily morning religious ceremony.

[9] A Sikh initiation ceremony, wherein a young Sikh will take religious vows and affirm a commitment to Sikhism.

just got up and started cursing at me and said, "Do you want to fight?"

I said no, but he came up to me, all the students gathered around both of us, and he started hitting me. He tried to punch me, so I put him in a headlock for twenty seconds to stop him. When I let him go, he started really punching me, so I started punching him too. Then the security guard came and took us into the dean's office.

When no one was looking, the kid said, "I'm going to get you outside school. Watch your back." My heart was beating fast. I knew something was going to happen, so after school, I took off running. When I was about three or four minutes away, I slowed down, turned, and started walking to the subway station. Behind me, I saw the Hispanic kid with a group. They were all behind me. I got scared and I couldn't do anything. I told him, "I'm sorry, I'm sorry."

I tried to ask people for help, but nobody came to help me. The kids behind him were big and seemed to be gang-affiliated. Some of them had flags that looked like they represented gangs, and they wore these flags around their heads like bandanas, or stuffed them in their back pockets.

I don't know what happened, but the Hispanic kid took my head and banged it into a metal pole. I just collapsed, and then all of them ran away. When I got up, my head was throbbing and bleeding.

By the time I got to the subway station, everyone was staring at me. I just wanted to get out of there as soon as possible and get home. I was so scared. I was crying and running and I didn't know what to do.

I wanted to go back to the dean's office, but I didn't go because I was intimidated by those kids. If I told the dean, the kid would be suspended, and then when he came back, he would pick another fight. I just wanted to leave everything alone, so I never told my parents. I've never told anyone until now.

I just kept going to gurdwara and it made me stronger. I started being strategic and thinking of different ways to avoid bullying. One of my strategies was to ignore them, to just forget what they say. They can call me whatever they want. I know who I am.

MAYBE THERE WILL BE A
SIKH PRESIDENT ONE DAY

In high school, I learned how to make friends. I was never good at communicating; I didn't know how to start off a conversation, and I'm still a bad talker today. But when I was sixteen, I just started talking to people, asking them questions. And it worked.

People still stared at me in high school. There were times when kids still called me "terrorist" and harassed me. One time in biology class, I accidentally bumped a girl's desk and her Arizona juice bottle spilled all over her. I said, "Oh my god, I'm really sorry." When I was getting tissues to clean it up, she came behind me and dumped the rest of the bottle all over my turban. My turban was wet for the rest of the day, and I felt so embarrassed. I thought, *I don't want to go through this again.*

But there were good moments too. I remember the day Barack Obama was elected president. Many of the kids at the school are African-American kids, and I had a U.S. history teacher who's also African-American. On that day, she was so happy she was crying. I saw that it was really different having an African-American president. I thought, *Maybe one day, there will be a Sikh president too.* Kids like me can't be president because I was born in India. But one day, there will be a Sikh president.

I WANT BULLYING TO END

Now I'm eighteen, in college, and I have good friends. I haven't been involved in much in my life, so I don't know what to do after college. But I still play tabla and now I'm an advanced player.

These days, I travel to Long Island to get to college every day. People at the train station stare at me, and sometimes they say things about 9/11, like, "That guy has a bomb." I always think, *What? Still? You still don't know what it's like to be us!?* But now I have tricks. I breathe deeply. I walk away. I keep myself away from the situation. I wait for the train.

If 9/11 hadn't happened, people wouldn't call me these names. They wouldn't think of me as a dangerous person. People would see a Sikh standing in front of them as just an ordinary person. They wouldn't be afraid and have bad thoughts pop up in their mind. They would respect our religion and respect the way we look. They would respect us.

Now that I'm older, I want to help Sikh kids. I don't want them to go through what I went through. I want to tell other kids that they shouldn't be afraid. If they are afraid, they should tell people. Now we have all of these organizations, like the Sikh Coalition, that are here to help them. I want to tell them: Don't give up. Look back in our Sikh history, how much we've been through, and gain strength from that.

I want to use my life to help end discrimination. Everyone should live in peace, whether they are Sikh or Muslim or Hindu. I want bullying to end.

I AM NOT ALONE

I just came back from the White House, where my mother and I attended the Conference on Bullying Prevention. When I arrived in Washington, D.C., I was very anxious about the meetings that were scheduled. At those times Tejpreet Kaur, the community organizer for the Sikh Coalition, kept me focused. All the way from New York to Washington, D.C., I was treated like a little brother by Tejpreet. She is a very benevolent human being. One thing I learned from her was to anticipate and think that there will always be a "next time."

First, I went to the Department of Education and met with the Asian Pacific Islander Movement (API). They interviewed me and asked me some questions in English and Punjabi about my personal experiences. Afterward, we settled down in a hotel, where I met a man called Rajdeep Singh. He works for the Sikh Coalition, and he helps pass laws and policies that help Sikhs.

The next day, we met Bryan Jung, Director of Special Projects for the Office of Public Engagement and Intergovernmental Affairs, who escorted us into the White House. He was very nice. He treated us like close friends and even gave us his number in case we got lost. Before the conference, we toured the White House. I went into the conference hall, and everything looked luxurious; I was astounded by its architecture. As we entered the main room where the conference was scheduled, we saw tons of photographers and news reporters. Once we were seated, First Lady Michelle Obama spoke, and then President Barack Obama spoke. I always used to watch President Obama on television, and I never thought I would see him in the White House. It was unbelievable! They were very supportive in their speech. With the help of the president and others, they launched a website (stopbullying.gov) that was created to support families and individuals currently experiencing these situations, including bullying and cyber-bullying.

I spoke after the conference. Speakers were divided into groups, and I was in the in-school policy group. We exchanged experiences, talked about obstacles we faced, and also solutions. After that, we went to the other hall for the closing. A few people came on stage and shared their experiences on bullying. There was one girl who talked about her brother who was bullied in school. He committed suicide, and it was very devastating to everyone. I heard about many people who had committed suicide from cyber-bullying and other forms of bullying. There were times when I was also helpless and couldn't do anything. But being at the White House with these people made me feel hopeful. It made me feel like I wasn't alone.

My mother was the happiest person there. She has always supported me during the bad times, and it was great to see her smiling. This experience meant a lot to my family, and I have learned a lot and hope to continue this work. I hope to participate in more events like this. I am prepared to contribute as much help as I can toward our Sikh community and let them know that there is hope and help available. I have a long way to go, but there is no limit for doing good things, there is no limit for eradicating bad things, and there is no limit for trying.

KHALED EL-MASRI

AGE: *48*
OCCUPATION: *former truck driver
and car salesman*

On New Year's Eve 2003, Khaled el-Masri was seized at the border of Serbia and Macedonia by Macedonian police who mistakenly believed that he was traveling on a false German passport. He was detained for over three weeks before being handed over to the CIA and rendered to Afghanistan.

Shortly after Khaled's release from Afghanistan, staff within both the CIA and the United States State Department reported the mistaken identity of their detainee to senior personnel, and German prosecutors issued arrest warrants for thirteen CIA agents allegedly involved in Khaled's abduction. However, cables disclosed by WikiLeaks[1] reveal that United States officials heavily pressured Germany to abandon the case. A February 2007 cable quoted the deputy United States Chief of Mission in Berlin as advising a German diplomat to "weigh carefully at every step of the way the implications for relations with the United States" if the agents were prosecuted. The German government withdrew the warrants five months later. The CIA analyst who advocated Khaled's abduction and argued against his release has since been promoted to run the agency's al-Qaeda unit.

---

[1] A non-profit organization that publishes private and classified media submitted from anonymous sources. In 2010, they released a number of cables by United States diplomats.

Currently incarcerated in Germany, Khaled has stopped speaking about his experiences. The narrative below is drawn from sworn and published statements Khaled made in the past.

My story is well known. It has been described in literally hundreds of newspaper articles and television news programs, many of them relying on sources within the U.S. government. It has been the subject of numerous investigations and reports by intergovernmental bodies, including the European Parliament. Most recently, prosecutors in my own country of Germany are pursuing indictments against thirteen CIA agents and contractors for their role in my kidnapping, abuse and detention. Although I never could have imagined it, and certainly never wished it, I have become the public face of the CIA's "extraordinary rendition" program.[2]

I HAD TO LEAVE TO GET MY HEAD TOGETHER

I was born in Kuwait on June 29, 1963. Both of my parents are Lebanese. I fled Lebanon in 1985 during the civil war and sought asylum in Germany. Before my asylum application was processed, I married my first wife, a German citizen. We lived together for ten years and were married for seven.

In 1995, I renounced my Lebanese citizenship, acquired by virtue of the nationality of my parents, and took up German citizenship. After my first marriage ended in divorce, I re-married in 1996. My second wife is Lebanese. Together we have four young children, ages three, five, seven, and eight years old, and a baby of seven months.

I trained as a carpenter when I first came to Germany. I then began working as a truck driver and subsequently as a car salesman. Around late 2003 and early 2004, I was made redundant from the car dealership. Since then I have been continuously unemployed and dependent on

---

[2] A covert United States program in which suspects are abducted and transferred without due process or trial to CIA "black sites," or detention centers of other nations, including those known to torture detainees. For more details, see the glossary.

unemployment assistance.

In the last few months of 2003, my wife and I had been experiencing marital problems. These problems were made worse by our living conditions. At this point I was unemployed and was living together with my wife and four young children in a one-room apartment. By December of that year, things had gotten so bad that I felt I just had to leave home for a while to get my head together.

I decided to travel to Macedonia. ADAC (a German automobile club, similar to AAA in the United States) informed me that the cost of living there was inexpensive and that hotel rooms were easy and cheap to come by.

On December 30, 2003, I purchased a round-trip bus ticket from Ulm to Skopje.[3] When I purchased the ticket, I had no set plans as to how long I was going to stay there, but I planned on remaining for at least a week before returning home again.

*

The bus left Ulm as scheduled on December 30. We traveled without incident through Germany, Austria, Slovenia, Croatia, and Serbia.

Around 3:00 p.m. on December 31, 2003, the bus arrived at the border between Serbia and Macedonia. As with all other border crossings we made during the trip, at the checkpoint the bus driver collected all the passengers' passports, mine included, to take to the border police for examination. After our papers were checked, everyone, except me, had their passport returned to them. The bus driver approached me and asked me to get off the bus and meet with the border official.

The official asked me a few routine questions. First he asked where exactly I was going to stay in Macedonia. I replied that I intended to find a hotel once I arrived, and that I had no specific one in mind. He

---

[3] Capital city of the Republic of Macedonia.

then asked me about the purpose of my stay in Macedonia. I said I was on a tourist trip and had planned to stay for about a week. As I did not speak any Macedonian, a fellow traveler translated for me and for the border official.

The official said that there was a problem with my passport, and resolving it might take some time. He suggested that I remain behind and let the bus continue on. He said that after we had resolved the passport issue, he would drop me off at a hotel in Skopje. The bus drove on without me. I had to then hang around waiting until about 6:00 p.m.

At this time I was taken to a narrow room, about eight meters from the border station. The room had a door and a big glass window facing the street where cars drove by. In the room there was a table, a desk, and a chair. I sat down on the chair with my back to the glass window. The official did not allow me to turn around. He also told me to put every item I carried with me on the table.

Afterward, he searched everything thoroughly. Once he had completed the search, a young man appeared. After an hour-long interrogation, another man turned up. He started a second interrogation, mentioning Islamic organizations and groups and asking whether I knew any of them. I said that I had heard of most of them. He then asked if I had anything to do with any of them. I replied that I had no involvement or even contact with any of them. He continued to question me about Ulm, asking me if there were any mosques in the area near where I lived, how many people attended their services, what nationalities they were, and if I had ever invited someone to Islamic activities at the mosque or if someone had ever invited me to them. I answered no to all these questions.

I was asked if there were any other activities in mosques apart from Friday services, and if I knew of any non-Muslims who had converted to Islam. He offered me alcohol, presumably to test whether I drank alcohol. I declined. He asked me if I prayed or fasted. I replied, "Sometimes."

The interrogation ended around 10:00 p.m. By this stage, some of the officers had gotten drunk; in less than two hours, the New Year would begin.

I was eventually taken out of the office and led on to the road leading toward Serbia. I saw three vehicles there, all without license plates. It was very dark and the fog was thick. The streets and the border station were deserted. My escorts were all dressed in plain clothes and were armed with guns. On our way, we saw a police barricade. We were allowed to pass quickly through it without stopping when my escort turned on a blue signal light.

A NEW YEAR

In Skopje, I was taken to a hotel. I subsequently discovered the name of the hotel: the Skopski Merak.

My escorts quickly walked me inside the hotel and over to the elevator. We exited on the top floor and walked into the room located opposite the elevator.

Three of my escorts remained with me. They locked the door. I asked them why they didn't leave. They said that they were going to be staying with me even when I was sleeping. I thought they just wanted to accompany me to my hotel and then leave me there, as they said they would when I was detained at the border.

I asked them if I was under arrest and they said that I wasn't, asking me if I saw any handcuffs on my wrists. They carried out another search of all my belongings. After this, three of them began interrogating me again. These interrogations were conducted in English, despite the fact that I have only a very basic grasp of the language. The three men asked many questions all at once, speaking at me and firing questions from all sides of the room. The interrogation lasted until at least 3:00 a.m. the next morning.

The men conducted similar such interrogations for the next three days. They observed my every move at all times. Even when I went to the toilet they asked me to leave the door open, although it was located in the same room where I was staying. When I was exhausted and tired of answering their questions, and after having been locked in this hotel room all this time, I demanded a translator. Then I asked to call the German embassy, a lawyer, and my family. All my requests were refused.

At one point I became so angry that I demanded to be released and attempted to leave the room by force. During this particular incident, we all raised our voices, each of us speaking in our own language. Communication was clearly impossible. One of the men pulled out his firearm and held it level with my head. The other two placed their hands on their holsters in a threatening manner.

*

The watch was divided between nine men; they changed shifts every six hours. On the fifth day, a man with a bag appeared. He had sheets of paper and fingerprint ink. He also had a camera and took a few photographs of me: right profile, left profile, and then frontal.

After about seven days, another official turned up. He appeared to be of a much higher rank than any of my guards. He brought an assistant with him. He was very respectful. He asked me about my condition and how the food was. He told me that I could order food from any restaurant if I didn't like the food that was being served. He also asked if the guards had treated me well. I thanked him and said that so far I was fine. He then told me that he wanted to and could end my current situation, and that he had a deal to offer me.

I asked him what kind of a deal. He replied that if I admitted that I belonged to the al-Qaeda organization they would send me back to Germany with a police escort. I refused and he subsequently left.

Two or three days later, his assistant showed up again and presented me with a list of allegations. He told me that he was certain that these allegations were true. He added that, based on these allegations, the case against me was no longer within their control, and that it had been referred to the Macedonian president. He said that the president had made a decision regarding my continued detention.

I was surprised by this turn of events and asked again to meet with the German ambassador or any other German authority. He told me that the German government did not want anything to do with me, and that I was wanted by them as well. One of the specific allegations against me was that my passport did not belong to me, and that I was wanted by both the Egyptian and German governments because I had been seen in Jalalabad, Afghanistan. After presenting me with these allegations, he left.

On the thirteenth day after my seizure, I began a hunger strike to protest my situation. A week later, I was told they would soon send me to the airport to fly me back to Germany. I did not eat again for the remaining ten days of detention in Macedonia.

At around 8:00 p.m. on the twenty-third day of my captivity, January 23, 2004, a video recording was taken of me. I was instructed to state my full name, that I had been treated well, and that I would shortly be flown back to Germany. I was then accompanied out of the hotel. Once outside, two men approached me. They grabbed hold of my arms and a third man then handcuffed and blindfolded me.

Before being blindfolded, I saw a white minivan, and in front of it, a black jeep. I also saw many people in plain clothes waiting around. I was placed in the jeep and it drove off.

THE MOST DEGRADING AND SHAMEFUL ACT

After about half an hour, the vehicle came to a halt. I was taken out of the vehicle and made to sit down on a chair, where I sat for about another one and a half hours. At this point, I heard the voice of the assistant who had come to see me with the high-ranking official. I was told that I would soon be taken into a room for a medical examination before being returned to Germany.

As I was led into this room, I felt two people violently grab my arms, one from the right side and the other from the left. They bent both my arms backward. This violent motion caused me a lot of pain. I was beaten severely from all sides. I then felt someone else grab my head with both hands so I was unable to move. Others sliced my clothes off. I was left in my underwear. Even this they attempted to take off. I tried to resist at first, shouting out loudly for them to stop, but my efforts were in vain. The pain from the beatings was severe. I was terrified and utterly humiliated. My assailants continued to beat me, and finally they stripped me completely naked and threw me to the ground. My assailants pulled my arms back and I felt a boot in the small of my back.

I then felt a stick or some other hard object being forced in my anus. I realized I was being sodomized. Of all the acts these men perpetrated against me, this was the most degrading and shameful.

I was then pulled to my feet and pushed into the corner of a room. My feet were tied together, and then, for the first time since the hotel, they took off my blindfold. As soon as it was removed, a very bright flashlight went off and I was temporarily blinded. I believe from the sounds that they had taken photographs of me throughout.

When I regained my vision, I saw seven to eight men standing around me, all dressed in black, with hoods and black gloves.

I was dressed in a diaper, over which they fitted a dark blue sports suit with short sleeves and legs. I was once again blindfolded, my ears were plugged with cotton, and headphones were placed over my ears. A bag was placed over my head and a belt around my waist. My hands were chained to the belt. They put something hard over my nose. Because of the bag, breathing was getting harder and harder for me. I struggled for breath and began to panic. I pictured myself like the images I had seen in the media of the Muslims that were brought to Guantánamo.

They bent me over, forcing my head down, and then hurried with me to a waiting car and then on to a waiting aircraft. They walked so fast that the pain in my joints was getting worse, as the iron of my shackles chafed against my ankles. When I tried to slow down, they almost dislocated my shoulder. In the airplane, I was thrown down onto the floor and my arms and legs were spread-eagled and secured to the sides of the plane.

During the flight, I received two injections, one in the left arm and one in the right arm, at different times. They put something over my nose. I think it was some kind of anesthesia. It felt like the trip took about four hours, but I don't really remember. However, it appeared to be a much longer trip than one to Germany.

I was mostly unconscious for the duration. I think the plane touched down once and took off again. When the plane landed for the final time I was fully conscious, although still a little light-headed. I was taken outside the aircraft. I could feel dry, warm air and knew immediately that the place where the plane had landed couldn't possibly be Europe.

That day, Khaled was not flown back to Germany, as he'd been told, but to Kabul, Afghanistan.

A SMALL, FILTHY CONCRETE CELL

After being removed from the aircraft, I was thrown down into what felt like the trunk of a vehicle. The vehicle drove for about ten minutes. I was then dragged out of the trunk and down a flight of stairs. My arms were raised high behind my back. I was marched so quickly that at times my feet hardly touched the ground. They pushed and shoved me against the walls of the building. Finally I was thrown to the ground. They beat me and kicked my head. Someone stepped on my head and neck with his feet, then removed my chains and my blindfold. I heard them leave and the door being pulled hard and locked behind them.

After adjusting my eyes to the light, I could see that I was lying in a small, filthy concrete cell. The walls were covered in crude Arabic, Urdu, and Farsi writing. In place of a bed there was one dirty, military-style blanket and some old, torn clothes bundled into a thin pillow. It was cold and dark. Through a small opening near the roof of the cell, I could see the red, setting sun. It was only then that I realized that I had been traveling for some twenty-four hours.

Through a small grille on the metal door of the cell, I could see a man dressed in Afghan clothes standing in front of the cell. I was very thirsty at this point and called out to the man for some water. The man pointed to a small bottle in the corner of my cell. It was a very old plastic bottle, dirty outside as well as in. The color of the water was greenish-brown. It stank. I could smell the water from the other side of the cell. After I held the bottle, the smell stayed on my hands for quite some time. I was extremely thirsty but when I tried to drink the water, it caused me to vomit. It was impossible for me to drink from this bottle.

That night, four masked men in black uniforms came to my cell, dragged me outside, and pushed me into a room close by. The room was bare apart from a table and some chairs. Three men in masks were sitting in the room when we arrived.

Speaking in Arabic with a Palestinian accent, one of them instructed me to strip naked, as a doctor was going to examine me. I undressed, but left on the diaper. I was instructed to remove this as well, and I complied. I was left standing naked.

I was then photographed, and blood and urine samples were taken by one of the masked men. I think he may have been a doctor.

The doctor wore a tight-fitting mask covering his head and extending down his neck. I complained to him about the unhygienic cell and the filthy water. He told me that the Afghans were responsible for the conditions of my confinement. He then asked whether I preferred Islamic or non-Islamic food. I told him I wanted Islamic food. Later I found out that he had made fun of me for this request, since the Afghan food was nothing more than the leftovers of the guards. All it consisted of was chicken bones and skin.

After the examination, which lasted about ten minutes, I dressed and was accompanied back to my cell. I had to search for the bed because the cell was so dark. There was no lighting. I found it almost impossible to sleep because it was so cold and I was in so much pain from being strapped to the unpadded floor of the airplane. I could not sleep on my right or left sides. Only after ten days was I able to sleep on my front or back. My discomfort was made worse by the nighttime cold in Kabul at this time, and I only had one blanket.

On the second night, four masked men came to my cell, bound my hands and feet, and dragged me into the interrogation room again. Seven other men were in the room. All of them were masked and wearing black matching uniforms. One of them yelled at me to come forward. He spoke Arabic with a South Lebanese accent. The man asked if I knew why I had been detained; I said that I did not. He then told me that I was in a land where there were no laws, and that nobody knew I was there.

On the desk in front of him was a file. He said that the file contained information about me and was the reason I had been detained in Skopje and flown to Afghanistan. He said that the file contained evidence that I had attended a terrorist training camp here in Afghanistan, and that my passport was forged. He interrogated me about these issues and my alleged association with important terrorists and other alleged extremists based in Germany.

I said that I had only heard of these individuals in the media, adding that if they wanted to determine whether I had ever trained in Afghanistan and whether my passport was a fake, all they had to do was speak with the German authorities, who would prove that I was a German citizen and that I had never been to Afghanistan.

I repeatedly asked him to contact the German government. I also asked why I had been taken to Afghanistan, when I was a German citizen and had no ties to this country. My interrogator did not answer.

In total, I was interrogated on three or four occasions, each time by the same man, and each time at night. In one of these interrogations, I was asked about telephone calls to Sudan. My interrogations were always accompanied by threats, insults, pushing, and shoving. Two of the men who participated in these interrogations identified themselves as Americans. During each interrogation, I demanded that I meet with a representative of the German government. My demands, however, were ignored.

HUNGER STRIKE

In March, together with several other inmates with whom I had been communicating through the cell walls, I commenced a hunger strike. We refused to eat or drink, and demanded to see an American commander or representative to complain and demand our basic human rights. Initially, there was no response to our demands. After six days, I became very weak and felt close to death. I started to drink again, but still refused to eat.

On the eighth day, one of the inmates met with an American official and handed him a note detailing some of our demands, including that our captors respect our most basic human rights, afford us access to a court to challenge our continued detention, inform our relatives of our whereabouts, and give us reading materials. None of our demands were met.

On March 3, I was interrogated by three unmasked American officials and a psychologist who also functioned as the prison's Arabic interpreter. This interpreter had a Syrian accent. The interrogation focused on my alleged associations. I was also asked about people associated with the multicultural center Multi Kultur Haus[4] and the Islamic Information Center (IIC) in Ulm.

On March 31, after twenty-seven days without food, I noticed people standing outside of the house and I shouted to them. I was taken to an interrogation room. After my hands and feet were shackled, I met with two unmasked Americans. One described himself as the prison director; the other was a more senior official whom some of the other inmates referred to as "the Boss." In addition, the Afghan prison director and the Arabic translator with a Palestinian accent were both present.

I was asked why I was on a hunger strike. I replied that I was protesting my abduction from Macedonia and my detention in Afghanistan. I said that I was also protesting my continued detention without charge or trial, their refusal to allow me access to a lawyer or my family or government, and the inhumane conditions of my confinement.

The American prison director demanded that I end my hunger strike. I responded that I would not unless I was released, brought before

---

[4] An Islamic cultural center in Neu-Ulm that was shut down by the Bavarian Interior Ministry.

a court, or permitted immediate access to a German government official. The only other circumstance that would bring my hunger strike to an end was death. The American prison director said that I was innocent of any crime, and that he would take that matter up with his superiors in Washington, D.C., but that he could not release me without their authorization. After this conversation I was taken back to my cell and continued my hunger strike. My health continued to deteriorate on a daily basis. I received no medical treatment despite my repeated requests.

By April 8, I was so weak that I was unable to leave my bed, not even to use the toilet. On April 9, some Afghans came to see me and tried to convince me to end my hunger strike, as they had noticed how much my health had deteriorated.

On the night of April 10, thirty-seven days into my hunger strike, hooded men entered my cell, dragged me from my bed, and bound my hands and feet. They dragged me into the interrogation room, sat me in a chair, and tied me to it. One of the men then grabbed my head. A tube was stuffed up my nose and some sort of liquid was forced directly into my stomach. After this procedure, I was given some canned food as well as some books to read. I noticed that the food boxes had blue and white labels and listed sodium and potassium as part of their contents. I could make out "USA" written on these boxes. I was also weighed at this time. The scale showed that, since the time of my initial detention in December 2003, I had lost more than sixty pounds.

Thirty hours after this force-feeding, I became extremely ill and suffered excruciating pain in my stomach. A doctor visited me in my cell in the middle of the night and administered medication. I remained in bed thereafter for several days, during which time my health gradually improved.

*

Around the beginning of May, the Afghan prison director took me to the interrogation room where I met with an American who identified himself as a psychologist. The psychologist told me he had come all the way from Washington, D.C. to check on me and ask me some questions. At the end of our conversation, he promised that I would be released from the facility very soon.

On May 16, the American prison director, together with a man in military uniform, arrived. The man in the military uniform spoke German and identified himself only as "Sam." He told me that he wanted to talk honestly with me about everything I knew. I said that I was more than happy to share everything I knew with him, but before I did, I wanted to know who from the German government had sent him. He told me in German that he could not respond to the specific questions I had raised. I then asked him if anyone in the German government knew I was here. Again he refused to respond. I then asked him if my wife knew where I was. To this, he replied no. I noticed that whenever he spoke he searched for his words. He seemed very nervous while the Americans stood beside him. After my questions, "Sam" began to interrogate me.

He asked more or less the same questions that I had previously been asked in Macedonia, and by the Americans as well, regarding my alleged associations with extremists in Neu-Ulm, Germany, and people who attended or preached at the multicultural center. In all, the conversation lasted for about two to three hours.

From our very first meeting, I was convinced "Sam" was a German citizen, and, from his accent, from the north of the country. Following my return home, I identified "Sam" twice: once on January 1, 2006, from a photograph in the online newspaper *Saar-Echo* (after I was notified of the article by its author, Frank Kruger), and again on February 20, 2006, from a police line-up. His name is Gerhard Lehmann and he is an officer from the German BKA (Bundeskriminalamt).[5] I am 90 percent certain that the "Sam" I met in Afghanistan and the man I identified in this line-

---

[5] The Federal Criminal Police Office of Germany

up one and half years later are one and the same.

"Sam" met with me three more times. On May 20, he told me that it might take them another week to assess whether or not I could be released. Upon hearing this, I became angry and told him that they kept promising my release and always postponed it. I said that I would begin my hunger strike again the next day.

On May 21, I began my second hunger strike. In the evening, the American prison director appeared together with "Sam" and an American doctor. "Sam" asked that I end my hunger strike and assured me that I would be on my way to Germany within the next eight days. He said that they were just clearing the security formalities for my transfer from Afghanistan to Germany. He explained that the flight would not go directly to Germany and that it would take many hours. He asked that I remain calm, not worry, and that I would be home soon.

I recall distinctly all of the dates mentioned in this declaration because I dutifully counted them from the first day of my detention. When I didn't have any paper or pencil to record the dates, I scratched the days off on the wall of my cell. Then, when I was issued paper and a pencil, I wrote them down. When the other inmates warned me that the guards would keep any papers in my cell when I left, I committed the dates to memory.

GOING HOME

On the evening of May 27, the American doctor and the American prison director came to my cell. The doctor examined me. The director then said that I was to be flown back to Germany the next day. He went on to explain some of the details of the transfer from my cell to the airport. The doctor requested that I not eat or drink after that night, as I wasn't going to be permitted to use the bathroom during the flight.

The next morning, May 28, the doctor and the American prison director arrived in my cell. I was handcuffed, shackled, and blindfolded before being led outside and put inside a jeep. I was driven for about ten minutes and then taken inside a large empty shipping container. They sat me down in a chair so that I was unable to see out and was forced to face the wall. From this position, I could hear the sound of an approaching aircraft.

Shortly thereafter, my blindfold was removed and I was handed the suitcase that had been taken from me in Skopje. I was also given two T-shirts. I removed the clothes I had been wearing and changed into some of the clothes that I had in my suitcase and one of the T-shirts.

My hands were cuffed again. My ears were plugged and headphones were placed over my ears. I was blindfolded again and led back to the jeep. We drove a short distance to the waiting airplane. Once inside I was chained to the seat.

The plane was much smaller than the one that had flown me from Macedonia. It had leather seats. I wasn't administered any injections before taking off. "Sam" accompanied me. I could also hear American accents around me. Although they were muffled, it sounded to me like there were at least two or three different people.

At one point during the flight, I asked if I could remove the headphones. "Sam" obliged, and they remained off for the remainder of the flight.

After telling me that there was a new president in Germany, "Sam" explained that we would eventually land in a European country, but that it would not be Germany itself. When he told me this, it heightened my persistent fear that I was not going to be flown home, but rather taken to another country and executed.

The flight took about six to seven hours. When the plane landed, "Sam" told me that we would part company there, and some other people would make sure I got back to Germany safely. I was blindfolded and handcuffed the whole time. I was then bundled out of the plane and placed in the backseat of a minivan-type vehicle.

*

I was driven in the car, up and down mountains, on paved and unpaved roads, for more than three hours. The vehicle came to a halt and I was aware of the three men in the car getting out and closing the doors, and then three men climbing in to the vehicle. All of them had South European/Slavic accents, but said very little.

The vehicle proceeded to drive for another three hours, again up and down mountains and on paved and unpaved roads. Eventually, the vehicle was brought to a halt. I was taken out of the car and before my blindfold was removed, one of my captors turned me around. He then removed the blindfold, sliced the cuffs from my wrists, gave me my suitcase and passport, and directed me to walk down a path without turning back.

I heard the car leave and began to walk as instructed. It was dark. No one was around. As I walked, I feared that I was about to be shot in the back and left to die.

As I came around a corner in the road, I came across three armed men. They immediately asked for my passport. When they saw my German passport, they said I was illegal and asked me what I was doing in Albania without the necessary authorization. I had no idea I was even in Albania.

We walked together a short distance until we came upon an old one-story building. The building had an Albanian flag on it.

Some time later another man appeared. He seemed to be a superior officer. He went through my bags and asked me what I was doing in Albania. He said that, from my appearance (I had grown long hair and a beard), I looked like a terrorist. When I told them the story of my arrest in Macedonia, transport to and imprisonment in Afghanistan, and eventual transport to Albania, they all laughed and said that no one would believe my story. The officer instructed me not to tell my story to anyone.

I asked if they could take me to the German embassy. The officer in charge said that was unnecessary; they would take me to the airport and put me on a flight to Germany.

The whole time I was with them, I sensed that they had been expecting me, that our chance encounter on the road was not an accident at all but rather planned.

The three men drove me to the Tirana International Airport in Tirana. We arrived at around 6:00 a.m. One of the men took my passport and 320 euros from my wallet and went in to the airport building. When he returned some fifteen minutes later, he instructed me to go through a door. On the other side, I was met by another man who accompanied me through customs and immigration controls and onto the airplane. Apart from an exit stamp in my passport, I went through these controls without further inspection. Only after the plane was airborne did I finally believe that I was going home.

*

The plane landed at Frankfurt Airport at 8:45 a.m. on May 29, 2004. I went through customs and immigration controls. By this time, I had lost a great deal of weight, something like sixty pounds. My hair was long and unkempt, and my beard had not been shaved since I arrived in Macedonia. Consequently, I looked nothing like the picture in my passport. The immigration officer questioned whether I was the same man, but after substantiating my identity with other documentation in my possession, he let me through.

From Frankfurt I traveled to Neu-Ulm and from there to my home village, Senden. I knew before I entered my house that no one was there and that no one had been there for some time. I went from my home to the cultural center in Neu-Ulm, where I asked for my wife and children. I was told that my wife and children were all safe and well and that they had all relocated to her family's place in Lebanon.

I called my wife and she returned to Germany with our children one week later.

IMPOSSIBLE TO RETURN TO A NORMAL LIFE

On June 20, 2005, I met with the American Civil Liberties Union (ACLU) in Ulm. I retained the ACLU to represent me in legal proceedings in the

United States. On December 3, 2005, together with my German lawyer, Manfred Gnidjic, I attempted to travel to the United States to meet with my United States lawyers and to attend a press conference. Although Mr. Gnidjic was permitted to enter the country, I was denied entry.

In December 2005, on Khaled's behalf, the ACLU sued former CIA Director George Tenet, along with other CIA agents and contractors, for their roles in his kidnapping, mistreatment, and arbitrary detention. El-Masri wrote in the LA Times *that what he wanted from the lawsuit was "a public acknowledgment from the U.S. government that I was innocent, a mistaken victim of its rendition program, and an apology for what I was forced to endure. Without this vindication, it has been impossible for me to return to a normal life."*

Despite the fact that Khaled's story was already known throughout the world, a judge dismissed the case in May 2006 after the U.S. government intervened, arguing that allowing the case to proceed would jeopardize state secrets. The ACLU appealed the dismissal in November 2006. At that time, Khaled was able to travel to the United States to hear the oral arguments. The United States Court of Appeals for the Fourth Circuit upheld the lower court decision that denied him a hearing in the United States. In October 2007, the United States Supreme Court refused to review Khaled's case.

I did not bring this lawsuit to harm America. I brought the lawsuit because I want to know why America harmed me. I don't understand why the strongest nation on Earth believes that acknowledging a mistake will threaten its security. Isn't it more likely that showing the world that America cannot give justice to an innocent victim of its anti-terror policies will cause harm to America's image and security around the world?

During my visit in November 2006, many Americans offered me their personal apologies for the brutality that had been perpetrated against me in their name. I saw in their faces the true America, an America that is not held captive by fear of unknown enemies and that understands the strength and power of justice. That is the America that, I hope, one day will see me as a human being—not a state secret.

AMIR SULAIMAN

AGE: *32*

OCCUPATION: *poet, activist, recording artist*

INTERVIEWED IN: *Irvine, California*

Amir started writng poems at the age of twelve, and got his big break in 2004 when he was invited to perform on the HBO show Def Poetry Jam. *There, he performed his poem "Danger" to an enthusiastic audience. After the show aired six months later, Amir went to San Francisco to visit his mother-in-law. There, FBI agents tried to question Amir, who refused to talk to them without legal representation. Amir soon discovered that agents had spoken to various friends and family members about his poetry. He also learned that they had visited the school in Atlanta where he taught and had attempted to obtain from the principal the names, addresses, and phone numbers of Amir's students. When he attempted to fly from San Francisco back to Atlanta, he was informed that he had been placed on the No-Fly List. In the following months, Amir took various measures to avoid FBI surveillance: he quit his job, moved from house to house, and only made calls from pay phones.*

I'm from upstate New York, Rochester. I'm an artist. I'm a Muslim. I'm a pretty serious man about serious things, so I tend to take things that aren't serious very unseriously, and make life light in every other way.

Growing up, I was the only black guy in the neighborhood. Education for my mother was the first thing on the list and what she was all about.

We couldn't afford private school, so we lived in the neighborhood where the good schools were. That left us in suburban neighborhoods that were basically all white. Like I said in my poem, "She Would Prefer a Broken Neck to a Broken Heart:"

> My mother kept us in good neighborhoods
> even though we couldn't keep on the lights
> so that we could go to the best schools
> so that we could learn to read and to write.
> Sometimes we would be so broke in the store
> that she would have to pick between the beans and the rice.
> So sometimes she would put ketchup on the navy beans
> so that it wouldn't seem that we were eating the same thing every night.
> Two jobs during the day and one at night.
> And the struggle I saw her enduring
> I never want to see in my wife.
> So I know that being a man is more than being a male.
> AND I'm focused I'm doing it right.

From first grade through high school, usually I was the only Muslim. I was in an environment that was maybe 2 percent black. I never had a black schoolteacher, never had a black janitor, a black principal, a black nurse, a black football coach, wrestling coach, track coach. I was almost always the only black person in the classroom. Up until the time I graduated from high school, I was hyper-conscious of blackness, and I made everyone around me conscious of it. I just became a super duper black radical. I knew even at that age that race had too much room in my consciousness.

*

I was born into a Muslim family. My mother and father were both from Christian families, and both of them went into the Nation of Islam. About two years before I was born, they made the transition to mainstream Islam. In that time, blackness and Islam were different than they are now. Not only did you not have to leave off your blackness to be Muslim, becoming Muslim was like the Eagle Scout of blackness. If a black man stopped drinking alcohol, started dressing well, took his life seriously, wanted to clean up the community, really loved his people, they would say, "What are you, Muslim?" That was the telltale sign that this person must be Muslim.

The first time I was called a "nigger" was in elementary school. You have to ask yourself, why does an elementary white school kid know the word "nigger"? If I got into a fight at school, the only thing I would not get in trouble for is if I'd say they called me a nigger. My mother was so big about manners, but she was like, "If they talk about your mother, or they call you a nigger, you have a green light."

I WANTED NOT TO "BE BLACK" FOR A WHILE

I went to college at North Carolina Agricultural and Technical State University in Greensboro. I wanted to go to a black college because I wanted not to "be black" for a while. I mean, so I could not be described as "the black guy" as I had for my whole life. I had to be something else, and I wanted to know what that something else was. I was still Muslim in college though; I was one of the few Muslims there. You don't have to wear your Islam the same way you have to wear your blackness.

When I went to college, I pushed further in my poetry career. That was a big part of my college years. I decided that this is what I wanted to do. Then it just began to grow, and I was known as a poet.

I got married in college. I graduated and I taught for a year in Greensboro. Then my wife and I moved to Atlanta and I started teaching there. The poetry scene was really bubbling. Almost every night there was an open mic. I knew that it was possible to do poetry full-time, so I was working toward that. I was coming up the ranks, paying dues, and it was really a competitive scene. Eventually I became one of the premier poets in Atlanta.

WHY DO THEY HATE US?

When 9/11 happened, I was teaching high school English at a small private school called Horizons School. I started in August, so the school year was just getting started. We were having an assembly, and one of the other teachers, Paul, was standing next me. He got a call that said World War III had started. We turned on the TV and, like everyone, I was in shock. It was total and utter disbelief. Obviously, the day became about that. We watched the news for most of the day and had informal discussions in the classrooms during our class time.

The next day, I was asked to give a talk about Islam at the school, which impressed me about Horizons School. I didn't want the whole conversation about Islam to just fit into this current context of terrorism, so I also talked about some of Islam's fundamental aspects, like the prayer, the fast, the hajj, what the Qur'an is and who the prophets are. I wanted them to understand some of the breadth of it.

Students asked questions, and it was a real back-and-forth conversation. I was very impressed by how open they were, about how desirous the teachers were to learn for themselves and for the kids to learn. Even at that point, I wasn't pulling any punches. They wanted to know things like, "What is jihad? Why would someone kill themselves? Why would people become angry with America?" These were really big questions. I remember the news headlines over and over again had the question, "Why do they hate us?" In the American consciousness there was this real feeling that there was no reason why anyone would dislike us, a real kind of childlike curiosity and astonishment.

The reaction to my talk was good. The school was really open-minded, so there wasn't any really hard-core judgment. That came a little bit later on in the year. There were a few occasions where I got some nasty letters from parents of students, saying, "Are you American or are you Muslim?" If you remember, at that point there was this almost drunken patriotism that had taken over America. Everywhere you went you were seeing flags, and there was this "we are Americans" spirit that sometimes turns ugly. I just wanted the students to not get deluded into this idea that the terrorists were Muslims who hated our freedoms, ideas like, *Oh we wear high heels and Muslims don't like high heels so they want to blow us up,* or *We drink Budweiser, and Budweiser is against Islam, so they want to kill us.*

I WANTED TO SAY THINGS THAT WOULD FORCE PEOPLE TO RESPOND

Once the U.S. government really started drumming up for war in Afghanistan, that's when my poetry started to come out like fire. It was different from what I was doing before, it had a different energy. It was way more overtly aggressive.

My poem "Brimstone" was the first in that series of poems that was really driven by this feeling of anger and injustice. I felt the need to write it because I thought that the Muslim leadership was being so apologetic, and that this made them look guilty. It made me lash out. I wanted to say things that would force people to respond.

Surprisingly, reactions to my poetry were just really good. I remember the first time I performed one of these new poems at a club. Going up, I was mentally preparing myself for the audience to become angry and throw things. But I recited the poem and they went crazy, clapping, clapping, clapping.

I produced more work like that. My career grew and my reputation grew. I was writing more stuff and I was invited to all kinds of places. I was really amazed by it. Then there was *Def Poetry*.

DANGER

In early 2004, some people that I worked with videotaped me and some of the premier poets in Atlanta. They sent in the tape to HBO's *Def Poetry Jam*, a TV show that Russell Simmons created. It was the biggest showcase for poetry, particularly of the hip-hop generation. It's black, white,

Asian, Latin, gay, straight, all across the spectrum. They also feature celebrities or poets from the generation before, so Sonia Sanchez, Alicia Keys, Dave Chappelle are invited as guest poets. It's that type of vibe.

I got a call saying that they liked me and wanted me to come that February. I remember being very, very happy and excited. Getting on *Def Poetry* was like getting an Oscar or something. I thought I was going to go on *Def Poetry* and do a great job, and everyone in the world was gonna see me do poetry. I thought this could be the means by which I could do art or my poetry full-time.

I decided to do my poem "Danger" for the show. I knew it was risky. The show is in New York, so these people experienced 9/11 in a different way than I did. They saw Manhattan on fire from their houses, and some of them may have known people in the towers. The day of the show, I had a certain level of resolution, like, *This is what I'm going to do.* But still thinking at the back of my mind, *Man, should you do this? Is it smart?*

I have a tendency for extremism. I don't mean political, Islamic extremist type things, but just going too far, whether it's working out, my art, whatever. I just always want to push the limit, and so sometimes, I have to be aware if I'm just pushing the limit just for the sake of it, or if it's something that will actually be of benefit for myself or the people in general.

On the night, the other poets that went before me, their poetry was very light and kind of funny and cute. Everyone was laughing, having a great time. Mos Def was hosting on the show, and he was telling jokes, and everyone was laughing and in a good mood, and I was thinking, *This is going to be so horribly tragic. This is going to be just a bad, bad look.*

I got on stage and introduced the poem. I said, "This poem has four reasons for being. Number one, it's a poem of desperation. Number two, it is a poem to remind those who would like to be reminded. Number three, it's a poem to remind those who would like not to be reminded. And number four, it's to inform those who don't know."

I recited:

DANGER

I am not angry; I am anger.

I am not dangerous; I am danger.

I am abominable stress, illiotic, relentless.

I'm a breath of vengeance.

I'm a death sentence.

I'm forsaking repentance,

to the beast and his henchmen.

Armed forces and policemen

that survive off of oil and prisons

until their cup runneth over with lost souls

That wear oversized caps like blindfolds

Shiny necklaces like lassoes

Draggin' them into black holes

I may have to holla out to Fidel Castro

To get my other brothers out of Guantánamo

The innocence on death row?

It's probably in the same proportion

as the criminals in black robes

That smack gavels

That crack domes

That smack gavels

That smash homes

Justice is somewhere between reading sad poems

and 40 ounces of gasoline crashing through windows

It is between plans and action

It is between writing letters to congressmen and clapping the captain

It is between raising legal defense funds and putting a gun to the
bailiff and taking the judge captive

It is between prayer and fasting

Between burning and blasting

Freedom is between the mind and the soul
Between the lock and the load
Between the zeal of the young and the patience of the old
Freedom is between a finger and the trigger
It is between the page and the pen
It is between the grenade and the pin
Between righteous anger
and keeping one in the chamber

So what can they do with a cat with a heart like Turner
A mind like Douglass
A mouth like Malcolm
And a voice like KRS?!

That is why I am not dangerous; I am danger
I am not angry, I am anger
I am abominable, stress, illiotic, relentless
I'm a death sentence
For the beast and his henchmen
Politicians and big businessmen
I'm a teenage Palestinian
Opening fire at an Israeli checkpoint, point blank, check-mate
now what?
I'm a rape victim with her gun cocked to his cock, cock BANG!
Bangkok!
now what?
I am Sitting Bull with Colonel Custer's scalp in my hands
I am Cinque with a slave trader's blood on my hands
I am Jonathan Jackson handing a gun to my man
I am David with a slingshot and a rock
And if David lived today, he'd have a Molotov cocktail and a Glock
So down with Goliath, I say down with Goliath

But we must learn, know, write, read
We must kick, bite, yell, scream
We must pray, fast, live, dream,
fight, kill, and die free!

Everyone was on their feet, and dudes were crying! When I went backstage, Kanye West was there, and he got up and gave me a hug and so did the other poets who were there. Russell Simmons came backstage, and it was amazing, really emotional. It wasn't even just like, "Oh, that was a hot poem." People were crying.

I was still kind of in the ether when everyone was congratulating me and everything. I had to give everybody a hug and everything because that was the polite thing to do, but I was in outer space. At that point in my career, the act of performing a poem like that was like an electric storm in my spirit. It was like conjuring lightning, thunder, and volcanoes in my heart. So it used to take me a while to recover from it. Usually I would recite the poem and then walk directly out of the door of the establishment and go outside, and it would take me sometimes an hour to recover to the point where I could have regular social interaction with people. So I had to walk out and get my bearings before I could really digest what just happened.

For some time I tried to figure that out, what part of the poem touched people the most, and what made it emotional. Even to this day, I don't know. I think the only thing I can attribute it to is just the sincerity, that although it can be seen as political, it's really just a man expressing for so many people. It still amazes me to this day, because it feels so personal and, particularly at that time, it felt so radical and so on the fringe, but all kinds of people engaged with it and enjoyed it.

IT'S LIKE TALKING TO THE DEVIL

The poem aired about six months later, on August 8, 2004. At that time I was in the San Francisco Bay Area to see my mother-in-law. Someone was getting married, so a lot of family had come to the Bay.

There's a recording artist in Oakland called Goapele. I was in a recording studio with her doing a song about political prisoners when I got the call that the FBI was at my mother-in-law's house. It was so strange. I wasn't in a rush to go talk to the FBI, so I finished this song and then I came back. I literally took hours recording. I was hoping that maybe if I just took too long, they would just go away. That didn't work.

When I got to my mother-in-law's house, two FBI agents were parked in a car outside, waiting for me. They met me in the door of the apartment building and one of them said, "I'm Agent So-and-so. This is Agent So-and-so. We're from the Federal Bureau of Investigation." He showed me a badge, and said, "We want to talk to you."

I said, "I don't want to talk to you without representation."

But they just kept trying to start conversation, and I just kept shutting them down, and so they gave up and left.

I really didn't want to engage them at all. I remembered stories that I had heard about the FBI, about how to kind of stonewall them. Don't enter into any conversation because it'll lead to questions like, "Were you here on such and such a date? Were you here on Thursday?" And you'll say, "Nah, I was here on Friday," but you really were there on Thursday, you just made a mistake. And then lying to a federal agent is a federal offense, and they'll leverage that to say, "Well, we can charge you with a federal offense unless you cooperate on XYZ."

So to me it's kind of like talking to the devil. Don't try to outwit him, just keep your distance before you get tied up in something that you don't know you're tying yourself up into.

*

Right before the FBI caught up with me in San Francisco, they'd gone to Horizons School with a grand jury subpoena for the names, addresses, and phone numbers of all the students that I had taught. The principal refused to hand them over. He never budged. I was really kind of surprised and proud of him.

They had also gone to other places and interviewed other people. While I was on the road, the FBI had visited some of the places that I had been to. Most of the information I got about their interests was through other people they were having conversations with. They'd talked to my brother and specifically asked him about my poetry. They asked him if it was anti-American. This was always one of my favorite questions, just because I never really mention America by name in "Danger."

As this was all happening, I was trying to get a grip around how big this was, what they were intending to do. I was thinking, *This trajectory ends where? With me in custody? With me dead? With me being "deported," even though I'm American? With me being kidnapped or "disappeared"? Where does this go?* All those things were happening in the Muslim community, so those were very real possibilities.

I was feeling a lot of stress, thinking I may have to leave all of life as I knew it and just disappear. As a black person, it's not totally strange for bogus charges to be brought up against you for ulterior motives. I'm thinking the Black Panthers, the Black Liberation Movement, the Black Liberation Front, those histories. That black consciousness and that black revolutionary narrative combined with the current political, social, and legal environment around Muslims, Islam, and terrorism made for what appeared to be a deadly recipe.

I knew that by the time I saw the FBI agents, at the very minimum, my phone had been tapped. They knew where I was staying—not just the city, but also the friends that I had crashed with. After that I only used pay phones. I was calling some people that I knew, friends and so on, and just listening to see if they had been talked to yet. I knew from hearing their voice, by intuition, if the FBI had come to talk to them, like if they were surprised or not to be hearing from me.

In the interim the FBI kept calling me on my cell every few days, up to twice a day, saying, "This is Agent So-and-so and I would like for you to talk to me."

I kept saying, "I don't want to talk to you without representation," and they were saying things like, "Lawyers just get in the way. It would be easier if you just came in and talked to us." That's the whole point—I *want* my lawyer to get in the way!

It's so crazy that they even said things like that, because that means it must have worked, at some point. I feel sorry for anyone that that actually worked on.

YOU HAVE TO TALK ABOUT IT ALL THE TIME

The day after the FBI came to my mother-in-law's house, I tried to fly from SFO back to Atlanta. That's when I realized that I was on the No-Fly List. At the airport, I went to the counter, gave the airline agent my ID and she put my details into the system. Everything was cool, and then something happened. She looked at the screen, then at me, and then at the screen again. She told me to hold on for a minute, and she went in the back for a long time.

That time I got special clearance and ended up being able to fly back to the East Coast, but it would happen every single time I flew for the next couple of years. Sometimes the agent wouldn't go in the back, and sometimes they would get on the phone right there at the counter and be on there for a long time. They would have to give my name and license number and where I was flying to, and there would be a lot of questions that they had to answer. They'd be on hold for a long time, and then they would get the green light if I could get on the plane or not. Sometimes the agents were kind of embarrassed about having to do it. Some seemed suspicious. Some seemed like it was a ridiculous thing they had to go through. Different agents saw it differently.

There were some occasions when I couldn't fly. The thing I learned about the No-Fly List is that it's haphazard vis-à-vis how you get on, how you get off.

*

I was just staying very, very low. I disappeared for some four months after the FBI found me in San Francisco. I had quit my job at Horizons School, and I was basically house to house and on the low, trying to get my bearings. I didn't want to go anyplace familiar, anyplace that I had already been. I remember not knowing who to trust. I was only making calls from payphones. I would perform, but I would not book gigs in advance; I would come unannounced and let everyone know I was alive.

I was invited to Nigeria in early 2005 and I turned it down because the situation with the Feds was so hot that it felt unwise. I worried that I wouldn't be able to come back, or that they would kind of outsource my questioning and that is always a bad look. My fear was, if they had some intention to do something with me in the United States and were being prevented by United States law, they could do it in Nigeria.

I ended up talking to the poet Sonia Sanchez and some of the people a generation older than me, who had gone through a lot of this in the Islamic movements and the Black Liberation movements in the sixties. Back then, that type of environment when the government was watching folks was prevalent. Their advice changed my perspective dramatically. They were all telling me, "You have to be out in front of people and you have to talk about it a lot. Talk about it all the time."

That's when I went on the offensive, because they said if you are by yourself and no one knows where you are, that makes it easier for the FBI because you're essentially making yourself disappear, you're doing half their job for them. So you have to be on the offensive and talk about it and write about it.

So I wrote a public statement describing what was happening. It was called "The High Cost of the Freedom of Speech." Around that time, I got legal representation and did a television show telling my story with the ACLU.

My position wasn't "I'm an American and therefore I have the right to speak and so I'm somehow petitioning for this right." My position was that my right to speak is God-given, that it's a truly inalienable right, and not just because some men agree that it's inalienable. I wasn't interested in surrendering that right, and I wasn't interesting in humiliating myself in front of people by begging for a right that they neither have the power to give nor revoke.

Once I realized that I needed to go out on Front Street and keep basically doing what I was doing and mentioning these encounters and stuff like that, that's what I started doing, and it brought me back out into the open. And the more I did that, the less visible attention I got from the FBI. Eventually they stopped calling me.

WHAT AM I DEALING WITH?

In mid-2005 I was invited to London to speak. I decided to go because things had kind of cooled off by then. So I'm in California, I'm getting ready to fly from SFO to the U.K. I get to SFO, I'm standing in line to check-in, and I get a call from my brother and he says, "They're waiting for you at the airport, they're calling to see what happened." And I'm like, "What are you talking about?" And it turns out that I had come a day late to the airport. I was supposed to fly the day before, so I'd missed it! The people that had invited me to London had been waiting at Heathrow for me for quite a few hours.

So while I'm having this conversation with my brother, I'm going up the line at SFO, waiting for my turn. At that point I have my ID out and I'm getting ready to put it on the ticket counter. And my brother says, "Yeah, they waited for you for a long time and asked about your flight, and ended up asking an airline agent about you. The agent told them that you'd been taken into custody in the U.K."

I put the ID back in my pocket and walked out of the airport, because I'm thinking, *Where did that story come from? Obviously I'm not on the flight and I'm not in custody.* It made me think that, on my way off the plane, the plan was to to arrest me.

I left the airport feeling confused, a little anxious. Again I was thinking, *What am I dealing with? Why would they do that and who is "they"? Is this like an international cooperation where not only is some guy waking up, sitting down at his desk with a cup of coffee, and opening my file, but is there someone in England doing that too? I mean, is this like Interpol at this point?*

My biggest fear was the same as when I first saw the agents—of being kidnapped, of disappearing, a rendition kind of scenario. I remember hearing and reading about this, and the whole Guantánamo Bay situation and all of that. And even the talk around the USA PATRIOT Act in the political arena, and just what that would give the government the right to do.

As far as any in-your-face "we're following you" stuff, I'm not experiencing any of that anymore. The more aggressive I got in my presentation, the more the FBI left me alone. But I do believe that, at a minimum, there is still a file at the FBI, and my phone is tapped and my email account is being hacked and all that kind of stuff. The internet, email, Twitter, Facebook and instant messaging make surveillance that much easier.

THE POWER OF LANGUAGE

The thing is, I don't know the reason why they stopped. I still don't really know what the logic was, or what it was even about, really. But the experience helped me to crystallize my resolve and my mission. The whole thing showed me the importance of what I do. Altogether that was a defining moment in my life. It taught me a lot about my art, it taught me a lot about my opposition, and it taught me a lot about the people who enjoy my art.

This whole scenario, as it's played out, has taught me about the power of language, of words and art, and that that power enlightens some people and inspires some people. And, like all power, it destroys some people. It builds and destroys. Invariably, every creative act, every act of creativity creates and destroys something at the same time. As light destroys darkness, as the voice destroys silence, every act of creation is an act of destruction. And so the question is, what will you create and what will you destroy?

RANA SODHI

AGE: *54*

OCCUPATION: *small business owner*

INTERVIEWED IN: *Phoenix, Arizona*

Rana and four of his brothers fled to the United States in the mid-eighties to escape the political and religious violence in Punjab, India. After years of working and saving money, the brothers opened their own convenience store in 1998 in Phoenix, Arizona, and then a gas station in Mesa, Arizona. Rana's older brother Balbir managed the gas station and was a liked and respected member of the community. On September 15, 2001, Balbir was gunned down on the forecourt of his gas station. His death was the first reported hate muder in the immediate aftermath of 9/11.[1] The following August, Rana learned that his brother Sukhpal, a cab driver in San Francisco, had been shot and killed in his taxi. Although police suggested that Sukhpal had been caught in a gang fight, Rana believes his death was also a hate crime. Rana spoke with us by phone from his home in Phoenix, Arizona. Speaking gently, he reflected on how his life had changed in the last ten years since his brothers' deaths.

Before September 11, 2001, I did not expect what we experienced in

---

[1] No exact statistics have been determined for the number of post-9/11 murders that could be attributed to religiously and racially-motivated violence. Estimates range from five to eighteen.

Pakistan or Punjab to happen here. I never thought we would be attacked for our turbans.

HOW DO YOU KEEP YOUR FAMILIES ALIVE?

I was born in 1957 in Punjab, India, in a small village called Passiawal. I'm the youngest in a family of eleven brothers and sisters. I am number eleven! I grew up with so much love from everybody—my parents and brothers and sisters. It was so much fun being part of a big family.

We used to farm sugarcane, wheat, rice, and all kinds of vegetables. I didn't work in the fields; as the youngest, I was the gopher. It was my duty to take care of my elder brothers and sisters as they farmed, running food and chai tea between our house and the fields.

I loved my childhood in that little village. As the youngest, everyone in the whole village took care of me. My parents would always push us to go to the gurdwara, the Sikh house of worship, a few hundred yards from my home. We kids went once or twice a month, but my mom and dad went twice a day: once in the morning and once in the evening to do seva (service) and paat (prayer).

When I was in high school, I saw a television for the first time. My father was the head of the village, and he bought a television for the whole village. It was my first glimpse of the outside world. Even then, I had not heard very much about America. I never imagined I would live there one day.

In 1984, the state of Punjab had asked for more rights, including water rights for farmland, but Prime Minister Indira Gandhi refused. Then some Sikhs started calling for a separate homeland for Sikhs. That's when it turned very bitter, and in June 1984, the Indian government attacked the Golden Temple.[2]

---

[2] A temple and Sikh holy site in Amritsar, Punjab. In June 1984 the Indian government launched a military operation called Operation Blue Star, which entailed a three-day attack on the Golden Temple complex. Almost five hundred civilians inside the temple were killed, and the holy buildings sustained serious damage. Following these attacks, Prime Minister Indira Gandhi was assassinated by Sikh bodyguards, and Sikh/Hindu violence continued to escalate.

People disappeared every day. Parents did not want to let their children out of the house. No one got arrested or punished for those disappearances. No one had answers. Then, on October 31, two Sikh bodyguards assassinated Indira Gandhi, and riots broke out the next day in New Delhi. Three thousand Sikhs were massacred in the capitol. My brother-in-law lost all his businesses after rioters burned them to the ground.

After the assassination, I felt a lot of discrimination against all sardars—turbaned Sikh men. On trains, people blew cigarette smoke in our faces. I was running a small family business at the time. The government imposed curfews for weeks at a time. With curfews lasting a month, how do you keep your families alive? The whole bazaar was closed for ten days and then two weeks, and business was very, very bad.

WE CAME FOR FREEDOM AND A SAFER LIFE

Our parents decided to send their youngest unmarried sons to America to make a new life. My brother Harjit fled first. He went to Los Angeles and he really liked it. In his letters, he wrote, "It's beautiful here. Los Angeles is the best city in the world. If you work hard, you have lots of freedom, including freedom of religion. You can do whatever you want to do." He lived near a gurdwara, which was just a couple blocks from his apartment.

I came here two years later, and then my brothers Balbir, Sukhpal, and Jaswinder came after me. We all worked at a 7-Eleven in Los Angeles and did lots of part-time work in flea markets, fabric stores, restaurants, and the taxi service. I worked the night shift at the 7-Eleven in a rough neighborhood, but I was never afraid.

We really enjoyed a wonderful life working here, and decided to bring the other brothers over to work. We all came to the United States for more freedom, a safer place, and a better life.

ALL OUR BROTHERS TOGETHER

In 1990, I moved to Phoenix and started working in a restaurant. My brothers and I opened up our own restaurant a few years later but we lost a lot of business, so I moved to San Francisco with my brother Balbir, and we spent some time there driving cabs.

Balbir and I lived in the same apartment. He was sixteen years older than me, and he took care of me more like a father than an older brother. Everyone knew that he had a very kind heart, and if anyone needed anything, he would take care of it. He was very social and friendly. He would get his friends together once a month and do paath[3] in his apartment and make langar[4] and feed all his friends.

Back in India, my parents selected a wife for me. They called me and said, "You're engaged. Your marriage is December 11, 1992." That's how I was married.

I brought Sukhbir, my new wife, to America in 1993. My daughter Rose was born in June 1994. They stayed in Phoenix with the rest of the family while I drove a cab in San Francisco. I missed Rose a lot, so I came back, and all the brothers except Sukhpal decided to make a home together in Arizona. My son Satreep was born a short time after in 1995, and the youngest, Bhavdeep, was born in 1998.

We owned our first convenience store in 1998 with our brothers Harjit and Jaswinder. Then in 1999, we decided to open our own gas station in Mesa. We bought some land and started building the gas station. We decided that Balbir would run the gas station, while the rest of us continued to work in our convenience store in Phoenix.

Balbir's wife stayed in India to help take care of his parents, and he'd send money home to them. In 2000, Balbir opened the gas station to the neighborhood while he worked on finishing the landscaping. He was still planting the flowers when 9/11 happened.

---

[3] Daily repetition of scriptural texts from the *Guru Granth Sahib*, the religious text of Sikhism.

[4] Free vegetarian food served as part of Sikh service.

TURBANED PEOPLE ON TV

The morning of 9/11, at around nine o'clock, I was getting ready for work when I got a call from my brother Harjit.

"Something's happened in New York," he told me. "Those planes hit the building and they're showing Osama bin Laden's picture on TV."

I turned on the TV and watched all those things with my wife, and she was scared for me. Half an hour later, Balbir called me. He said, "They're showing turbaned people on TV. We should be careful when going outside."

I went to work anyway and noticed that people who came into the store were treating me differently. They were upset about what had happened. They said things like, "Go back to your country."

A friend said to me, "You guys need to be very careful, because there are a lot of rumors going around the community about Sikhs getting attacked, and you may get hit very soon. They're showing bin Laden's picture on TV, and he looks like a sardar."

The next day, a Wednesday, Balbir and I were driving in our car together and people yelled at us because we were wearing turbans. We thought that this was getting serious, and we had to do something.

I remember meeting a Japanese American man who told me stories about what happened to Japanese Americans in this country during the war when he was a little boy. He still remembers living in internment camps in Arizona.[5] This is what happens in times of crisis. It happened here during World War II. It happened in India in 1984, when Sikhs were killed in retaliation for the prime minister's assassination. And it was happening around us now, in the United States

So that afternoon, we called Guru Roop Kaur Khalsa, a Sikh American community leader. We said, "We need to do something, otherwise Sikhs are going to get hurt."

---

[5] In a response to the attack on Pearl Harbor in late 1941, President Roosevelt began a domestic mass-incarceration program targeting people of Japanese descent, many of whom were United States citizens or legal permanent residents.

Guru Roop proposed that we call the media and tell them about our religion, our turban, our community, and that 99 percent of people who wear turbans in America are Sikh. We decided to invite the media to come to the gurdwara on Sunday, so that we could show the larger public our community.

On Thursday morning, Balbir called me and said, "You shouldn't go to work today because you're wearing a turban. Either you work in the back where no one can see you, or you don't go to work at all."

"Where are you?" I asked.

"I'm working."

"That's not fair. Why is it okay for you to work but not me?"

"I work in a safe neighborhood in Mesa," he said.

In the nine months since the gas station had opened, Balbir had built relationships with so many clients in the area, and everybody loved him. He would give candy to the children and let people fill their tanks for free if they were low on cash.

That night, Balbir cooked dinner for me at his house. He said, "I really want to go to New York to help those people." He wanted to join the rescue efforts in some way, to help recover people from the rubble, but our brother Harjit told him he couldn't go because he didn't have professional experience.

He never thought anything would happen to him.

WE DIDN'T KNOW WE WOULD
BE THE FIRST TARGET

On Saturday, September 15, 2001, Balbir went to Costco to buy flowers for the landscaping in front of the gas station. In the checkout line, he paid $75 to the New York Relief Fund. Honestly, I believe he donated whatever he had in his pocket.

He called me around 2:00 p.m. and said, "Bring me a couple of American flags. I want to put them in my store."

I checked my neighborhood stores and couldn't find any. They were all out of stock. So I told him that I would just see him at a friend's party that night.

At around 2:45 p.m., an employee from Balbir's store called me and said something had happened at the store. I immediately thought it was a robbery, something very common in convenience stores. He told me that there had been a shooting, that bullets had hit my brother, but still I never thought, *This is a hate crime,* or *Balbir has been killed.* I locked up my store and went straight there.

I arrived at the gas station at around 3:15 p.m. When I got there, I saw my Balbir laying facedown on the forecourt. Nearly a hundred people were gathered around him. The police would not let us go onto the property, they had taped it all off. I saw my brothers and cousins and everybody crying. I saw all these things at once, so I still couldn't imagine what had happened. Then I started crying very badly too. I turned to my brothers and cousins, and they tried to comfort me. I had so much attachment to Balbir. It was very emotional for me.

By the time I got there, everyone had figured out what had happened. It was a hate crime. At around 2:30 p.m., Balbir had been standing on the forecourt talking with Louis Ledesma, a landscape worker, when a black pickup pulled up and the driver shot him. He didn't try to shoot anyone else standing there—only my brother, because he had a turban.

Sikh community leaders from around the country began to call me to offer condolences—Kirtan Singh from Los Angeles, Dr. Rajwant Singh from D.C., and many others. I became the default spokesperson for the family, so I had to keep myself calm. I had never done this in my life. I'm not a spokesperson. But something happened. Our natures help us rise to the occasion. We learn in the moment how to move forward. Time moves us to do what we must do.

Neighbors who heard the news came straight to the gas station. Around two hundred people held a candlelight vigil through the night. People said to me, "You go home and take care of your family. We will stay here." This made me feel stronger. It made me feel part of the larger family, part of a larger community. This incident has built more respect in my heart for people in this country.

So I went home and stayed with my family. Everything happened quickly after that. The next day, we found out that a man named Frank Roque was the murderer. When the police arrested him, he'd yelled, "I'm a patriot! I stand for America all the way!" He'd complained that he was being taken in while "those terrorists run wild!" Someone who kills someone else because of who they are is not a patriot. I think that person is a terrorist, just like bin Laden.

We held a press conference the next day in the gurdwara and invited the mayor of Phoenix and the attorney general to come and speak with the community. The attorney general made a strong statement to the media that we would not let these incidents happen in our state. The mayor offered us the civic center for a memorial for Balbir.

OUR FAMILY BECAME
PART OF AMERICAN HISTORY

The Sunday after Balbir died, we held a big memorial service with three thousand people at Phoenix Civic Plaza. Everything happened professionally. It was just so well coordinated and well done. Guru Roop Kaur Khalsa and the whole Sikh community, with the support of local government, helped our family remember his death and educate people about what had happened.

Local officials had invited my family from India: my parents, Balbir's wife and sons, and my cousins too. The United States embassy in New Delhi had called my parents immediately and issued them a visa. They were the first to walk off the plane, and someone met them and took their passports and cleared them in immigration. I can never forget this level of support from the government. It was amazing.

Balbir was not a famous person. He was just a middle-class businessman who owned a gas station. But the government took this case very seriously because it was the first reported post-9/11 hate crime.

The memorial service itself was very touching. People showed up with cards, candles, and flowers. We still have boxes and boxes of cards for our family. Now, almost ten years later, some of the boxes are in Balbir's family's home, some are in my brother Harjit's home, and others are with me.

I was just checking my files for the gas station the other day and we found one of those boxes with videocassettes from the memorial service. I think we should make a room, like a library, and put all the items together to make sure they're never lost, so that we can access them when we need them.

I remember someone from the East Coast sent an American flag for my family. We still have that flag. The man had received this flag from the military when his father died in the Vietnam War. In his letter, he wrote that he wanted to honor my brother with this American flag. He said that my brother had gone to work and died in the line of duty after 9/11 due to hate. "He's our hero," he said. It was very touching.

Someone else wrote a poem about Balbir. And other people have created rap songs, country songs, and comics in his memory. Just last month, one of my brothers saw Balbir's picture in an art gallery in Las Vegas. He bought it and put it on his mantle.

Our governor put Balbir's name in the 9/11 memorial in the State Memorial Park. It's like my brother, my family, have become part of American history.

AT LEAST WE GET JUSTICE HERE

During Frank Roque's trial for murder, they played the audio recording of the 911 call that my sister-in-law, who was working in the store, made after Balbir had been shot. They also showed video recordings, photographs, and other evidence, including the image of my brother's body lying down on the ground. It was a painful thing for my family to experience again. It was like going through the day of his murder all over again. One time, Balbir's widow fainted outside the courtroom.

Frank Roque was found guilty of first-degree murder. He got the death penalty, but the sentence was later commuted to life in prison. From the beginning, I didn't feel that Frank Roque should be killed or get the death penalty. I don't believe in it. I don't think you should ever take a life.

If Frank Roque spends his life in prison, then so many people will come into contact with his story during his life cycle. People can learn that he killed someone out of hate, and that he's spending his life in prison. So actually, he's a source of education, even though he's in jail. People can learn from it, that what he did was wrong.

I lost my brother, and it's very painful. But at least we get justice here; people are arrested and punished. Twenty-seven years after the 1984 persecution of Sikhs in India, there's still no justice. Many perpetrators never got punished. Although the Prime Minister of India is a Sikh, and this has raised awareness, people still can't forget what happened. So the response to Balbir's murder gives me comfort and makes me proud to live in this country and in this community. You feel like a person.

IT WASN'T AN ACCIDENT

On Sunday August 4, 2002, less than a year after Balbir died, I got a call that my brother Sukhpal had been in a very bad accident and might not survive. Sukhpal had been driving a cab in San Francisco, sending money home to his wife and children in India. Although Sukhpal had stayed in San Francisco, he was planning to move with us to Phoenix.

I went to San Francisco and found out that it wasn't an accident, it was a shooting. He was driving his cab in the city and was hit in the back of his head by a bullet, then his car crashed into a pole. It wasn't a robbery; nothing was taken from his pockets.

The police said that he was in the wrong place at the wrong time, that maybe he was passing through a gang fight and got hit by a stray bullet. But there had been lots of attacks on Sikh cab drivers in the city. Two weeks earlier, Sukhpal's friend, also a turbaned Sikh, had been pulled from his cab at a red light and beaten. I believe Sukhpal's death was a hate crime too.

On September 14, we had a large memorial in Mesa for Sukhpal. We had a celebration in the park, and two thousand people showed up. The media covered the event well and conveyed our message of peace to the community. After that we had another memorial service in San Francisco. But I don't think as many people know about Sukhpal's death as they do Balbir's. Ten years have passed and people still know the story of Balbir Singh Sodhi. Sukhpal's death is still not resolved as a hate crime. Many people like Sukhpal have faced beatings, assaults, and other kinds of racism, but there's not enough evidence to show that it's a hate crime.

HIS DEATH HAD TO MEAN SOMETHING

I had lost two brothers in eleven months. I wasn't feeling anger, but sadness.

I thought, *This is happening all over again to our family.* Then I found Balbir's diary and I read his very last entry. He wrote, "God, I'm blessed by you, and I'm happy with my life, and I'm ready to give my life for your work." Maybe God wanted to use Balbir as a messenger to bring the whole community together.

One night, both brothers appeared to me in a dream. Sukphal told me, "We are happy where we are. You should be happy." That dream changed my thinking a little. I felt that everybody has to die, but it's the way they die that's important. We respect their lives, and people will remember them their whole lives—it's a big honor to die like that. It's a sad thing, but after 9/11, I look at their deaths that way.

Sikhs have lived in this country for more than 100 years, but our community is still not recognized. When people see the turban today, they still don't know who we are. However, organizations like the Sikh Coalition, the Sikh American Legal Defense and Education Fund (SALDEF), and United Sikhs are doing work to spread the word and educate other communities. Even the prime minister of India called Bush after Balbir's death and said that he was concerned for the Sikh population in America.

When I met with the Anti-Defamation League here in Phoenix, they encouraged me to tell my story and work against hate crimes. They helped me come out and speak and educate people. Now I travel the country to raise awareness about Sikhs and tell my brothers' stories.

Last Saturday, I spoke to 250 high school students. We are working toward educating more people. On April 12, we have 200 students coming to learn about our culture.

This has been sad for our family because we lost so much. But on the other side, we are now doing so much to educate our fellow Americans in Congress and around the country about Sikh culture. All of this has happened after Balbir's death, so I think his death had to mean something to us.

I think that it's an important part of life to take care of our extended community and to work to understand one another better. And when I say "community," I don't mean the Sikh community but the whole American community.

If we had a better family, a better community, and a better country, all these incidents wouldn't have happened.

Bad things happen when people don't know about each other. That's how I feel. I try to do whatever I can do to make our future better.

IF NO ONE STANDS UP

Arizona just passed a new law called S.B. 1070. It allows local police to stop anybody anytime and ask their status.[6] So the police can stop me anytime and say, "Show me your license. Show me your status."

---

[6] Signed into law in April 2010, this state law makes the failure to carry immigration documents at all times a criminal offense, and gives police the power to detain anyone they suspect of being in the country illegally.

How can you feel American if the police stop to check your identity? How many times can a person be stopped before they feel like they are not seen as American? What does an American look like?

This law has encouraged hatred for immigrants. I have seen those effects in Phoenix. I have experienced it myself.

Last Sunday, I was driving at 11:30 a.m. My wife, my son, and my sister-in-law, Balbir's widow, were in the car. A guy in the car next to us showed us the finger. He came in front of the car, slammed on the brakes and tried to crash into my car. I have no idea what I was doing wrong. He just saw me in my turban.

This kind of racism always happens when something comes up in the news. Every time there's a new event—the Iraq war, the London bombings, the Madrid bombings, S.B. 1070, the Park 51 controversy[7]—there is a resurgence of racism, and Sikhs are often the first targets.

This hatred still exists. I'm wondering how it will end. If no one stands up, then it will happen again and again and again.

I still go to work at Balbir's gas station, just like he did. And to this day, I have never taken my turban off.

THE KIND OF COURAGE WE NEED

Last month in Washington, D.C., at the ADL in Concert Against Hate event, I met a female teacher from South Philadelphia High School who protects Asian-American children who are being bullied and beaten at school. One time, a crowd was trying to attack six kids, and she stood between them. She said, "No one can touch them." That's the kind of courage we need.

Every time we have a crisis, we learn and get better, right? During World War II, they put Japanese Americans in camps and treated them

---

[7] Controversy around the construction of an Islamic community center, also known as Cordoba House, to be located two blocks from the site of the World Trade Center. For more details, see the glossary.

badly. What happened after 9/11 was bad, but see the difference? Things have changed: the government is different, people are different. So we are becoming a more educated country.

When Barack Obama was chosen as president, it gave me hope. Did anyone think fifty years ago that our nation would elect a black president? This is America today. Obama received more of the young vote than anyone else. I feel that our new generation is more understanding. Our new generation understands what we need to do.

I felt very encouraged from neighbors, from government. I lost my two brothers, but I feel like I made hundreds more brothers. That makes my heart open, and I feel proud to be part of this community. After all this happened, I don't have anger in my heart, because of the way the community rose up and joined us. We received thousands of greeting cards and flowers from all over the world, just for my brothers. It was amazing. It was a big honor to my family and my brothers.

The most memorable event I did was at the Kennedy Center in Washington, D.C. last November. Twenty-five hundred guests came to that event. The Anti-Defamation League honored me as a community leader and educator. They also honored five families who had sacrificed their lives to protect and educate other people.

The death of my brothers changed my life. When I first came to this country, I was focused on my dream: my house, my business, my family. I never thought about the larger community. But now the community is my extended family too. We need to evolve and be part of our extended family. Now I'm totally changed. I am inspired to do something.

HANI KHAN

AGE: *20*

OCCUPATION: *student*

INTERVIEWED IN: *Foster City, California*

Hani was born in New York to Indian and Pakistani parents. She grew up in Foster City, California. Hani spoke to us about being fired from Hollister (a clothing store chain owned by Abercrombie & Fitch) after refusing to remove her hijab, a head covering traditionally worn by Muslim females. After taking her story public, Hani received hostile comments and death threats, and found it difficult to secure another job.

I am an American-born Muslim. I am the typical American girl. I hang out with my friends, I have fun, I listen to Taylor Swift. It's just a piece of fabric that sets me apart.

There comes a point where you can't be a flip-flop anymore. I'd been wearing the hijab since kindergarten, but I didn't start wearing it full-time till I was in high school. For me, the hijab represents modesty, and it represents how women in Islam want to be viewed—for what they have to say, for their personality, for their intelligence. I had to find that conviction inside of me.

In October 2009, I applied for a job at the Hollister[1] store at the

---

[1] An American retail clothing store owned by Abercrombie & Fitch.

local mall. A lot of my friends had after-school jobs at the mall. If you work there you get to see your friends, and they come and visit and kick it with you.

At the interview, the manager asked me about my hijab. He said the store had a beachy, laid-back vibe and told me what the dress code was: the colors were navy, grey, and white. I said, "It's fine. I have those three colors."

He said, "Then it won't be a problem."

*

I'd been working there for just over four months, when one day, on February 9, 2010, the district manager came into the store. He didn't acknowledge me. *Pretty standard*, I thought, since he's district manager and he has to oversee a lot of things. All day I was going in and out of the stockroom to the floor, so I wasn't really paying attention to him. It was pretty much a normal day.

Six days later, the next time I was in for work, the district manager was there again. He said he would like to put me on the phone with human resources (HR) corporate.

I spoke with a woman from HR, who said, "We recently became aware of the fact that you wear a headscarf."

I said, "Yeah, it's part of my religion. I've been wearing it since I was hired."

Then she told me that my hijab didn't conform to their store policy, that no headgear is allowed—no caps, scarves, anything like that.

It was frustrating. Because I was put on the phone with her, she didn't get a chance to see me. I wanted her to see that I was wearing jeans, I was wearing company colors, and that the only thing different you'd notice about me was that I was wearing a scarf.

She said, "Well, will you be able to conform to our store policy?"

I told her that wasn't acceptable. I said I was not going to take off my scarf for work.

Then she let me know that they had to talk to their lawyers, and that I would be taken off the schedule until further notice. She was trying to be cheery, but it sounded like she really wanted me to understand what was happening.

I went to clock out. I was crying, because I'd never had a negative experience regarding my hijab before, even after 9/11. The store managers could see that I was upset, and I let them know what had occurred. One of the managers was studying to become a lawyer, and he said that this was unjust.

I called CAIR[2] the next day and went to talk to a lawyer there. She gave me handouts about civil rights and the Constitution, and about religious gear being accommodated at the workplace. She said, "When they call you in for the next meeting, take that with you."

The week after the first incident, I went in and I gave the district manager the handouts. He glanced at them but he didn't say anything. I guess he realized I was talking to someone at that point.

He put me on the phone with the woman from HR again, and again she let me know about their "beachy vibe" dress code. She asked me explicitly, "Would you be able to take your headscarf off when you come to work?"

I said, "That's not acceptable. It's a part of my religion, and it's a part of who I am. I've been wearing it for so long, I'm not going to take it off for you." Then she told me I was no longer working for their company. I think they were prepared for what was going to happen, because the district manager already had my last paycheck ready with my name on it.

THE GIRL WHO'S STIRRING UP TROUBLE

The lawyer at CAIR told me we could file a complaint with the EEOC[3]

---

[2] Council on American-Islamic Relations, a civil rights group. For more details, see the glossary.

[3] Equal Employment Opportunity Commission, the government agency that enforces federal employment discrimination laws.

and let the public know the injustice that had occurred. I said okay. I thought, *We can either let this injustice slide by and it's going to happen to the next person, or we can take action about it.*

So CAIR sent out a press release about my situation, and the next day I was interviewed by all the local TV stations, including CBS, KTVU and ABC. It was really fast—one station would come, and then I would get a call that another one was on their way. My face was blurred out. I wanted to remain anonymous because of personal safety, but also because I was going to try to find another job. I didn't want people to recognize me and be like, "Oh, that's the Hollister girl, that's the girl who's stirring up trouble."

The day after the TV interviews, a hate letter was sent to the CAIR office saying I should go back to my country. It said someone should behead me and wrap me in a pig carcass and bury it in a mosque.

Some people wrote comments online saying I was sent in to be a spy. They said I wasn't wearing the hijab at my job interview and that I started wearing it after. I don't know who at nineteen would go, "I'm gonna infiltrate a company and I'm gonna take them down."

There were also people who wrote, "Go back to your country." But this *is* my country. I was born here, you were born here, so this is *our* country. How are you going to tell me, just because I wear a scarf, to go back to my country? I don't have anywhere else to go back to.

*

Hollister and Abercrombie & Fitch declined to release a statement. A friend from work let me know that nobody at work was allowed to talk about the situation and that, funny enough, they had to sign a new policy stating that no headgear was allowed.

After the story went public, they offered me my job back, but they said that I would be working exclusively in the stock room. I refused, because that's like you're not good enough to stay in the front, you're going to stay in the back. I thought that was segregation at best.

I've tried hard to find another job, especially in retail. But since Hollister is the last thing on my resume, people want to know why I'm no longer with the company. Although nobody's mentioned it to me, I feel like they're aware of the situation. I went in for two interviews at the mall, and when I called them, there would always be an excuse, like, "Oh, I'll have the store manager get back to you," and then the store manager never got back to me.

I'm worried, especially in this economy when it's hard enough to find a job.

*

I don't want to be known as "that Hollister girl." I'm not ashamed of it, but it's not something that I'm publicizing. But I do feel proud of myself that I actually took the step. I just didn't want to be a quiet bystander. I know a lot of people are letting cases slide because they don't want the attention.

I think my generation and the next generation are not going to be afraid of the hijab. I'm studying Political Science at UC Davis, and I'm hoping after I'm done with undergrad I can go to law school. I don't want to work for a corporation. I want to be helping people, so that's where I'm hoping to go with my future.

What happened made my identity stronger. It made me realize how important the hijab really is to me, and why I need to continue to wear it.

ZAK MUHAMMAD REED

AGE: *45*
OCCUPATION: *firefighter*
INTERVIEWED IN: *Toledo, Ohio*

Zakariya Muhammad Reed was born and raised in Toledo, Ohio where he still lives today. Zak spoke to us about how his life changed after his conversion to Islam in the late nineties and his marriage in 2004 to his second wife, Razan. Originally from Lebanon, Razan grew up with her family in Toronto, and she and Zak would make regular trips to Canada to visit her parents. During one of these trips in 2006, Zak and Razan were stopped at the United States–Canada border. There, Zak was detained for over four hours and questioned about his conversion to Islam. This was the first of many incidents of detention, interrogation, and harassment he and his wife would experience over the following years.

My parents were from Polish-German descent. I grew up in Toledo, Ohio in a close, tight-knit family with three sisters and a brother. My given name is Edward, but my family started calling me Zachary, my grandfather's name, because my dad, my uncle, and his son were all called Edward!

I met my second wife after I had converted to Islam. She told me that the name Zakariya exists in Arabic. I said that was perfect, and so I changed my name legally to Zakariya. I also changed my middle name to Muhammad. I wanted an attachment to the religion, and for people to know who I am, maybe in a more subtle way.

When I changed my name, and people at work asked me what they should call me, I'd say, "You can still call me Ed," whatever they were comfortable with, because they'd known me as Edward for so long. But everyone else is to call me by my chosen name.

NO IDEA ABOUT ISLAM

My family was very much blue collar, working class. My father worked for A.P. Parts, an auto manufacturer. He made mufflers for automobiles for thirty-five years.

When I was a junior in high school, one of the kids I was going to school with, his dad had one of the only construction firms in the area. They were in the process of building a mosque in Perrysburg, which was lavish. I remember going out there and visiting it. I had no idea about Islam at all. But there was this beautiful structure, and nobody had objections to it, even though nobody really knew what it was.

IS THIS REALLY WHO I WANT TO BE?

I joined the military in 1984. We didn't have money, so joining the military was the only way I was going to college. I made arrangements to go and join the Air Force, and I went to boot camp and tech school. It wasn't working out for me. Thank God it was the late eighties, because they were letting people transfer out if they wanted to. So I got trained, went over to the Air National Guard, and I ended up spending twenty years over there.

At the same time I was doing my Guard duty, I went to school full-time at Bowling Green State University. I had also been working a part-time job in a clothing warehouse in Toledo through college, and then I took a full-time position there. Two firefighters worked there on their off days. They told me, "It's a good job, you should check it out. Good benefits, good pay, it's a lot of fun." I took the test and passed it in '95. I was hired in '96.

I got in trouble when I first started the job. I was married to my first wife and wasn't particularly thrilled about it, so the fire department was perfect for me. There was a lot of going out, a lot of getting in trouble and doing things I shouldn't have been doing.

I have a daughter from my previous marriage. When she was born, that really set me on a different course. It settled me down a little bit. When you have a child, you have to start thinking, "What am I doing? Is this really who I want to be?"

Around that time, I can't tell you why I was possessed to start reading the Bible. I was at this bookstore, and I just picked up the Bible and bought it. I was still carrying on, don't get me wrong. It wasn't like I had this epiphany. My goal was to start reading it and getting introduced to who I was. And then I started picking out some inconsistencies in there, and I started making a checklist of things that didn't make sense to me, like original sin and all this other stuff.

So I was on this quest or whatever. One day I was working out in the basement of the fire station, and there was this book. It turns out that it was a Jehovah's Witness book. What they did was, they took all of the world's faiths and they wrote three or five pages on each one and why you wouldn't want to be part of them. I thought, *Okay, cool.*

I always thought I should contact the author of this book and tell him he might have made a mistake, because the way he wrote the part on Islam was in such a concise and informative way about this particular faith, that it actually piqued my interest.

I WANTED TO KNOW MORE
ABOUT THIS ISLAM THING

I took a class at university to learn more about Islam. It was basically outlining Christianity, Judaism, and Islam. It was a terrible class. A Muslim lady taught it, and she was terrible. There was a guy in class, I think he was from the Emirates. I would ask him about something she'd taught us and say, "Is this true?" He would say, "I don't know, she's nuts. If you are really interested in this, you should go talk to somebody. Why don't you go talk to this guy up in Detroit, Mohammad Ali Elahi?"

Mohammad Ali Elahi was an imam at the Islamic House of Wisdom. I made an appointment to go talk to him and off I went up there. I don't really know what possessed me to do it. I remember walking in the place thinking, "Ugh, what did I do? What was I thinking?" There was Arabic everywhere. I thought, *How do I know where to go?* It turns out they have school there, and they're teaching the kids Arabic, so that's why all the signs were there.

So I sat with the imam and he was just the nicest man. I went through my questions, one after the other. The big things were about the idea of the Son of God and Jesus as God and the Trinity—things that just never made sense to me, from creationism to original sin and all this other stuff. For the very first time, I was getting answers back to stuff I had in my heart all along. When he explained the philosophy of Islam it really hit home. He explained that Islam is a religion of justice and logic. There isn't this notion of, *Well, we do these things because we have faith, and that's the way it's supposed to be.* No, it isn't that way. It's more like, *There is a reason and a logical explanation for things, and I'm going to tell you what it is.* This is why we believe it.

The Iman also said that Islam only means submitting yourself to the will of God. So in effect, Moses and Abraham, because they submitted themselves to God, they were Muslim—not by title, but as a way of life. Sometimes people don't want to hear this. But it just hit me wave after wave after wave with how beautiful it really was.

We said our goodbyes and I walked out completely confused, my head spinning. On the way back I was thinking, *This can't be. Of all the things, this is the faith that I understand?* I didn't know any Muslims then. I certainly didn't know any white Muslims. I thought that it was going to be odd, that I was going to be a freak.

I met with the Imam several times afterward. Then I started going to the Friday prayers. Once I showed interest in it, I thought they would pull the full-court press and say, "All right, we got one!" It was just the opposite. Instead, the Imam said, "I don't want to push you into all of this. You need to know what you are doing."

A CONVERT

It was probably eleven years ago when I finally professed my faith.

I started praying at work. The fire station I worked at was quite big at the time. The dorm room was pretty much unoccupied during the day. For a while there, I was praying without anybody there. Before that, I was sneaking into the apparatus floor where we kept the rigs and I would pray out there.

At first glance I don't look like the average convert. Most people who convert to Islam embrace not only the philosophy, but also try to look like how a traditional Muslim would look. I wasn't able to do this. I can't have a beard and be a firefighter, but when I'm off work for any length of time I always wear a beard. As far as the clothing, I've never felt comfortable with what is typically viewed as Islamic garb. Because of these things, it might seem to those who don't know me that I'm not sincere in following Islam. Nothing could be farther from the truth. Islam is my faith, and I live by the conditions set forth by it. The conversion has been hard for me. It's taken me a long time to have Muslim-Arab friends. I've had trouble fitting in because of my appearance—I look more like a FBI agent than I do a convert to Islam. The way Muslims are treated in this country, it's no wonder I'm not trusted by the Muslim-Arab community. So it's really been hard.

AN ARAB WOMAN

My wife Razan and I first met on the internet, while she was living in Toronto, Ontario. She and her family are from Lebanon. I think she finally sent me a picture on Valentine's Day, something really sappy like that. When she sent the picture, I said to her, "I'm jumping in my car and coming there!" I got in my car, went to Toronto, and I met her and her family.

We got married in Toledo, down at the courthouse, on February 9, 2004. Our religious marriage was a year prior to that. There was a long road to convince her family. I had all these strikes against me. I'm twelve years older than her, I'd been married before, I was a convert. But they got to know me and they approved of our marriage, and now I think I'm closer to her family than I was to my own folks. Since then, my wife and I have had three sons and a daughter. I'm completely absorbed into her family, and there's no American/Arab/white, it's none of that.

WE EITHER GET SYMPATHY OR WE DON'T EXIST

9/11 was tragic. At the fire department, we were deeply affected by the loss of the firefighters and everything else. I still have a "Remember the Firefighters" sticker on the back of my helmet.

At that time, there were stories of people having their hijabs pulled off and generally ignorant things that people would say. It was just ignorance; they wouldn't do anything violent against somebody. I personally didn't have any of it, but I could feel it.

It got bad after 9/11, and then after the Iraq war it just got even worse. When people find out you're a Muslim and you're a nice person, it's almost like, "Oh, you're kidding me. You're Muslim? Too bad, you guys are so nice." I remember I was with my wife and son at Wal-Mart, this had to be in '06. The checkout person, a middle-aged woman, was looking at my son, saying, "You are just the cutest thing, you're so sweet! How old are you?" And then she asked him what his name was, and we said, "Muhammad." The woman didn't say another word to us, and just continued checking us out. She didn't have a look of shock on her face, didn't have a look of disgust, a look of anything. It was just like the entire conversation prior to that never existed.

LIKE WE DO IN THE DESERT

The first time I was detained at the United States–Canada border was in November of 2006. We would go up once a month to visit my in-laws. At that time, it was my wife and my boys. One of them was still an infant, and the other one was about two.

We came over the Ambassador Bridge in Detroit, and we pulled up at the border at around 6:00 p.m. We gave the officers our passports. They swiped our passports and one of the guys looked up at me, closed his little door on his booth, and the next thing I know, the whole car was surrounded with officers.

An officer came up to our window. He had his hand on the gun on his hip. He said, "Put your hands on the wheel. Turn your car off and put your hands on the wheel." I turned the engine off and I asked, "What's this about?"

No answer.

The officers took me around the back of the car and had me straddled and frisked. Then they took me into the main office of the United States Customs and Border Protection at the Ambassador Bridge. I was led through the main registration area into a hallway where I was frisked again. They had me undo my trousers because they wanted to make sure I had nothing in my waistband. Then they uncuffed me and led me into a storage room.

I was scared. I was thinking, *Something isn't right*. The officers took me into this room that was probably as big as a closet. I sat in there and one officer came in and interviewed me, asked me all these questions about my address, who I saw in Toronto. He asked me if I ever went by another name and I told him, "Yeah."

He asked, "Why did you change your name?"

I said, "Well, it was a personal choice. I'm Muslim and I changed my name."

Then he wanted to know why I would convert to Islam. I thought it was a ridiculous question. "It was a personal choice," that's all I said.

At that time I used to wear a little pin. It said "God is great" in Arabic. The officer was curious about this pin.

"What is that?" he asked. "What is that pin you have on?"

I said, "It's a religious pin."

He asked, "What religion is that?"

I said, "I told you, it's Islam."

He said, "Okay." And he just kind of looked at me and then he got up and walked out.

An hour went by, then two hours. The door to the interrogation room was open, and there were two guards sitting outside. I could hear my son crying in the waiting room down the hall. I could hear, "Baba, baba, I want baba." Every time I heard that, I just got infuriated because there was no reason for this whatsoever.

Finally I asked the guards, "What's going on? Can somebody please tell me?"

They answered, "Hey dude, we don't know anything."

That's when this other guard came out and said that the detention facilities at the border were too "cushy." He said to him, "They're lucky we don't treat them like we do in the desert, where we put bags over their heads and ziptie their hands together."

Now I was getting really hot. I tried with my faith to control my temper, but I was getting pissed and I wanted to talk to somebody. So the same guy who interviewed me before came back in and sat down. He asked me the same bunch of questions he'd asked me before, and then he left.

I sat there for another two hours. Then an officer came in and said, "Follow me." I went out to the waiting room to my family. By that point, my wife had come completely unhinged; she'd had these two babies there for four and a half hours, at nighttime. They wouldn't even let her go to the car to get a diaper bag to change their dirty diapers.

They'd taken my wallet and my cell phone. When they gave them back to me, everything in my wallet was rearranged, so I knew they had gone through everything. My phone had been gone through as well; the contacts list was open. I snatched my stuff, and off we went to the van.

The van was trashed. My kids' portable DVD player was broken. The window was chipped. We had a Qur'an and it was just thrown on the floor. I had lectures and stuff and Learn Arabic CDs I listened to in the car. They were just thrown all over the car.

I just came unglued. I slammed the door and shouted, "What are you people doing? What is wrong with you? Nobody's telling me what I've done and yet you've gone and treated me like a criminal!" The next thing I knew, there were ten officers and they're all, "Sir, calm down, calm down. You don't want to go down this road."

I wanted somebody to say, "Sir, we're sorry. We'll fix it." I remember there was a female officer who gave us a form and said, "Fill this out and we'll pay for your DVD player."

We did fill it out. We never heard from anybody about it after that.

NOT A RANDOM THING

As we were leaving, my wife and I were chatting about the line of questioning. The officers were asking me about why I would change my faith, what the pin meant. Plus, the Qur'an thrown on the car floor really started to get us talking. It wasn't until halfway home that we realized this had something to do with me and my faith.

About three weeks later, we went to Toronto again, and very much the same thing happened on the way back. It was then that my wife and I realized that it wasn't a random thing, that something was wrong.

Soon after that second incident, we attended a panel meeting at the local library about religious profiling. On the panel was a lady from the Council on American-Islamic Relations (CAIR).[1] My wife stood up and told the story of what had been happening to us. After the meeting, the lady from CAIR came up and said, "Maybe we can be of some service," and so we took her contact information.

In the meantime, we went back up to Toronto a third time. On the way back we decided to be sneaky and come in through the tunnel instead of taking the Ambassador Bridge.

---

[1] An organization whose work focuses on protecting civil liberties. For more details, see the glossary.

It was me, my wife, my mother-in-law, and the two boys. This time I got pulled out of the car by officers, thrown onto the hood of the car, and handcuffed. My kids were screaming in the backseat, everybody in the car was just screaming and crying. I said to the officers, "I was born and raised in this country! I was in the military!"

For some reason I kept thinking this meant something to somebody.

"I volunteered for Desert Storm. I was the first one there from my community, I couldn't wait to go. Then I became a firefighter. This ought to mean something!"

No, of course it didn't mean anything.

*

The officers put us in a big holding area for detainees. My wife asked if they had a place where she could change our baby son because he had a messy diaper. It was like it was the first time they'd ever stopped anybody and this kind of question had been asked. They almost had to have a conference call to respond. "Is she going to be able to change this child?" "Do we have facilities?" "Is it okay?" "What are the ramifications if we allow her to change this child?" It's a huge roadblock in their day.

*

Later we did this again—going through the tunnel because the interrogation room there was so much bigger and nicer than the first one. The interview process became the norm. Every time we got stopped, I would have to go into the same office and answer the same questions, and then that was the end of it. The officers knew who I was toward the end. They'd say things like, "Okay, you're still a firefighter. You're still having problems."

The officer who did the questioning, he was a major or something. He started seeing us regularly. He'd say, "I know, man. I know what you're going through and I know it's messed up. It's not their fault. A red flag comes up and they have a protocol they have to follow."

At one point the major had me and my family gather in the interrogation room. My wife said, "What do we do?"

He said, "I can't tell you what you've done and I can't tell you how to fix it. But if I were you, I'd contact somebody."

He was trying to guide us. My wife said, "Who? The president? Our state representative?"

He pointed at us, as if to say, "Yes."

THE SYSTEM IS BROKEN

I contacted Marcy Kaptur, my representative of Congress, but she got absolutely nowhere.[2] Then the woman from CAIR, whom we met at the library panel, suggested I go to Cleveland and tell my story. There was a contingent at one of the mosques there, and Senator Voinovich, the former senator of Ohio, was there to discuss profiling. So I went there and told my story, and they took down all my information. I never heard from them again. I contacted current Senator Sherrod Brown and never heard anything back from him either

*

I took all the Muslim people off my phone for fear that they would be connected to me and whatever I was wrapped up in. Whatever the government thinks I have done, just by having their name on my phone, it could implicate them in some way. So every time I crossed the border, I'd start taking everybody off my phone.

---

[2] On January 5, 2007, Representative Kaptur wrote to the Congressional liaison at the immigration service. She noted that Reed was an "honorably discharged veteran and United States-born American citizen" who had "no criminal record nor has he exhibited probable cause to make law enforcement think he may be associated in any way with anti-American elements." She concluded: "I would request that your office act to prevent Mr. Reed from experiencing further delays and detentions and do what you can to update his record in the computer."

PATRIOT ACTS

Each time I was stopped I would fill out this IBIS form.[3] It's supposed to be a critique on your detention. And if you think you're erroneously being stopped, you can request information as to why you're being stopped. The form says they can give you information on how to stop that. Of course I never heard back from these people at all.

After the fifth time we were stopped at the border, my wife and I took separate cars so she wouldn't get stopped. I couldn't have her and the kids go through it anymore. It was just tearing them up.

"Traumatized" may be too strong a word, but these kids had been affected in such a way that any time we got into a toll booth they were just terrified. They would ask, "Baba, do we have to stop at the border?" These kids have shed more tears at that border than anywhere else.

THE FEAR IS THERE

I've gotten to the point when I go to a ballgame, I can't even stand for it anymore. I can't do it. How can I pledge allegiance to the flag? I'd be a hypocrite. I just can't describe how hard it's been, how angry and sad the whole thing is. How do I raise my kids? What do I tell my kids?

If we go buy a house, is it going to affect our mortgage? Maybe not, but that fear is there. Everything we do, there's always the thought in the back of my mind, *Is this going to affect me in some way?*

*

Probably two and a half years ago I was going through paramedic training, and I just happened to be over at the station riding a live squad. I got a call from my wife. She said, "Hey, I've got two FBI agents sitting

---

[3] The Interagency Border Inspection System (IBIS) is a federal database used at United States international borders to identify criminal suspects, including suspects of terrorism-related activity, when they attempt to pass through border checkpoints. IBIS data is often used in combination with other federal law enforcement databases.

184

in our living room. They asked if they could come in and I thought it had something to do with our case, that they were going to be able to help us. Now they're snooping around. It turns out they're asking if you happen to know about an assassination that took place in Syria."

I said, "What? Just put the guys on the phone."

One of the agents got on the phone, and I said, "You guys get out of my house right now."

By the time I got there, they had gone.

After they came to the house I just, I really stopped making any attempts at all to do anything about it. It seemed completely lost at that point. I thought, This is just the way it's going to be. So we stopped going to Toronto. It was after twenty times or so of me getting stopped. Instead, the folks have been coming down to see us.

That's where I sort of fall short in my faith I guess, because I'm not willing to sacrifice everything. I mean, I keep feeling in my heart I should press on with this, but at the end of the day, I look at my kids, and I think, *I can't do it*. I'm weak. I feel sort of ashamed of myself in a lot of ways, that I've let them win because I have too much to lose.

We've made strides to move. We started this once we realized that this was a pattern. I started working on papers to potentially emigrate. I would go scrub toilets in Canada, as long as I don't have to put up with this anymore. Why do I want to be in this country that clearly doesn't want me, clearly doesn't appreciate the service that I've put in toward it? What's the point of me being here?

GHASSAN ELASHI

AGE: 57
OCCUPATION: *former charity co-founder and
vice president of a web-hosting company*
INTERVIEWED IN: *Marion, Illinois*

Ghassan Elashi, a co-founding member of the Holy Land Foundation for Relief and Development (HLF), was sentenced to sixty-five years in prison for providing material support to Hamas[1]. Following a 2007 mistrial, Ghassan was among the five HLF members convicted in November 2008 on all 108 counts against them, including support of terrorism, money laundering and tax fraud. The HLF was not accused of directly financing terrorist violence, but of supplying funds to Hamas-controlled charitable societies and committees. The U.S. government has argued that providing humanitarian aid to victims of war or natural disasters is a crime if provided to or coordinated with a group labeled as a foreign terrorist organization.

Ghassan had two convictions prior to the HLF case. In July 2004, he and his four brothers were convicted of export violations. They were found guilty of making illegal computer shipments to Libya and Syria through their computer and web-hosting company InfoCom Corporation. In April 2005, Ghassan,

---

[1] Founded in 1987, Hamas is the largest and most influential Palestinian militant Islamist organization. Hamas was placed on the first United States list of Specially Designated Terrorist Organizations in 1995.

his brothers Bayan and Basman, and Infocom Corporation were each found guilty of conspiring to send money to Mousa Abu Marzook, identified by the U.S. Department of Justice as an investor in Infocom and a leader of Hamas. Ghassan contends that all three convictions were politically motivated, and that he is innocent of providing support to Hamas. He is currently incarcerated in a Communications Management Unit (CMU)[2] within a federal prison, and as such, his communications are severely limited. He shared his story by written answers to our questions.

Voice of Witness has published seven books in its series, many of which have included the testimonies of previously convicted narrators, and narrators who have confessed to crimes of which they have not been convicted. We have printed these narratives in the service of illuminating larger issues of civil and human rights. Although Ghassan's narrative has provoked strong debate and difference of opinion among the editors in the Voice of Witness series, his story is included in this collection because he was found guilty under a law—material support for terrorism—that has come under fire from civil rights, civil liberties and human rights groups for criminalizing, and branding as terrorism, acts that include those that are nonviolent, or are without violent intention.

To be a Palestinian means to be one of the millions of refugees worldwide who were expelled from their homeland. To be a Palestinian means to often be looked upon with suspicion.

It means waking up in the morning to find the occupying forces building a wall to separate your home from your farm in the West Bank. It means waiting hours at checkpoints manned by teenaged Israeli soldiers as you attempt to reach your college in Nablus. It means fearing your wife will give birth in a taxi at a checkpoint on the road

---

[2] As part of the Bush Administration's War on Terror, self-contained areas known as Communications Management Units (CMUs) were created within federal prisons. CMUs severely restrict and monitor all outside communication for inmates suspected of ties to terrorism.

to a hospital in Ramallah. It means not getting a permit to build a house, while new immigrants from Russia are building homes on land confiscated or stolen. It means having your home demolished along with an entire neighborhood, under the guise of securing illegally built settlements. It means not having enough water to drink. It means being detained along with thousands of other Palestinians for years and years without being charged.

For me, it means being imprisoned for sixty-five years in the United States for feeding Palestinian widows and orphans.

NO COUNTRY TO RETURN TO

I came to the United States as a student in July 1978, a year after my brother Bayan came to pursue his graduate degree in computer engineering. A year later my other three brothers and my sister joined us. I finished my masters degree in accounting at the University of Miami in Florida in December 1981.

Being a Palestinan, I felt I had no country to return to. So after graduation, I joined my brother Bayan in establishing a computer company in Los Angeles that manufactured, assembled and designed one of the first Arabic-based personal computers. I joined the company as a financial manager.

In 1985, I traveled to Jordan and married Majida Salem, a Palestinian high school English language teacher. Later on, when I was blessed with children, my wife and I enrolled them in an Islamic school and brought them up with the teachings of Islam.

I applied for permanent residency in the United States and became a citizen in 1992. Then I, along with my four brothers, moved from Los Angeles to Richardson, a suburb of Dallas. This decision was based on the availability of a full-time Islamic school in Richardson, which all my children and my brother's children attended. In Richardson, we started a new computer and web-hosting company called InfoCom Corporation.

I had every intention of considering the United States the place to spend the rest of my life.

A DREAM COME TRUE

The Holy Land Foundation for Relief and Development (HLF) was begun by members of the Islamic Association for Palestine (IAP).[3] Those members worked in their own capacity to establish a foundation to help Palestinians.

Assisting the Palestinians took a jump start during the 1987 Intifada[4] of the Palestinian people in the West Bank and Gaza. The first Intifada was extensively covered by the media, showing the brutal treatment by the Israeli forces against unarmed civilians. A large number of the injured and killed were children and teenagers.

It was obvious to me that the Palestinians would be in need of emergency and development help for a long time. In 1989, I joined Shukri Abu Baker, Mohammad El-Mezain, and Ahmed Agha in establishing the HLF separately and to provide aid to Palestinians living in the West Bank, Gaza, Lebanon, and Jordan. We decided to become an independent charity to be run professionally with full-time-staff, offices, and a network of volunteers nationwide. It took a little over a year to get incorporated as a non-profit and tax-exempt charity.

We concluded that the best way to start was to coordinate with an Arab-Palestinian charity based in Israel, which was recognized by the Israeli government and licensed to conduct charity work inside the West Bank and Gaza. We picked the Islamic Relief Agency (IRA), and they welcomed cooperating with us and representing us in the area.

The HLF was a dream come true. The sky was the limit for us. It was

---

[3] The IAP was founded in 1982 as an Islamic advocacy group to inform and educate people in the United States about the plight of the Palestinians under the Israeli occupation.

[4] An uprising against the Israeli occupation of the Palestinian territories.

the means through which we were able to repair some of the damages that the occupation was causing. We provided hope and assistance to thousands of Palestinians who lived way below the poverty level and enabled them to eat the basic food ration, and get health care and education. It was the most rewarding volunteer work that I have ever done.

Although the HLF's main aim for us was helping the Palestinians in the West Bank, Gaza, and refugee camps in Lebanon and Jordan, we also provided aid for disaster and war-torn relief work in the United States, Bosnia, Turkey, Albania, and Kosovo.

Through the HLF, we were able to bring to life the important concept of zakat,[5] or charity, in Islam.

The charity grew from $300,000 in 1989 to close to $13 million in 2000 and 2001. It became the largest Muslim charity in America, with offices in San Diego, New Jersey, Chicago, Jerusalem, and Gaza.

By this time, I had become a citizen and was blessed with six children. My life was divided between my work, my family, and my volunteer time at HLF.

A RELENTLESS CAMPAIGN

The HLF faced unusual challenges from the Israeli government and its supporters in the United States who sought to eliminate all the charity work we were doing.

The campaign against the HLF first surfaced in 1993, when the Anti-Defamation League (ADL) issued a report about Islamic fundamentalism in the United States. The report referred to a mail fundraising campaign by the HLF, soliciting donations to help the families of dead Palestinian "martyrs," and stated that such aid provided support to extremism and terrorism.

This led to the closing of our office in Jerusalem in 1996 and the lob-

[5] For more details, see the glossary entry on the Five Pillars of Islam.

bying of U.S. Congress, the IRS, the State Department, the Department of Justice, the FBI, and the Attorney General's office of New York State to revoke our tax exempt status, shut us down, and even prosecute us.

Despite all these challenges, morale was always high, and the HLF continued to grow. We established new offices in the West Bank and Gaza that directly administered charitable programs, as well as several programs through different Zakat Committees.[6]

In 1996, the *Dallas Morning News* published a report by Gayle Reaves and Steve McGonigle with the headline PAPER TRAIL LEADS TO HAMAS.[7] That year, Senator Charles Schumer of New York held a press conference, calling upon the Department of Justice to investigate the IAP and HLF for links to terrorism.

At that time, new legislation authored by Senator Schumer[8] made it illegal to provide charity aid to any organization or country listed as a terrorist organization. The HLF, along with representatives of major Arab and Muslim national organizations, met with representatives from the Department of the Treasury to voice their concerns regarding the law and its impact on their charity work. The meeting ended without resolution.

In 2000, the HLF received an order from the New York Attorney General's office to provide a list of its major donors and aid recipients. Several months after providing this list, the HLF was shut down by an executive order by President Bush.

---

[6] Zakat Committees are charities that distribute the zakat, or donations to help the needy. For more details, see the glossary entry on the Five Pillars of Islam.

[7] The article presented evidence of what the authors called "a pattern of personal, financial, and philosophical ties" between Hamas and two nonprofit groups, Holy Land Foundation and the Islamic Association for Palestine. It cited court filings, business records, materials from the nonprofits, and interviews. In the article, Ghassan was quoted as calling the accusations "guilt by association".

[8] The Material Support Law, enacted as part of the Anti-terrorism and Effective Death Penalty Act of 1996.

THE LOCAL FACES OF TERRORISM

Between September 5 and September 8, 2001, close to eighty government agents raided the office of Ghassan's and his brothers' computer and web-hosting company InfoCom. The raid was based on suspicions that the company was shipping computers to Syria and Libya.[9]

On Tuesday, September 11, 2001, the World Trade Center was attacked. It was shocking. I was watching the events live on TV at my mother's house. I did feel that it would be a disaster for Muslims in America. I expected that mosques would be attacked. I just felt that it would not even be safe to walk in the streets, especially for Muslim women wearing the hijab, such as my wife, my daughters, and my sisters-in-law. I feel that as we move further from 9/11, the situation of Muslims in America is getting worse and not better.

But I did not really think that it would have any negative impact on the HLF. We are an Islamic charity with projects basically in Palestine. I did not see any relationship. But I guess my feeling was wrong.

After 9/11, the local media was knocking on the doors of both InfoCom and the HLF offices, looking for interviews and any knowledge of who was behind the attack. A local TV station reported that an FBI agent was looking into the possibility that the 9/11 attack was a reaction to the FBI raid on InfoCom a few days earlier. HLF and InfoCom became the local faces of terrorism.

The White House announced its intention to fight back against "Islamic terrorism," a term which I personally have challenged for a decade, because Islam disapproves of the killing of innocent civilians for political gains. A few weeks later, the White House announced its intention to declare several national and international organizations and individuals as terrorists, and to keep a list with the Department of the

---

[9] Ghassan and his brothers were subsequently tried in court for export violations, and sentenced in October 2006 to seven years.

Treasury. Among the HLF founders, the feeling that things were closing in on us surfaced again.

Then, around December 1, George Salem, the HLF lead attorney at that time, informed us that the White House and the Department of the Treasury were moving toward adding the HLF to the list of Specially Designated Terrorists.

Since George Salem's phone call, we were expecting at any time to hear from the government or the media. On December 3, 2001, at around 5:00 p.m., the HLF received a phone call from Judith Miller at the *New York Times*, who was seeking comments regarding the expected next-day announcement by President Bush of the HLF listing. Shukri Abu Baker and I left the office, not sure if we would be able to come back the following day.

The next morning, after dropping off my children at school, I drove toward the HLF office and noticed a few police and FBI undercover cars. A representative of the Department of the Treasury's Office of Foreign Assets Control (OFAC)[10] had delivered an order to freeze HLF assets, and asked Shukri for keys to the office.

They had movers empty the office of computers, desks, file cabinets, video tapes, chairs, coffee makers, microwaves, tables, projectors, Palestinian artifacts, American and Palestinian flags, pictures, posters, office supplies, bookshelves, books, telephone sets, routers, modems, TV sets, all personal belongings of employees, couches, plants, pots, printers, prayer rugs, and credit card processing machines. The only things they left were the refrigerator and the carpet!

We came to find out later that neither OFAC nor the FBI had a search warrant or a court order to enter our office and seize all its contents.

George Salem, along with another lead counsel, flew to Dallas, and we agreed we would hold a press conference in front of the HLF office the next day. Before the press conference, we met Salem and his partner and

---

[10] OFAC handles investigations of material support of terrorism. For more details, see Appendix III: United States Counterterrorism After 9/11.

we talked briefly about our next options. But then Salem said that he and his firm would not be able to continue to represent us in regards to the OFAC seizure, or with challenging the decision to add the HLF to the Specially Designated Terrorist list.

I listened to his decision carefully and did my best to control my reaction. I informed him that his firm's decision to withdraw was a real-life example of hypocrisy. How could we trust him after this most cowardly decision? Of course they refused to come down to attend the press conference, and Shukri and I were left to confront the press on our own.

At the press conference, reporters referred to a report compiled by an FBI assistant by the last name of Watson. The Watson Report recommended the listing of the HLF as a Specially Designated Terrorist. Apparently OFAC or the FBI had circulated it to reporters before even handing us or our attorneys a copy.

Ghassan and the HLF board of directors decided to challenge the Specially Designated Terrorist listing in court. The district court in Washington, D.C. did not rule in their favor, and stated that the executive branch had the power to determine such listings. The court did rule that the seizure of assets violated the HLF's constitutional rights.

The HLF board of directors then filed for an appeal with the appellate court and lost the case.

A KNOCK AT THE DOOR

In July 26, 2004, two and a half years after the listing and the freezing of HLF funds, United States prosecutors filed an indictment against me and other HLF members: Shukri Abu Baker, Mohammad El-Mezain, Mufid Abdel Qadir and Abdulrahman Odeh. Together we were charged with 197 counts, including conspiracy to provide material support for Hamas.

On that day I woke up, as usual, two hours before sunrise to do qiam prayer, or night prayer. Then, around 6:15 a.m., I went to the local mosque to join other Muslims for predawn congregation prayer.

I came back from the prayer and lay down in bed for a few minutes. Then I heard a knock at the door at around 7:00 a.m. I jumped to the door, wondering who was there at this early hour of the day. When I asked who was knocking, I heard a man's voice saying, "Richardson Police. Open the door Mr. Elashi, I need to talk to you."

I felt uncomfortable opening the door right away. I answered, "I did not call you for help. What do you want to talk to me about? Just talk to me from behind the door."

He said, "I am not sure if you are Mr. Elashi, I cannot see you. Just open the door."

I then told him to move a few steps to his right and he could see me through the kitchen window. He did what I said, and I saw that behind him was an FBI agent, who flashed her badge and ordered me to open the door immediately.

I then called them liars—the Richardson policeman said he wanted to talk to me, when in fact he was being used as a front by the FBI. I left the kitchen to change my clothes, and after about a minute I came back to the door dialing my cell phone, in an attempt to reach my attorney, Tim Evans. I got his voice mail and left him a message informing him that I was being arrested by the FBI.

At that time, the FBI agent threatened me. She said that if I did not open the door they would break it in. I opened the door and stepped outside. They asked me to turn my back to them and I was immediately handcuffed and escorted to an undercover FBI car parked at the front of the house. There were a few other undercover FBI cars, a couple of Richardson Police cars and a few FBI agents standing around the house.

Once they put me inside one of the cars a female agent approached my wife Majida, who by that time was standing outside with my oldest daughter Noor, who was eighteen years old. The agent asked her if she could get her permission to search our house.

Majida then asked the agent if she had a search warrant. When the agent said no, Majida said, "Then I will not allow you to search my house."

I then shouted at the FBI agents, saying, "You are a bunch of WASP racists!" Then I looked at Noor, who was seeing her father being hand-cuffed and taken away forcefully. I said to her, "Don't worry Noor, keep your head up high because your dad did nothing wrong."

Then the car drove away, heading toward downtown. When I asked why the agents were arresting me, they said that I would know later. Then I heard them talking about the Attorney General, Mr. Ashcroft, that he would be making a press conference announcing the indictment and arrest of the HLF members.

I thought, *Here we go, another political stunt against Muslim individuals and organizations. What happened to the fact that you are innocent till proven guilty?*

EVIDENCE

At the trial, the prosecutors focused on the killing of Israeli soldiers and civilians by Palestinian elements, and specifically Hamas, as opposed to the actions of the HLF or the defendants themselves.

One government witness testified in detail about suicide bombings claimed by Hamas, and prosecutors were also allowed to present to the jury numerous images and statements made by individuals other than us. For example, they showed pictures of the aftermath of suicide bombs, and videos of Palestinian school ceremonies in which children played the roles of suicide bombers, complete with suicide belts. None of the videos came from the HLF's files. The videos depicted events that happened years after the HLF closed, and there is no evidence that the defendants attended these ceremonies.

Yet all attempts by our attorney to show the jury fundraising vid-eos demonstrating the HLF's charity work were met with objections from prosecutors and the judge. The judge even deemed the evidence irrelevant.

At one point, the prosecutors exhibited a letter sent to the HLF by the imam of an Islamic center in a suburb of Los Angeles. The letter referred to my visit to the center in the early 1990s, soliciting donations for the orphan sponsorship programs. The letter quoted a saying from the prophet Mohammad, Peace and Blessing be upon him: "'Me and the sponsor of an orphan will be close to each other in paradise just like this,' and the Prophet raised his hand and held together the index and middle fingers." I got very emotional and cried. An act I was praised for ten years before—of being involved in the sponsorship of a Palestinian orphan—was now being used as evidence to prosecute me.

The prosecutors concluded by exhorting the jury: "Don't let the defendants deceive you into believing that they did what they did to support widows and orphans. The reality is that by supporting Hamas, they helped create widows and orphans. Find them guilty."

STAR WITNESS

The star witness for the prosecution was an anonymous expert who worked with the Israeli Secret Intelligence. His trial name was Avi. We were not allowed to know his real name. He was escorted by two guards and two lawyers, and on many occasions, he did not answer questions before consulting with his attorney. Prior to serving the Israeli Secret Intelligence, he served with the Israeli Defense Forces (IDF). Our attorneys were not allowed to question Avi about the time he served in the IDF. They could not search his background since his real name was not disclosed to us. They could not question his credibility or challenge his claims. He was immune from perjury. This is the first time in history the U.S. court had allowed an expert witness to testify with an anonymous name.

Prosecutors and Avi played a game of identifying a magazine-size portrait of almost every board member of all the eight Zakat Committees listed in the indictment. He claimed to gather his information about the Zakat Committees from police reports, intelligence resources, and from surfing the internet on weekends.

Some he would claim were Hamas members without presenting any corroboration or proof. Then he would conclude that all Zakat Committees in the indictment were not only controlled by Hamas, they *were* Hamas. He said that he could "smell Hamas"!

None of these Zakat Committees were, or have since been, listed on the

U.S. list of terrorist organizations during the period that HLF sent funds to them. I remain a firm believer that the Zakat Committees have never been controlled by Hamas. The Israeli occupation authorities gave licenses to some to build hospitals, and USAID-affiliated organizations based in the United States have provided aid to these exact same Zakat Committees. A CIA officer had even previously vetted these Zakat Committees, prior to visits to these Zakat Committees by the U.S. counselor in Jerusalem.

The prosecution objected to the admission of these facts, claiming they were hearsay.

IN GOD'S HANDS

The verdict was announced on October 22, 2007. My daughter Noor sent an email to members of the community, appealing to them to show up. The court was full, and additional room was provided to accommodate the supporters. I recall whispering to my lawyers that my feeling was that there would not be even one single guilty count.

It was a hung jury on all counts for me and Shukri Abu Baker. It was a joyful day to hear that none of the five defendants were found guilty on any single count out of 197 counts. The joy was very clear on the faces of our attorneys, families, and the entire community. The prosecutors were stunned and shocked.

Prosecutors then asked the judge to poll the jurors. The judge agreed, and one of the jurors changed their mind. Suddenly there was confusion in the court. Some of the marshals told us that they have never seen such a thing in their lives. The judge then ordered the jurors to go back to the deliberation room and come out with a final verdict. About fifteen minutes later they came out and each one sat at his chair. The judge then polled them again. This time one of the jurors changed their minds on Abdel Qadir's total acquittal verdict, and on Odeh's verdicts. The final verdict then was a hung jury on all counts for all defendants, except Elmezien, who was acquitted on all counts, with a hung jury on one count. The judge then announced a mistrial. A mistrial meant of course that prosecutors decided to retry the case.

Upon interviewing several jurors, the defense learned that, during deliberations,
the prosecution had provided the jury with approximately one hundred pages of
their theories and interpretations of the evidence, including Powerpoint slides,
videotapes, and diagrams drawn on large boards, depicting Zakat Committees
and HLF as part of Hamas. Criminal courts procedures prohibit having such
demonstrative exhibits in the jury room at the time of deliberation.

The verdict of the second trial was on November 24, 2008. We were all found guilty on all the counts. In the courtroom, I attempted to assure my wife Majida, my children and my mother by pointing my finger up—a sign that it is all in God's hands.

In May 2009, I was sentenced to sixty-five years in prison. Prior to my sentence, I spoke to the judge, prosecutors, my family, and the community for about ten minutes. I announced my firm belief that I was innocent of all the charges, and that helping Palestinian orphans and widows was my only intent. I said that there was nothing more enjoyable in my life than the time I'd spent doing my volunteer work at the HLF. I said, "I am really honored and privileged to have the chance to serve the people of the Holy Land and the world, and provide them with hope."

A CAGE

I have been in prison since April 16, 2007. I stayed in the general population in Seagoville, near Dallas, until the day of the verdict. Then the warden decided to place me and my other co-defendants in solitary confinement.

When one is held in solitary confinement, the prison guard escorts him outside into a caged area in the open air, just like the cage that houses an animal in the zoo. It is cross-wired metal on all sides, including the top. Usually I got this opportunity for one hour in the morning, five days a week, regardless of outside temperature. Sometimes I had the chance to go out only two to three times a week, because there were not enough guards to escort me.

It is not an easy task for one to accept being in a small, solitary-confined room. It is 7 × 8 feet, with a six-inch-high glass window at least seven feet from the floor. The room has a 200-watt light with a switch outside the room controlled by prison guards, and another 60-watt light that is always on, even during the night.

While I was in Seagoville, my family visited me at least once a week for about two hours at a time. In September 2009, the officer at the visitation room filed an incident report against me after my youngest son, Omar, who has Down's syndrome, ran toward me to get a last hug after we had been told the visit was over. He was nine years old at that time. The disciplinary offices found me guilty of disobeying an order, and suspended my family visitation for six months.

A few months later, during the Muslim holiday of Eidul Adha, I got a one-time permission for my family to visit me. The rules did not allow more than five visitors at a time, so my two sons Mohammad and Osama were waiting outside. That same officer then refused to allow them to come in, in exchange for Omar and one of my daughters. When I attempted to explain the matter to his superior, he insisted he would not allow my two sons to come inside, otherwise the visit would be terminated. Majida was worried about keeping our sons outside any longer and decided to leave.

I then stood and shouted at the officer, telling him that he was abusing his authority and that he was evil, preventing me from seeing my children. I was again disciplined by the prison administration for "initiating a riot and engaging in a demonstration," and my family visitation was suspended for another six months.

In April 2010, I was transported to a Communication Management Unit (CMU) in Marion, Illinois, and my co-defendants to the CMU in Terre Haute, Indiana. We joined about forty other prisoners, about 60 percent of whom are Muslim.

COMFORT

Ever since I was imprisoned, I make sure to communicate with my family, even with all the limitations imposed on me now, and discuss with them all of their problems, all of their dreams. When I was in Dallas, I used to see my wife and most of my children at least once a week for two hours at a time. Writing letters and sending them postal mail was another way of keeping in touch with them. I also had three-hundred minutes of phone calls a month.

Nowadays, since coming to Marion CMU, email is the primary way of communicating with them. Now I am allowed two fifteen-minute calls a week and two four-hour non-contact visits a month. I am in constant contact with my wife, Majida, especially lately with the email. She writes to me constantly about issues related to our children. Attempting to do my role as a father remotely through writing emails is not an easy task, but I make sure that I always get involved fully, writing to them and sharing my opinions. I engage myself with my children and write to them, advising and sharing with them my opinions in issues related to their lives and studies.

But there is also time for fun stuff. My son Mohammad is a forward on his high school soccer team. He is sharing with me the scores he is getting. We also had a few emails related to the soccer World Cup of 2010.

I believe the trial that I went through with my family and extended family, combined with our faith in God and His Mercy and Wisdom, have made us all grow stronger and wiser.

*

I have never had the slightest doubt about what I've done. The HLF work in Palestine was very much needed to remedy the suffering of the Palestinians. I challenge any decent human being to ever doubt or regret such work.

In mid-June 2010, the White House announced a $400 million aid package for Gaza and the West Bank. This is meant to improve Palestinans' access to clean drinking water, create jobs, build schools, and address healthcare, housing, and other needs. This is exactly what the HLF was doing in the West Bank and Gaza.

HOPE

Today is January 1, 2011, and the case is still in appeal. Meanwhile, public awareness about our case is being spread by our family members. I am in constant communication with my daughter Noor, and she always updates me on her attempts to speak in support of her father and the HLF5, as we are now called. We also have support from other legal entities, such as the Muslim Legal Fund of America, the National Association of Defense Lawyers, and the Center for Constitutional Rights (CCR), who filed amicus briefs in support of our case.[11] My hope is that, by the will of God, we win the HLF appeal and the case gets dismissed. I hope that the frozen funds of the HLF by the United States Treasury will be released and become the seeds to continue the work of aiding the Palestinians.

My hope is that I will be able to join my wife and family, and continue my role as husband and father.

My hope is to be able to hug my mother every morning, to be charged with her love and care.

My hope is to be able to complete the memorization of the whole Qur'an and to teach others how to recite it correctly. My hope is to be able to make hajj, the annual pilgrimage to Makkah, and visit the Prophet's mosque in Madinah[12] with my wife.

My hope is to see my children successful in what they have embarked on, for Noor to continue her writing, for Huda to become a pharmacist, for Asmaa to become a speech therapist, for Mohammad to be a lawyer, for Osama to own a farm, and for Omar to lead a joyful life.

I hope and pray to God to protect and bless them all.

---

[11] For more details about these organizations, see the glossary.

[12] Located in Saudi Arabia, Madinah is regarded as the second holiest city in Islam. For more information about the hajj, see the glossary entry on the Five Pillars of Islam.

SARA JAYYOUSI

AGE: *15*

OCCUPATION: *high school sophomore*

INTERVIEWED IN: *Washington, D.C. and Detroit, Michigan*

Sara was nine years old when her father Kifah was arrested in March 2005 and charged with providing material support to terrorists[1] and with conspiracy to murder, kidnap, and maim in a foreign country. The charges against him were a result of charitable contributions he made to an organization in Bosnia in the 1990s. Prior to his arrest, Kifah had been Chief Facilities Director for the Washington, D.C. public school system, and then an adjunct professor at Wayne State University. He had also served in the United States Navy. When he was convicted in 2007, the judge noted for the record that there was no evidence linking Sara's dad to specific acts of violence anywhere. The judge also said that he was "the kind of neighbor that people would want in a community." In June 2008, Kifah was transferred to the federal Communications Management Unit (CMU)[2] in Terre Haute, Indiana.

---

[1] A term usually associated with the crime of aiding terrorism or supporting a terrorist organization. See glossary.

[2] As part of the Bush Administration's War on Terror, self-contained areas known as Communications Management Units (CMUs) were created within federal prisons. CMUs severely restrict and monitor all outside communication with inmates suspected of ties to terrorism.

It feels so good letting someone else know about this. It's the best feeling in the world. You feel like you're educating someone on something that is really inhumane, something that's not supposed to be going on.

It's like you're letting them in on a secret, but it's not a good one. Carrying secrets around is horrible. Lately I've been feeling like there is a hole in my chest or something.

*

I was born on November 30, 1995, in Irvine, California. I grew up mostly in Detroit, Michigan. I am the fourth of five siblings. My oldest brothers, Kareem and Mohammed, are fraternal twins. They're twenty-five. My older sister Reem is nineteen. My younger sister Maryam is fourteen.

My parents are Hedaya and Kifah. My mom is half-Egyptian, half-Palestinian. My dad is fully Palestinian. But I feel Palestinian because I speak the Palestinian dialect and the food in our house is mostly Palestinian. And my dad always told me, "You are Palestinian!"

I just feel so cool being Palestinian. It means that I have people, people who are really brave because they are sticking to their land. They're not leaving, and they are not giving up at all. I wish I could be as strong as they are.

VERDICT

During my dad's trial, my sisters and I had been going to court four or five days a week for four months. We used to go almost every time when we weren't in school. Court was a new experience for me. At first it was confusing, but it got easier, like a routine. It bothered me to hear the way the government spoke about my dad in a negative tone, but I was mostly fine with going. I liked to hear how, throughout the trial, more good things were said about my dad than bad things. I remember one of his friends from the Navy talked about how much they appreciated his work, what a good man he is, and how there was nothing bad in his record.

I liked seeing the people who loved my dad, who came to bear witness to how great he was. My dad was a great and honorable man in society.

I never doubted him, ever. I just knew he had been taken, and he wasn't supposed to be.

On August 17, 2007, my dad and mom were going to court on the last day of the trial. That was the day the verdict was to be delivered. *High School Musical* was playing on the Disney Channel, and my sisters and I had never seen it before, so we were super excited to watch it. We made popcorn and got situated around the TV. As my father and mother were getting ready to leave, my dad told us to come hug him before he left. He was holding his brown leather briefcase. He has had it as long as I can remember. He took it with him every day of the trial.

So I walked up and gave him a hug really fast and pulled away. I wanted to hurry back to the TV because *High School Musical* was starting in a couple of minutes! I didn't know that was the last hug I was going to give him for a very long time.

My parents told us they would both be back in three hours. They had that much hope that my dad would be found innocent.

Four hours passed with me and my sisters watching *High School Musical*, playing on the computer, and messing around. Then we all started to get worried, and we didn't want to be alone. So we called my mom's friend, and she picked us up and took us to her house, where we swam in her pool. We just left a message on my mom's cell phone telling her where we were going. We swam for two hours with my mom's friend's kids.

I was carefree and super happy; it would be the last time I felt that way.

Suddenly, my mother appeared on the patio outside, next to the pool. Her face was red and puffy. I was freaking out because my dad wasn't beside her, and she was holding his briefcase in her hands.

She sat us all down when we got out of the pool. She said our dad had been found guilty.

I burst out crying. She said he wasn't going to come back. And I knew, from her holding his briefcase, that he really wasn't coming back.

Before she told us all this, it had felt so hot. But then suddenly I got cold. I was shivering, a lot. I was in my wet bathing suit; it felt like snow.

Then I felt this pumping in my head. Everything was weird, it was all going wrong. I felt like my family had been put on pause, like everything else was moving, except us. I'd never felt that kind of pain in my life before.

I remember going back in the pool because I didn't want anyone to see me crying. I remember my big sister came after me, hugging me.

I cried a lot that day, more than I have ever done.

When we got home, my dad's clothes were still were where he had left them in his room. That made it even harder for me.

That night, I remember me and my little sister piled in with my mom and we slept next to her. I've never seen my mom so sad before.

We still have my dad's briefcase. It has his smell in it. A cologne that smells really sweet and manly at the same time.

HANDPRINTS ON THE GLASS

Sara's father was sentenced to twelve years and eight months. He began serving his sentence in Florida. On June 18, 2008, he was transferred to the CMU in Terre Haute, Indiana, and was then moved to the CMU in Marion, Illinois.

After he was put in the CMU in Terre Haute, telephone calls were every Wednesday and Sunday for fifteen minutes. The thing about telephone calls is that we share them with my grandparents, so we get every other Wednesday but every Sunday. When he was in Terre Haute, we would visit him whenever we had a break at school, so every few months, but we've only been to Marion once because it's a lot further to get to. We always have non-contact visits with a heavy glass in between us.

I have not touched my father since December 2007. If I had known, I could have made that hug longer.

Now, when we travel to Terre Haute, I stay in the car most of the time because my mom and I get stared at a lot for wearing hijabs. Like when we enter Olive Garden, everyone turns around. I can just hear them talking and whispering. I imagine them saying, "Isn't that a terrorist?" or "*Oooo*, look, it's an Arab."

I don't know what they say exactly. I'm glad I don't.

I just don't feel safe. I hate stares. I hate angry people.

*

The CMU visits are horrible. The visitation room there is so, so small, and it's hot and uncomfortable. It's surrounded by Plexiglas, and we're separated from my father by a Plexiglas wall in the middle of the room. We are all locked in. I wanna break that Plexiglas wall.

We have to use a black telephone to talk to my father through the glass. Running through the glass are all these wires. The wires reflect on the glass, so it's checkered and I don't get a clear view. I can't even see my father's full face.

I want to see his face clearly. I want to notice the littlest things, down to every little dimple or freckle, so I can keep it in my head and remember them until the next visit. In Florida, I got to hug and kiss my dad. I got to smell him and see him as he is, without a checkered pattern from a glass on his skin.

One time we asked if we could hug him on a holiday, and the guards said no, because they didn't have enough security. It's not like he's gonna kill us or hurt us. I mean, we are his daughters. It hurts so much knowing that he's right there but you can't touch him at all, like he's an animal, like he's gonna hurt you.

When it's over, you hear the guard's keys rattling on the door. That sound hurts so bad. All you see at the end of our visits are the handprints on the glass.

WHERE HE'S SUPPOSED TO BE

If my dad had died, I would accept it more; at least with that you grieve for a while but you get over it. But I can't get over it, every day that he's not here. I know where he is, and he's not supposed to be there.

I just can't accept this. He didn't do anything wrong. He was so kind, he wouldn't even let us step on ants. He would always say, "Don't step on their hills. They a have a life too." He wouldn't let us kill any bugs, he'd take spiders in a piece of tissue and let them out outside.

Everything's really hazy because I'm trying to forget every day that he's not here. I'm trying to forget yesterday too, which was just a day without him.

*

Before, I always felt like life was easy, like clean, fresh air. But when this first happened, it was like smoke afterward. It feels even worse now. It's like I'm going through steam, and I can't breathe because I'm not seeing him where he is supposed to be—in the living room, or on trips to the lake, or taking me to school, or at the dinner table, or during Eid.[3]

*

I gave up dancing and drawing because I lost interest. I also lost interest in worrying about my looks and what I wear. Now I love to read books because it gives me the chance to escape my hectic life and my sadness. I am able to step into a life where I don't have to worry about my dad every second of every day.

I also like writing poems because it is the only way I can tell you how I'm feeling and why I am the way I am. I can write poems that you will think about long after the last word. When you read my poems, you are basically reading the shedding of the weight on my shoulders.

I want to be a writer and a literature teacher for high school kids. I love English; I want it to be a part of my future.

Now I see myself as a stronger person. Before, I used to cry about

---

[3] Islamic holiday marking the end of Ramadan.

the littlest things, like when someone insulted me. But since my heart was torn once, and I have felt how bad the blow was, I feel prepared for anything. I can withstand anything.

UZMA NAHEED ABBASI

ANSER MEHMOOD

AGES: *Uzma, 40's; Anser, 51*
OCCUPATIONS: *small-business owners*
INTERVIEWED IN: *Karachi, Pakistan*

Uzma and Anser moved with their three children to the United States from Karachi, Pakistan in 1994. Anser entered the United States on a business visa, started a small trucking company, and stayed after his visa expired. The family lived in Bayonne, New Jersey, and Uzma and Anser's fourth child was born there in 2000. On October 3, 2001, FBI and INS agents came to Uzma and Anser's home to question them about two of Uzma's brothers who were wanted on credit card fraud charges. The FBI had also received a tip from a transportation company that Anser worked with, saying that he did not want to deliver to Washington, D.C. on September 11, 2001. Anser was taken into custody and immediately classified by the FBI as being "high interest." He was taken to the Metropolitan Detention Center in New York, where he spent months in solitary confinement.

Anser's lawyer was informed by government officials that the FBI agents who searched his home had found a license to carry hazardous materials, box cutters, a flight simulator program, and three Pakistani passports in his name. Anser's explanation was that his trucking company required him to have the hazardous materials license, and that he used the box cutters for his job. The flight simulator program was a video game used by his children, and of the three passports, two were expired and one was valid.

Anser's treatment was part of a policy called PENTTBOM.[1] Under this policy, Arab, Muslim, and South Asian males brought to the attention of authorities during the 9/11 terrorism investigation, and who were discovered to be non-citizens who had violated the terms of their visa, were arrested and treated as "of interest" to the government's terrorism investigation. They were subjected to a blanket "hold-until-cleared" policy. Although they could have been removed promptly from the United States because of their immigration violations, pursuant to this policy they were instead further detained until they were affirmatively cleared of terrorist ties.

In February 2002, with her husband facing deportation, Uzma decided to return to Pakistan with her children. In May of that year, Anser was deported to Pakistan for using a non-authorized social security card.

UZMA: I NEVER FELT LIKE AN OUTSIDER

Never before 9/11 did I feel like a "Muslim" in America. Never. In fact, nobody ever thought to discuss religion at all. If you were a Muslim, Hindu, Christian, whatever, you had complete freedom to go to the mosque, or church, or wherever you wanted to go worship. It was never an issue, not in the kids' school, not with our neighbors, not in our community.

I didn't think that 9/11 would lead to what it did and what it's like today.

*

I was born in Sahiwal, Pakistan, and educated in Bahawalpur. I came to Karachi in 1986 after I married.

---

[1] PENTTBOM is the codename for the FBI's investigation into the 9/11 attacks. Its name stands for Pentagon/Twin Towers Bombing Investigation. The investigation was launched on September 11, 2001 and was the largest criminal inquiry in United States history, involving 7,000 of the FBI's then 11,000 special agents.

My husband is my first cousin, my maternal uncle's son. He was a businessman when we married. Before that, he was a first officer in the Merchant Navy.

Karachi, even back then, was always an uncertain situation. One can't ever really say that they can live in Pakistan with complete peace of mind. Though I've heard it was once a very peaceful city, ever since I've been in Karachi I've only seen trouble, really.

When I first got married, life was wonderful, Mash'allah. But then my husband wanted to go to America to find work. My brother already lived over there, and he invited my husband to come as well. We didn't think at the time that we were moving there permanently, we had no such plans. We just went with two bags.

Back then it wasn't like it is now; it wasn't difficult to stay in America. If you had a visa and you went there, you could stay with no problems. My children and I had multiple-entry visas.

Anser worked so hard, and Mash'allah we were well taken care of, we were very happy. We loved our weekends together. My husband always gave us 100 percent of his time. He never had any activities of his own actually, except for his work. After work he was home with us, and it was the same on the weekends. We always got to be together.

What I liked most about America was that we never felt any discrimination. I never felt like an outsider; everyone always respected us so well. In return, we followed all their rules.

The only thing is that we never tried to get our papers while we were there or immigrate formally; we just didn't think that way. We never felt any hurdles or any necessity for it. Also, I didn't want to leave my own country forever.

ANSER: WE'RE THE ONES WHO HAVE TO COMPROMISE?

I was born in Lahore, Pakistan. But I used to live right here in Karachi, in this house we're sitting in now.

The reason we needed to emigrate was because of the local mafia. My company manufactured medical equipment. I had about twenty-seven electro-medical engineers working back then, in 1989. But because of the local mafia taking money from us every day, the business didn't take off.

One day, I decided I couldn't do it anymore. I would give them money once a week, not every day. They agreed to take the sum of four or five thousand rupees[2] once a week, and then they went away. But they came back the very next day. That day, we were shipping cardiac monitors and defibrillators to the Pakistan Army in Rawalpindi. Back then, the stuff was worth almost 4.5 crore rupees.[3] The mafia came and tried to extort money from us again, but we wouldn't give it to them. So they set fire to our goods and burned them.

I went to the police station to register a First Information Report, but the police told me to compromise. I thought, *It's our goods that got burnt and we're the ones who have to compromise?* So that's when we decided to close the business.

Once I closed shop, I just left the country.

America was wonderful. People helped me out a lot. I left Karachi with nothing, and at first the only job I found in America was as a taxi driver, so that's what I did for a while. After that, I started a small trucking company under the name Unique Trucking Company. Eventually I had a house, my own cars, my trucks. I was able to achieve all that with the guidance of helpful Americans. Allah's blessings were with me, but those people helped me a lot. They didn't discriminate about who lived among them.

I had great friends. Pakistanis, Americans, all kinds of friends. We're still in touch; they still call me, some come and visit. All my friends regret the injustice that I've suffered. They all feel bad that it happened.

---

[2] The Pakistan Rupee fluctuated greatly in 1989. Five-thousand rupees would have been the equivalent of $235–$269 US, depending on the month. At the time, the World Bank estimated the per-capita GNP at less than $400 U.S.

[3] At that time, the equivalent of $2.12–2.42 million U.S.

Before 9/11, there were no restrictions on practicing my religion. It was absolutely free. If I needed to say my prayers, nobody had a problem with it at all. Nobody had any such issues. They didn't care if you were Muslim or Christian or whatever. All that happened only after 9/11.

UZMA: THE SKYLINE HAD CHANGED

When 9/11 happened, I was getting the children dressed for school, which was right across the street from us. As soon as they left, my tenant, who lived upstairs, came down and told me that one of the towers had been hit. At the time, I had no idea what had happened. When I turned on the TV, it looked like a minor accident, so I thought, *It'll be okay, they'll be able to put out the fire and take care of it.* I didn't know how much damage had been done.

My father-in-law was staying with us, so I woke him up, made him a cup of tea, and told him once he was ready that we'd go and see what happened. We lived in New Jersey, right across the Hudson River from the Twin Towers. Right after breakfast, we got in our car and had driven about fifteen minutes when we heard that the first building had collapsed. It was only minutes later that we heard that the second one had collapsed, too. We couldn't believe our senses. We couldn't believe the towers were gone.

That day, we were so upset about what had happened. Like everyone else, those buildings were familiar to us. We went past them all the time. We'd even had a family portrait taken on top of the World Trade Center, and had read up on the history of the towers. I'd read that they were earthquake resistant, made of very strong material, so I just couldn't believe that in a minute, such great buildings were just gone.

When we got closer, we saw the skyline had changed. It didn't look like Manhattan at all. There were just clouds of smoke where the buildings used to be. We were standing outside, looking up at it, and there were some people staring at us with these strange looks. Instantly, people's attitudes toward us changed. They were saying, "These are the people." I didn't understand why they were talking about us that way.

Later that day, I needed something from the store, and the same thing happened there. For the first time, I felt like I was looked at differently for being a Muslim. I wondered what had happened all of a sudden. That very day, we felt like something had changed.

My children suffered a lot that day. They saw everything from their school. And they suffered a lot when the FBI took away their father without any reason. After that happened, our whole life changed.

ANSER: EVERYONE WAS CONSCIOUS OF US BEING DIFFERENT

On 9/11, I was driving one of my trucks to Philadelphia to pick some stuff up at a warehouse there. When I got there, the warehouse guy said to me, "Do you know the country has been attacked?" I was surprised, I had no idea. It was when I went inside and saw the World Trade Center and the Pentagon on TV that I realized what had happened.

Everyone around me was calling home and telling their loved ones that the country was under attack. Nobody really knew what was going on. I also called home. That's when I learned that my kids had seen the buildings collapse. My load was canceled that day, so I turned around back toward the New York area. On the way back, there was a massive traffic jam. It normally didn't take me very long to get back, but I reached home at 8:00 p.m. that night.

The idea never occurred to me that, because of that event, people would see me differently as a Muslim. But I saw huge changes. We lived in a very white neighborhood, and my kids went to a school with mostly white children. The day after 9/11, these kids started telling my kids they were responsible for the Twin Towers being hit. Then my neighbors started asking me funny questions. Nancy, a neighbor who used to spend hours at our house every day, questioned me about my religion. She asked where we went to pray, and she wanted to know who my friends with beards were. Everyone had suddenly become conscious of us being different, and they were interested in where we went and who visited us. From the second day, we felt these changes.

All I can say is, people changed.

UZMA: THEY SHOULD HAVE TAKEN ME INSTEAD

On the morning of October 3, 2001, I was lying in bed with my one-year-old sleeping next to me. I wasn't feeling too well that morning, so I'd told my husband to get the kids ready for school while I slept on. Later, when I awoke, I was amazed to see men in FBI jackets all over my room. One of them was going through my closet.

I ran downstairs with the baby and found about twenty-five people all over my house—they were in the basement and even down our street. They were searching our house, picking up things and throwing them aside, acting crazy. God knows what they were looking for.

One of the agents asked me my name. I replied, "Uzma Naheed."

He told me, "Look, you already made a mistake. You didn't tell us your full name." He said I had only told him my name was Uzma Naheed, when my passport said Uzma Naheed Abbasi.

I didn't understand, so I asked them what the problem was. I said, "There's nothing wrong with that, I usually don't go by Abbasi." I told them it's no big deal, that people often refer to themselves by their short names. I asked another agent his name, and he told me his first name, and I said, "See, you didn't tell me your whole name, did you?"

Then they asked me this and that, about what my husband does and how he lives, I don't even remember anymore. First they questioned me and then they questioned my husband, but anyway, there was no charge on my husband at all. They charged me with something to do with my brother Ahmer. They had arrested him just a week before. He was an illegal immigrant and had some issue with his credit card, I'm not sure what. They told me they were going to arrest me on his behalf. So I said, "Okay, you do whatever investigation you need to do."

One of the women there told me to take off my jewelry and get ready to go with them. So I said, "Okay," I went to the bathroom and took off my jewelry and got ready to leave with them. Just as we were leaving, my little baby started to cry. He cried so much that Anser told the agents that the baby was very attached to me, and that he wouldn't be able to stay without me. He said, "You can't take his mama away now," even though they were only going to take me for a night or so, to question me. Anser said he wouldn't be able to care for the baby alone, so he told the men to take him instead for questioning, to leave me behind.

They hadn't found a thing at our house. They only wanted me to go with them because of some trouble with my brother. They had already questioned Anser at the house for almost an hour and a half, and found nothing wrong with his answers.

But they took him away. They should have taken me instead.

At the time I thought, *Oh well then, he'll just go instead of me and they can ask him whatever they need to.* But when I looked down from the window, I saw they had handcuffed him.

That surprised me. Why would they need to handcuff him? My children were about to come home from school, and I didn't want them to see their father that way. Why should they have to remember that image?

When my children came back from school they were surprised to see the house the way it was, with things thrown all over the place. They wanted to know where their papa was. I just told them, "He's coming."

When they took my husband away, they'd given me a phone number to call him at, and promised he would be home in a day or two. At the time, I didn't know anything. I had never lived alone or done anything alone. My poor children were worried too.

I called my mother and my father-in-law in Pakistan right away. I told them some FBI people had come and taken Anser away. Of course, then they became worried too. But I told them, "It's nothing to worry about, he'll be back by tomorrow."

That's what I had been told, anyway.

All night I called that number they had given me, but nobody answered.

*

The next morning I became really anxious. I hadn't had any communication with my husband, and I didn't know where he was. I only had that one number.

I tried to go about my routine the following day, but I became really frightened, because I still couldn't get through on that number and my husband still hadn't called.

On the third day, I ventured out; I went to the city with my children. I told them we would go to a police station there and see if there was any news of their father. But when we got there, I couldn't even talk. I wasn't even sure what to ask the police, about where my husband was, why he had been taken away, what was going on. I just didn't understand where to begin.

Nobody would talk to us. The police just told me that if it was an FBI case, they had nothing to do with it.

I couldn't stop crying. My children kept saying "Mama, don't cry, don't cry, why are you crying?"

I thought it was time to go meet a lawyer. Our community at the time was mostly Jewish. There weren't many Muslims there. I had nobody I could ask for advice. Our neighbors had become suspicious of us and refused to talk to me. There was just one Egyptian lady, who lived in the apartment below us. She was the one person who was always very nice. Other than that, I had nobody to go to. I had only one brother in America, but he had been arrested too. He didn't have any real charges against him either; he was just one of those people they picked up on the street randomly in those days and jailed.

*

I hired a lawyer to find my husband for me. He told me his fee was $300. Two or three days later, I found out through someone else that Anser was at the Metropolitan Detention Center in Brooklyn.

I went back to the lawyer and said, "I want my money back, I already know where he is and I was only paying you to find out. I don't need your information anymore." I had no money as it was, and I had children at home and no job.

The lawyer said, "Do you think this is a laundromat, where you can demand your cash back?" He hadn't given me any information, any help; he just took my $300.

I went to another lawyer, one we had hired for my brother. He was in Manhattan and I knew him, he was also Pakistani. I told him I needed his help. So he arranged a lawyer for me, someone who would stay in touch with me and help me out. Through him, I found out Anser had been charged with an expired visa and was due to appear in court in a week or so.

Slowly, people started appearing who could help me. The Islamic Circle of North America (ICNA)[4] people helped me so much. They would always go with me when we knew Anser had a date in court. They also came to know that I was living alone with my children, with no source of income. I didn't have much of a bank balance. It wasn't like Anser and I had saved that much money, so they helped me with financial support.

ANSER: SOLITARY CONFINEMENT

From my house the FBI took me to a place on Varick Street, in Manhattan. There were a lot of people there. On the way, the officers had told me, "We'll let you go by evening," since it wasn't really me they wanted. They

---

[4] A community organization and advocacy group focused on supporting the American-Muslim community.

kept me all night, though, and in the morning they took me to the Metropolitan Detention Center. They kept me there for seven months.

One of the officers told me I was there because of the World Trade Center attack, but during that whole time, they never once came to me for interrogation.

For four months, I was in solitary confinement. I was kept in a twelve-by-six cell and was video monitored at all times. A urinal and wash basin were in the same cell. I could be seen through a glass window in the door.

There were guards outside my cell. At the beginning, they didn't let me sleep. If they knew I was falling asleep, they would loudly rattle their keys or bang on the door to keep me awake.

I wasn't allowed to see anybody else or know who else was there. I wasn't even allowed to make a sound, let alone talk to people.

On February 6, 2002, I was taken downstairs to general population, where they kept me with other prisoners—murderers, dacoits,[5] etc.

Prisoners there used to be terrified of being kept in solitary confinement, so all the other prisoners, even the huge ones, were afraid of me. They figured I must have done something really bad to have come from solitary confinement.

UZMA: THERE IS NO ANSER MEHMOOD HERE

I went to see Anser after they moved him out of solitary confinement. By that time, I'd got a very good lawyer through ICNA, called Marty Stolar. But now they had put Anser with, oh, such criminal people! People who had murdered others!

Anser was in chains and handcuffs, wearing those orange clothes. He looked so weak. There were video cameras all around us. He asked me if the kids were okay. But truth be told, I was so busy running around after lawyers, I had no time to see what was happening to my children. The poor

---

[5] An Anglo-Indian colloquial word for bandits or robbers.

things would get themselves ready for school, come home themselves, make food and eat themselves, do their homework alone. They even looked after their baby brother. Living alone all those months had been very difficult.

The kids were in public school. My eldest son Umair was in eighth grade, Uzair was in seventh grade, and Harris was in sixth. The other students there really tormented them. They kept telling my kids things like, "You people are terrorists," because of what had happened to their father. They had a lot of problems in school and got into a lot of fights because other kids were making their lives miserable. They would get upset when people bullied them. They would get angry and tell me that other kids called them names. I told them to forget about it and not go outside too much. But of course they still had to go to school, where kids would keep teasing them.

Even their teachers had become strange with them. They said Umair had mental issues, and for me to send him for counseling. This wasn't true. He was a very intelligent child, he did really well in school, but the teachers had also come down to petty discrimination. When they made me take him for counseling, I saw that all the other kids there had developmental issues, the kind of kids who can't hear or speak properly. And there was my son, a smart eighth-grader. But they told me if I didn't send my son there, they wouldn't let him stay in school. They even made me pay a fee for the counseling, $150 or $200. I had no money at all, but they harassed me until I paid.

*

My neighbors discriminated against me a lot. They picked on me in little ways, like demanding that I clear my footpath of snow, little things like that. They knew I was alone with young children and couldn't always get out and do it immediately, but they would harass me and say, "Come out and do it!"

I tried putting up my home for sale once, but whenever anyone would come to see the house, the neighbors would tell them all about our circumstances before they even had a chance to come in, and then they wouldn't be interested anymore.

I didn't have any friends or neighbors that I could count on there. I had always been absorbed in my family and children until then. There were a couple of other Pakistani families who lived some distance from us. They were very good people who helped care for my baby a lot. Sometimes I had to be out all day, and I didn't want to leave the baby with my kids; they were too young to watch him for so long.

I was out talking a great deal after the FBI took my husband away. I don't think any other women had come out yet to talk about it. I told everyone, I told the media what had happened, how the government had blamed us without any reason. They'd just started calling us terrorists, when we were just ordinary citizens. The same way everyone saw what had happened, we witnessed it too. The same way everyone grieved for what had happened, we did too. I don't know how they involved us in their accusations.

*

My children would go with me and visit Anser. Once we went on Eid.[6] On Eid day, the ICNA people told me that prisoners were allowed to see their relatives for religious holidays. They told us to get ready, that they would come and pick us up. So I got my children dressed nicely and we cooked food to take with us. We thought we'd see him and we'd all eat together there, as a family.

But when we got there, one of the guards said to me "What Anser Mehmood? There is no Anser Mehmood here."

They often did that with me. I would call them and they would give me a time to visit. It took a long time to get there—I had to take a bus and then a train, and I had to change subways many times. When I got

---

[6] Eid al-Fitr marks the end of Ramadan, and Eid al-Adha—occurring approximately two months and ten days later—marks the end of the hajj period.

there, they would let everyone meet their relatives, but when my number came, they would say, "There's nobody here by that name. Go away." Then I would have to leave.

When I went with my children on Eid, we waited outside in the car for a long time. We kept going in and asking about Anser. Eventually the guards started saying they would let us meet him in an hour, then two hours. We had been there since morning, and then it became evening. The children didn't eat their food; we kept thinking that we would eat together, with Anser.

Finally, they just told us, "There is no Anser Mehmood here." It was so cold that day and the baby was with us, but they didn't even let us come inside. My poor children went home crying. We had spent all of Eid sitting in that car.

I DIDN'T WANT TO RAISE MY CHILDREN WITHOUT A FATHER

Our lawyers told me that the government probably wouldn't let my husband go, and that even if they did, they would deport him. They gave Anser a choice: fight or leave. He decided not to fight, and to be deported back to Pakistan. All the lawyers told me I should get immigration papers made for myself and my children, so I could stay if I wanted to. But I didn't want to raise my children there without a father. I decided I couldn't fight it all alone anymore. I thought it would be best if we went back to Pakistan, so we left, in February 2002. Yesterday was exactly nine years to the day since I came back to Karachi.

Marty had told me that within a week of my return, Anser would be sent back to Pakistan. Instead, it took about three months. The day Anser came home, the whole family went to the airport to pick him up. When he arrived, he was so weak, so weak.

Everyone here was just amazed that a man who couldn't kill a fly was being kept for terrorism allegations. Anser was known for never so much as raising his voice at anyone.

The truth is, your problems are always your own. Nobody can really share them with you. I suppose having my family around me makes a difference, in that there's someone to ask after you. But nobody can really help.

*

My children still haven't adjusted to life in Pakistan. Their upbringing was all in America, their education was there. Everything here is different. On the one hand, we're telling them to live one way, but on the other hand, they've grown up in a different way. Anser and I knew what we would have to deal with, so we were mentally prepared. Their academics were affected. Their lives had been disrupted. We had a lot of financial problems here as well, and our children saw a lot of hardship. All the dreams I had for them were spoiled.

My children still want to go back to America. It feels like they'll run away as soon as they get a chance! From what I've been hearing since I returned, about families having to go through what we did, facing the kind of injustice that I faced, it's not a one-off situation. It's still happening.

ANSER: LIFE IS CARRYING ON

At least the Americans released me. If it had happened in Pakistan—if I had been suspected of blowing up the World Trade Center while I was here—I believe I would not have been released.

I had my home here. My family was here when I came back. There are many changes in Karachi. Now, economically and politically, Pakistan is in a terrible state. If there used to be one person extorting money a few years ago, now there are three. Now even the Sunni Tehreek[7] comes to collect money.

---

[7] A sectarian Islamic political organization based largely in Karachi, and often associated with promoting traditional Islamic beliefs and practices.

Now I am in my rhythm. Currently we are a little short of funds, but by God's grace my earth-moving machinery business is in practice. I am fine here. Life is carrying on.

YASIR ALADDIN AFIFI

AGE: *20*
OCCUPATION: *student; computer salesman*
INTERVIEWED IN: *Santa Clara, California*

Born in the United States to an Egyptian father and an American mother, Yasir grew up in Santa Clara, California, until he was thirteen. He then moved to Egypt for five years before returning to the United States in 2008 to continue his education. In October 2010, during a routine oil change, Yasir discovered a tracking device under his car. Two days later, FBI agents came to his apartment. They demanded the tracking device back and questioned him about his travels in the Middle East. During the questioning, Yasir learned that the agents had been collecting detailed information on him, from his upcoming travel plans to the fact that he was looking for a new job. Since Yasir's interview with us in 2010, he has sued the government over the tracking action, claiming it was a violation of his civil rights.

When my parents split up in 2003, my dad won custody of me and my two younger brothers Adam and Sherief. After the divorce, he decided to move back to Egypt. I guess he'd just had it because he probably started to get homesick. He'd been away for twenty-five years and only visited his family once or twice a year. Also, his parents were very old and not in great health, and he wanted to make sure they were cared for.

I was thirteen at the time. At first, I thought moving to Egypt with my dad was a horrible idea. I didn't want to go, but during my time there I learned a lot of things, like family virtue, family values, and dignity. In Egypt, families are a lot tighter than they are in the United States, and they care about each other a lot more. That was the vibe I felt when I was there. There's a lot more support from friends and family members. People wish others well there, and they want people to be the best for everybody and not just for themselves.

What I didn't like about Egypt was that you could sense the oppression everywhere you went. I felt it in conversations, I saw it on people's faces. Everybody had their own problems, and too many of them. People were not happy. There's just too much of a poverty line. There aren't enough job opportunities there, the education system is wrecked, and the political system isn't as great as it could be.

I missed the United States a lot. I missed my friends and my neighborhood in Santa Clara where I grew up. It was a peaceful, friendly environment, a really nice neighborhood. We had been happy there.

*

In 2008, we came back to the United States together—me, my dad, my brothers, and my dad's new wife, an Egyptian woman. We were here to visit for a week and a half. My dad wanted us to come back so that my brothers and I could visit our mom, since we hadn't seen her in so long.

At that time, I was eighteen and studying linguistics at Ain Shams College in Egypt. Linguistics was the only available subject in English that I could take. While I'm really good at reading and writing in Arabic, I found Arabic history and Egyptian history at the university level too difficult. But I realized I was wasting my time at college in Egypt, and that I had better options back in California. So, during that week and a half in Santa Clara, I set up a job and I found an apartment for the fall. I wanted to show my dad how badly I needed to stay in the United States to continue my education, and that I had all the conditions available for me to stay and work and study.

He eventually accepted it. He wished me the best of luck, he told me he would always stay in contact, and then he flew back. Soon after he got back to Egypt, he had a heart attack and passed away. It felt horrible. I felt bad that I wasn't there, but what could I do? I went back to Egypt and stayed for almost a month to get everything situated, to make sure my brothers were in the same school. My aunt—my father's sister—took them in. Every day I think about bringing my brothers to the United States. The plan is to bring them here when the youngest, Adam, turns eighteen next year.

NO PLACE FEELS LIKE HOME

Two weeks after returning to the United States, I started my first year in college, studying business marketing. I love it. Now I'm a sophomore. At the same time, I work for a computer company doing commercial sales.

I work full-time because I have to. I feel the need to be a better person and to be financially stable enough to support my brothers. If I need to help them out in any way, I can be ready.

I like Santa Clara. I like the people, the community, the weather, the job opportunities, and the education system. I know most of the people in this community and they know me, and there's moral support. If I ever need advice, I can have that within a second. It's an American-Muslim community, with a vast mix of Americans.

No place feels like home, yet. Not even Santa Clara. But it comes the closest.

AN ANONYMOUS TIP

In the spring of 2010, I got a call at work from my roommate. He told me he'd just had two FBI agents knocking on the door who wanted to speak to me. So I got a name and number and I called them up. I said, "Hi, this is Yasir Afifi. How can I help you?"

The agent said, "Hey, Yasir. Oh, it's nothing, we just received an anonymous tip from someone who said that you may be a threat to national security."

I said, "Great! How can I help you?"

I didn't think there was an anonymous tip. It was so slick off his tongue, I was sure it was just something the FBI said to people. I think I fit some type of profile for them—I'm Arab-American, I'm Muslim, I fly to Egypt a lot to see my family, and I'd just recently come back from Dubai for a computer expo.

The agent said, "Well, we just want to sit down and ask you a couple of questions so we can put this to the side."

I replied, "I'd love to cooperate and answer any of your questions, once my lawyer tells me that's the right thing to do."

He wasn't too happy to hear that. Then he said, "Okay, whatever, that's fine. I'll be waiting for your phone call."

I didn't really have a lawyer, so I called a prepaid legal service. This was a service I could call any time to ask legal questions or understand my rights. The lawyer there told me, "You don't have to answer any questions. You don't have to sit and talk with that FBI agent." She said, "These are your rights, and you don't have to do anything unless they have a warrant or some evidence against you."

Once I understood that, I asked her to call the FBI agent and to push him away. So she called him and told him, "Mr. Afifi understands his rights, and that he doesn't have to answer any of your questions."

I didn't really care how they'd react. I wasn't tempted to go in and prove myself. I understand that the FBI are professionals, not your friends, and so I have no reason to speak with any FBI agent. And that's my right.

Fortunately they never called me again after that. I thought it was going to be the last I'd hear from them.

A REGULAR OIL CHANGE

About six months later, in October, I took my car to my mechanic in Santa Clara for an oil change. As the mechanic was elevating the car on the hydraulic lift, I noticed that there was something like a piece of string or wire coming out from the back. Then, when the car was fully elevated, I noticed this black device under the back of the car. I asked the mechanic to pull it out, and he handed it to me. He was somewhat freaked out.

There was a big, black rod attached to something that looked like a walkie-talkie. I wasn't freaked out because I had an idea of what it was—it looked like a tracking device! I didn't think it was normal at all, and I had a feeling it was the FBI who'd put it there.

When I got home, some of my friends and I Googled the serial number of the tracking device. What came up was "Federal Property Tracking Device GPS, $1500, $4,200, $3,200." I was thinking about selling it. I'm a salesman, that's what we do!

But in the end I didn't think it'd be a great idea to sell it. I wasn't going to do anything with it until a lawyer told me what I should do. As my friends and I were Googling the information, my friend posted a blog about it on Reddit, the social network site. He posted this comment: "Me and my friend went to the mechanic today and we found this on his car. I am pretty confident it is a tracking device by the FBI but my friend's roommates think it is a bomb. Any thoughts?"

Within two or three hours we'd made the front page on Reddit and received maybe 3,500 comments. We even started getting calls from the ACLU.

A lot of people wanted to talk about this. Most of them were just random people giving opinions, but one person actually found out what exactly this device was—its real name, its authentic cost, who it is and isn't supposed to be sold to.[1]

Family and friends told me to just live my life normally, to not do anything differently. They said, "You're going to school and you're working. You're a perfectly normal person who happened to find a tracking device on your car. Just relax."

---

[1] The tracking device has been identified as an Orion Guardian ST820, made by the company Cobham. Cobham sells the device exclusively to military and law enforcement personnel.

And that's what I did.

Until now I don't know exactly why the device looked so rudimentary and unsophisticated, but I can only guess that maybe I'm not a priority on their list. I think the FBI are as smart as they get, and if they didn't want me to find the tracking device, I probably would have never found it. Maybe they were just trying to scare me or somebody else, if not the whole community.

A VISIT FROM THE FBI

Two days after I found the device, the FBI showed up near my house.

That day, I came home from work at around five o'clock. One of my friends and my roommate were in the living room, just chilling, watching TV. My roommate said to me, "There are two people standing next to your car."

I had somewhere I had to go anyway, so I changed my clothes and walked out to my car.

There was a man and a woman standing at the back of my car, to the right of it. They were standing exactly where the device had been.

As I walked by I said, "Hi."

They just stood there and played stupid.

Right when I opened the car door, the man said, "Hey, did you know your tags are expired?"

I replied, "Yes, I know that. Does that bother you?"

He just laughed it off and looked the other way, so I got into my car and started the ignition. As I started leaving the complex, I saw two brown, unmarked SUVs pull in. They turned around, pulled a U-turn, waited, and then followed me for about ten seconds.

When I got into the street they started flashing their lights, so I pulled over. Then I realized there were *three* cars: one small and black, a Caprice, I believe, and the two brown SUVs. The man and woman from before were in the black Caprice. I was feeling pretty intimidated.

A police officer wearing an FBI vest came up to my window and said,

"Did you know your tags are expired?"

I said, "Yes. Is that why you pulled me over?"

After I showed him my license, registration and insurance, he asked me to come out of the vehicle and speak to the man and woman from the Caprice, who were standing beside him. The man showed me his FBI badge. His name was Vincent, and the woman was called Jennifer.

Vincent asked me, "Do you know why we are here?"

I said, "No, but I have an idea. Would you mind *telling* me why you are here?"

Then he asked, "Were you at a mechanic's shop last Sunday?"

"Yes."

"Where is the device that you found under the car?"

I asked, "Are you the person who put it there?"

"Yes, we put it there."

"Okay, how can I help you?"

He said, "We need that device back right now."

I replied, "Do you have a search warrant or anything proving that this is your device?"

Then Vincent got a little frustrated, and he said, "Yeah I can get you a search warrant. I'll get it for you within an hour."

I asked him, "Why didn't you bring it with you just now?"

And then Jennifer started coming into the conversation with a real soft tone, and she was very charming, very sweet. She told me, "You know, we're just trying to help you. We need this device back and then we'll leave you alone. It would be helpful if you cooperated."

I said, "I am cooperating with you. And I don't mind answering any of your questions."

I just felt like Vincent was much more intimidating, and she was the nice one, you know, really sweet and everything. She said, "What happened to the device? Did you do anything to it? Did you lose it?"

"Nothing happened to the device," I said. I told them I'd thought about selling it. I think they thought it was funny. Then they asked me for the device a couple more times, and finally I told them, "I don't mind giving it to you. It's in my living room. Follow me."

I walked them back to my house. Vincent, Jennifer, and four cops waited for me directly outside my door. As I opened the door to my house, Vincent was about to step inside my living room, but I asked him to stay outside while I got the device. He said, "Sure."

So I went in and picked up the device, and then I handed it to Vincent. I said, "Is this what you wanted?"

He said "Yes! This is what we needed."

"And is there anything else I can help you with?"

"Yes, we'd love to just, if you don't mind, ask you a couple of questions."

I told him I'd be more than happy to answer all of his questions. I hadn't spoken to my lawyer, but at the same time, it didn't make any sense for me not to answer their questions. I knew that I wasn't doing anything wrong, so I didn't want them to say, "Why are you avoiding our questions?"

The seven of us walked around the complex as Vincent and Jennifer asked me questions. I was confident in what I was doing, so I felt no pressure. What I expected was what happened; the questions were pretty simple. Vincent asked me, "Have you ever been to Yemen, for any type of training? Do you know anybody there?"

"Never been to Yemen," I replied. "I've only been to Egypt and Dubai."

Then he asked me if I had ever been to Syria or Iran, and if I'd ever been in any type of training. I told him no.

After we'd been walking for about a couple minutes, the four cops walked back to their car. It was just me, Vincent, and Jennifer, so I tried finding out why they were here by asking them some simple questions myself. The more I asked, the more I understood from Jennifer how much she knew about my personal life. She told me things like, "I like your taste. I like these restaurants that you're going to," and "We know that you're flying to Dubai in two weeks."

She also knew that I was looking for a new job. The only way she could have known all this was either through my phone or email. So,

I was 100 percent sure they didn't only have a tracking device under my car—they also had my phone and email tapped.

Jennifer could speak Arabic, but I couldn't get her to talk too much in the language. I was trying to figure out where she was from, trying to find out more information about them, but hers wasn't an accent that I could identify, and I can pick up accents anywhere. For the past two years, my job every day has been to talk to Arabic business owners across the world, all of whom have different dialects. All I can say is that Jennifer's was just clear Arabic, clear enough for me to understand that she wasn't Arab. She said she was Lebanese, but I didn't really buy that.

It ended with them telling me, "We appreciate your cooperation. You've been great. Sorry to bother you; you're boring. No need to call your lawyer."

I thought by "boring" they meant that I wasn't too significant or important to them. Nonetheless, as they left, I thought, *Let me call my lawyer right now and find out what she thinks of all this.*

Not a lot of people find a tracking device under their car. I'd have to say I was more confused than scared, and maybe a bit pissed, too, about them invading my privacy.

STOPPED AT THE AIRPORT

Fortunately I didn't hear from the FBI again, but I have other problems. Each time I leave the United States I don't have problems; the problems usually happen when I come back to the United States.

For example, I got stopped when I came back to the United States from Egypt about two weeks ago. Right when I stepped off the plane, there was an officer standing there waiting for me. When he saw my passport he said to another officer, "Oh! That's him!"

I had no idea why they stopped me, but I gave them my bags and they walked me to the Border Patrol Office. There were a lot of people in there of different ethnicities, but most of them were Arab. Many of those people came and left before me. Some were there for thirty minutes, some were there for an hour, some were there for two hours. Even with my dad, every time we flew back into the United States from Egypt we would be stopped for some type of interrogation. After an hour or sometimes two, they would just give him back his passport.

Finally, the officers brought in my check-in bag and asked me if they could open it and search it. I told them, "Go ahead." They only found my clothes and my belongings. Then they asked me simple questions like, "What were you doing in Egypt? What are you doing in the United States? Why are you coming back?"

I had to stay for almost four and a half hours before they finally gave me back my passport and told me, "You're good to go."

TOTAL INVASION OF PRIVACY

I think the FBI are probably still watching me. I have no idea if they'll put another device under my car, but after that visit I did change my phone number. I just hope I never have to get another call from them.

The total invasion of my privacy bothers me. Two people, or maybe more than two people, know my whereabouts every day. They know what I'm doing, who I'm talking to. I understand that, as an American citizen, you're not supposed to be subjected to that. You're not supposed to invade another person's privacy.

I hope people my age, or Muslim-American youth, can use me as an example to understand what their rights are and how to assert them, to be confident in what they are doing as long as it's not anything wrong, and to never be intimidated by any federal agency.

*

On 9/11, I was ten years old and on my way to class in Santa Clara. I remember my mom crying. I remember school being closed that day. What I mainly remember about that day is that all of America was struck. A lot of people were hurt. At that time, when people were looking at

Islam as an extremist view, it was probably a moment for the Muslim community to help out and speak up about what Islam really is.

As a country, we can get past this by understanding the true meaning of Islam, by not exaggerating what extremists are doing in the world, and by not blaming their negative actions on Islam. Our religion does not teach these actions. It's a peaceful way of life, that's the way I look at it. We all believe in one god, and we all support each other, we all pray, and we all ask for forgiveness. And we try to live an ordinary life, to better ourselves, to be humble, and to be good to everybody.

I am not particularly religious. I pray, but not as much as I should. I do attend mosque every week for Friday prayer. But I have a lot of other priorities now; I'm working and studying full-time, and it's hard for me to devote another good part of my time to religion, even though I want to. I hope maybe one day to be a little bit closer to God.

FAHEEM MUHAMMAD

AGE: *28*
OCCUPATION: *marketing manager*
INTERVIEWED IN: *Santa Monica, California*

Faheem Muhammad was born in Karachi, Pakistan and moved to the United States in December 1991. Growing up in Southern California, he was an avid basketball player and dreamed of playing for the NBA. On December 20, 2009, during an annual road trip, Faheem and six of his friends were detained and questioned by Nevada police for praying in a commercial parking lot.

My friends and I try to do a road trip once a year, just try to get away from everything. Being busy individuals with school, work, or whatever, we make a point of it. We all came through the same Muslim Students Association (MSA)[1] and found Islam at the same time, so in a sense, we kind of grew up together. In the group there was an Indian, two Pakistanis, two Lebanese, one Egyptian, and a Jordanian. But we are all Americans.

The last trip I'd gone on with these guys, we went to a volcano up north. It was snowy and we went up to the top of the mountain, and we didn't feel like walking down, so we just kind of just slid down on

---

[1] A Muslim advocacy and support group organized through chapters based at colleges and universities. For more details, see the glossary.

the side—300, 400 feet on snow with nothing but our jeans! It was a fun trip.

For the 2009 trip, we stayed in Las Vegas, and then we drove up to Mount Zion National Park in Utah, which is about three hours' drive from Las Vegas. On the last day we took the tour of the Hoover Dam, and around, 2:30, 3:00 p.m. we were headed back. By that time, we were all hungry. We're like, "All right guys, let's eat, make one stop, and then just head back," because the next day everybody had to work. So we stopped at a Chili's in the city of Henderson, just outside of Las Vegas.

The time for Asr, afternoon prayers, was coming up, so we ordered and told the waitress, "We're going to go pray. We're not, like, trying to ditch!"

She said, "Yeah, sure, take your time."

Anywhere we're at, we'll stop to pray. If we're already somewhere, we'll go off to the side, without blocking anyone or anything, and pray. We've done that so many times. So that day we prayed right outside of Chili's on the sidewalk. By the time we got back in, the food was there. We ate, everything was cool.

After we ate, we stopped at a gas station and filled up the van for the last time. By then, it was Maghrib, evening prayer time. So we parked the van, and then we prayed in the parking lot.

After we were done praying, we started getting in the van, but then two cop cars pulled up with their high beams on and blocked us.

One of the cops got out of his car and said, "Do you know what's going on? Do you know why we're stopping you?"

My friend, who was the driver, said, "No, we just got done praying."

They told all of us to get out of the car. When we got out, they had their guns drawn. They weren't pointing at us, but they were still drawn and pointing downward.

They told us to sit on the curb. That's when I quietly took out my cellphone and started filming. So we were sitting on the curb, and the cop asked us again, "Do you know why you guys are being stopped?"

I really didn't, I was just so confused.

The cop said, "We had two calls. One said that there's suspicious activity, seven guys kissing the ground, and the other call said that there might be prayer."

They told us to give them our driver's licenses. There were people filling up their cars, and cars going by,

One of my friends said, "Do you think every time a Muslim prays it's suspicious activity?"

One of the cops replied, "Well, we don't know what you're saying. We don't know if you're repeating the same thing, or if you're standing there in the corner saying, 'I hope I kill a cop today.'"

They were being friendly, but in a condescending way. It seemed like they were kind of egging us on.

This is the funny part. Then a third police car came and the cop said, "Man, today's been so hectic, it took me an hour to get here. There's a robbery going down, right down the street, some store is being robbed."

We said, "Hey, if you guys need to go handle that, go ahead, we'll wait for you here."

They said, "Oh no, no, no, we have other people over there."

So they ran our licenses and then they went one by one asking us questions: who we are, where we live, what our addresses are.

I was pissed off because we told them repeatedly that all we were doing was praying. There was a robbery going down, and yet the seven of us were being sat down on a curb like criminals, feeling like second-class citizens.

Then the sergeant said, "Next time, if we come upon someone who's praying, is it better for us to wait until they're done before we start talking to them, or is it rude?"

I was just kind of going nuts at that time. I thought, *Is this guy really asking us this?* I said, "Look, my frustration is, you're supposed to protect and serve us. But you guys don't even know who the hell I am. Whoever you report to, maybe we can suggest them to bring in an organization that will do sensitivity training for you guys and get you the basic training on what Islam is."

He was pretty receptive. I know there are cops who wouldn't put up with that at all, but he was listening to what I was saying. He admitted that their police department didn't receive any sensitivity training whatsoever. I then offered to hook them up with contact information for organizations that have come down and done trainings for the L.A. Sheriff's department. At least they walked away with a phone number, email, all that stuff, to get training.

Then they asked us, "Can we search the van, or not?"

We were thinking, *Uh, catch-22*, because if we said no, then they were going to think, *What the hell are you hiding?*

So we told them, "Go ahead and search the van."

They didn't search through our stuff, they just looked through the glove compartment, asking us where we stayed and stuff like that.

Toward the end, the sergeant finally found out I was taping the whole thing. He said, "I hope this doesn't end up on YouTube. I don't want to see my ugly face up on the internet."

After the incident, Faheem and his friends contacted the Council on American-Islamic Relations (CAIR). They explained what had happened and showed them the video. CAIR began an investigation, which revealed that the police officers involved had run Faheem's and his friends' names through the FBI Terrorist Screening Center. In March 2010, CAIR filed a misconduct complaint against the police officers involved.

FARID RODRIGUEZ

AGE: *72*
OCCUPATION: *custodian*
INTERVIEWED IN: *Brooklyn, New York*

Farid came to the United States in 1975 from his native Colombia. After 9/11, he found that his Arabic name had changed from oddity to liability. Similarly, his unclear immigration status had come under increased scrutiny. In May 2004, Farid was arrested by immigration officers and placed in federal detention for three months at Passaic County Jail, New Jersey. Having previously served a brief sentence in federal prison in the mid-eighties, Farid witnessed a deterioration in prison conditions and in the treatment of undocumented inmates after 9/11. Farid shared his story with us at his home in Brooklyn.

All identities have been changed to protect the parties involved.

My name, Farid, has always been foreign. It's not a Spanish name, and how it arrived in Latin America is as mysterious as why it was given to me. It wasn't common in Cali, Valle Del Cauca, Colombia, where I was born in 1938. And now it stands out in New York City, where I have lived for half of my life. Now my name is associated with people and cultures that some Americans think hate the United States.

I had never met another Farid until my early thirties, in Cali. He was a truck driver, and he told me he too had never met another Farid. It wasn't until I had been living in the United States for almost thirty years, when the Twin Towers were turned to rubble in 2001, and when stories about Arab and Muslim people dominated the television news, that I realized that my name came from the Arabic language.

My last name, "Rodriguez" wasn't given to me by my father either, and it never belonged to my mother. I was born out of wedlock, and my mother died when I was around three years old. She worked in a textile factory, and like other garment laborers, I think she died of a lung disease. My father lived in another town, and I was raised in the homes of different relatives. At one point, I lived with my father for almost two years. I ran away several times from his home as a young child, and eventually lived with an uncle.

I remained nameless until I was old enough to start school. I was about six years old when the school's nun asked for my last name. I said "Rodriguez" because that was my Uncle Francisco's family name. He was my mother's cousin, but I called him "Father." He raised me in my parents' absence, but he traveled for long periods while working in other regions of the country.

After September 11, the name Farid started appearing on television, and was usually the name belonging to someone accused of plotting against the United States. It was around this time when I started to feel a connection with Arab people, because they were the target of suspicion and stereotypes because of where they were from. I dreaded that something similar could happen to me.

I LOVED THE USA BEFORE I EVER CAME HERE

I had started loving the United States long before I came here. In Colombia, I had seen many American movies. My first job was working in a movie theater when I was about ten or eleven years old. So when I arrived in the United States in March of 1975, I wasn't shocked at what I saw because I felt as if I had already seen everything before—the skyscrapers, the street corners and the subways. When I arrived, I liked everything about living in the United States, especially the transportation system. I owned a small bus company in Cali, but the roads here were something else, especially the bridges and tunnels. I often asked myself, H*ow did the people who built these bridges so wide know that in the future there would be so many cars?*

I started working soon after landing in New York. I cleaned apartments. In Colombia I earned money easily, $1,000 per month. But here I earned only $700 per month, and that was after working very hard.

I kept delaying my departure date, and I overstayed my visa. I had fallen in love with New York, and with my new wife. By 1976, I had gotten married and my wife had given birth to our first daughter, Diana. At first we struggled, living uncomfortably in a basement. But eventually we rented our own apartment. We were progressing financially. We didn't want to leave the United States, and I didn't even want to think about Colombia. I didn't care that I had left everything behind, because I thought that I would rebuild a business here. But I never developed a plan for getting ahead. I just thought there would be time in the future to do so.

*

Since my wife and I wanted to stay here, we began applying for our residency papers. My family returned to Colombia for about eight months while waiting for our immigration interviews. Once we received our green cards, we returned to New York as permanent, legal residents, and our lives continued to Americanize. I bought a 1979 Camaro, food-shopped at Pathmark, and accompanied my wife on shopping trips to Delancey Street on the Lower East Side of Manhattan. My wife and I attended Sunday mass in English, wore blue jeans, and walked in sneakers. I liked that I could wear the same outfit in the day as in the evening. We also enrolled in English language classes.

In 1980, my wife gave birth to our first son, Leonidas, and we were very happy. We were living in a spacious one-bedroom apartment in Sunset Park, Brooklyn. I liked the people there. They came from everywhere; they were Irish, Italians, and Russians. Some were born here and others were born outside of the country. Today there is tremendous ethnic and religious diversity in Brooklyn, including South Asian, Arab, and Muslim people. They are all American to me.

Most of the South Asian, Arab, and Muslim people I have met have been through work. Since 1986, I have had a custodial job cleaning offices. One of my friends there was Youssef from Morocco, who, like me, worked as a custodian. He was a tall, lean man. Educated. He spoke English, French, and Spanish. I liked how he pronounced my name with an accent on the "I" and I imagined it was how my name was supposed to be enunciated. Twice I visited him at his home in Astoria, Queens for dinner. I realized how much I liked their food. We sat on the floor and ate different kinds of fresh, soft meats, rice, and carrots, similar to Latino food. He left the job before 9/11, and we lost touch.

There was another man, an urban planner, one of the many executives who worked in the buildings I clean. He carried a straw mat with him and would go a couple of times every day to a desolate corner in the building's main floor. He would unroll his straw mat, take off his shoes, kneel, and bow down. I was very curious about it, and I would sometimes watch him discreetly from the end of the hallway. Sometimes I think he knew I stood nearby. And it could be that he didn't mind that I saw him because it was as if he were praying for both of us. I would let the janitors know not to clean near the area where he was praying.

After the World Trade Center attacks, people do not pray so openly. I've never seen anyone do it again at work.

So many other things have changed since 9/11. People took note of my name, mainly my co-workers. The other custodians started calling me Farid Osama.

In the past, white Americans were delighted to learn that I was Colombian. They had heard what a hard-working people we were. But after the attacks, many people are thinking, "Is he one of us? Or is he illegal? Because he looks illegal." In the 1970s through to the 1990s, nobody ever asked for my legal papers or treated me as a foreigner, even after I was arrested in 1983.

In 1983, Farid was arrested and later pleaded guilty to the possession of illegal narcotics in St. Paul, Minnesota. As a result, he served twenty-six months in federal prison, mostly in Danbury, Connecticut. According to court records, Farid stated that he had accompanied his employer to purchase cars for the auto-repair shop where Farid worked as a mechanic and assistant. Farid denied any participation in a drug scheme or awareness of his employer's involvement. Almost thirty years later, Farid's story remains unchanged.

NOT HIDING, NOT IN PLAIN SIGHT

When I came out of Danbury in 1985, the government began the process to deport me. There were several court appointments, but I missed one when I showed up to court on the wrong day. As a result, I was deported in absentia.[1] My lawyer suggested that I get a job, and said the government would probably never physically deport me. Luckily, I had already found my custodial job. It had health benefits and decent pay.

But over the next few years I was still bothered by the uncertainty of my legal residency. So I contacted another lawyer in 1993. He told me there was nothing I could do to fix the situation because the immigration laws had become stricter. He said we had to wait for the laws to change again and then apply for an official pardon. In the meantime, the best thing was to not bring attention to myself.

In those days the police weren't searching for illegals, so I never felt like I was hiding. But looking back, I see that I was. I remained under the radar. I didn't drive in the evenings, avoided places where I would be asked for my identification, and rarely traveled outside of the metropolitan area. I was disciplined about going straight home after work, and I never spent time in bars. With the exception of my wife's friends, I avoided most people. My past conviction became a secret that

[1] In absentia is the classification for a trial at which the defendant is not present. The United States Constitution maintains a person's right to be present at their own criminal trial.

I couldn't share with anyone. After all, who would believe that I, a Colombian man in the 1980s cocaine era, never intended to commit a drug crime?

But after September 11, the attitudes of many Americans toward the undocumented changed drastically. There were new, stricter laws, and a lot of discrimination. Suddenly the police in other cities were stopping people just for looking foreign—or really, Hispanic—and asking for their documentation. The idea that the police could randomly stop someone on the street seemed anachronistic. It reminded me of what happened in places such as the one I had left behind so many years earlier. It wasn't supposed to happen in a society such as the United States, which values personal freedom and that has laws guaranteeing that its citizens can live without fear of the authorities. Although up to that point I hadn't known anyone personally who had disappeared or been deported, I was reading in the Spanish-language press about sudden raids on factories where undocumented people had been openly working for many years. In the months following the attacks, it was clear that there was suspicion and anger toward immigrants. But most of the mania, I thought, was sprouting in the states near the borders or in rural towns. I never imagined that New York City, whose strong economy depends on undocumented workers' underpaid labor, would get carried away by fear of immigrants.

*

Then the resentments against immigrants reached New York. While working at my custodial job, I saw the proof. Because of my office building's proximity to a nearby courthouse, I could see the prisoners that the police were bringing to the courthouse. Before September 11, the people who were taken to the court house's central booking were American or Americanized, meaning they spoke English without a foreign accent or were of European descent. After September 11, these people were indigenous-looking men, which is to say that they looked Mexican, Central American, and therefore possibly "illegal." Their wrists and ankles were often handcuffed, but these young men seemed nonviolent. Instead, they looked scared, not understanding what would happen to them next. They were arrested in groups, which I hadn't really seen before either. And from what the other janitors and doormen were saying, the charges were often small, such as jumping the subway turnstile.

Around the same time, we heard rumors that these undocumented men were first being sent to Rikers Island prison, and then moved to other prisons for deportation. But I knew something was different when I repeatedly saw groups of people gathered outside of the courthouse. They were the family members of the detainees. And they would stop me, when I took a break outside or when I threw out the garbage, to ask if I could help them find their relative. They approached the other janitors as well, and told them about their predicament. The police weren't giving information about where their relatives had been sent, and they were frightened. That was when I knew that circumstances for immigrants had changed after 9/11. People were being deported, and it was happening quickly.

In the months after 9/11, I read articles in the newspapers about hundreds of Arab and Muslim people who were stopped for small violations before being deported. I remember reading that the government asked Muslims and Arabs to report themselves, and to be unafraid of deportation. But the ones without papers were usually deported.

*

One morning, on my way to work, I saw a bunch of men under the elevated train who were facing against the wall of a brick building. There were eight or ten of them. I had never seen people rounded up that way before. It became clear that after the terrorist attacks the government was allowing law enforcement to find undocumented people. That was when I realized I could be detained at any moment because I looked Latino. It was as if we were all suspected of being in the country illegally, or of wanting to hurt the country in some way.

I began to change my behavior. For starters, I took the morning shift at work, which began at 5:00 a.m., a time when there are fewer people and fewer police on the street. I avoided places where the police gathered, such as accident scenes. I also stopped driving just in case the police stopped my family.

Then one day, on May 10, 2004, I remember it was a warm day, I was sweeping an area on one of the upper floors, when a secretary approached me. She said two men were in the supervisor's office asking for me. When I went to the office, the men showed me an old passport photo of myself and asked if that was me. Then they said they were from the immigration office, and that I had a problem that wasn't resolved so they were going to arrest me. Then the shorter of the two officers said, "Take out whatever is in your pockets."

So I took out some papers, my keys, and my green card. I had never stopped carrying it because for so many years I wasn't sure about my legal status or which remedies I could take. Right away he grabbed them. Then the other officer said, "Come with us. Don't worry, this will be resolved quickly."

Many of the workers were curious about what was happening and had gathered outside of the office. Luckily the officers didn't handcuff me. It would have added to my shame. And just like that, I went. The kinder one of the officers said to me, "You've been in this country so long. Why didn't you ever fix this problem?" And I told him that I was waiting for the law that would supposedly pardon me.

Being in a car with government authorities felt surreal. Ever since 9/11 happened, my worst fear had been of being singled out on the street and being deported. When I had shared my concerns with my wife in the past, she would say, "Stop being paranoid." But she had been naïve. In a way, the immigration officers showing up to my job was worse than being stopped on the street, because it affected my reputation at work.

As we drove away, I looked at the building where I had worked for almost eighteen years, and it became smaller in the distance. I thought I would never see it again. When I asked the immigration officers where they were taking me, they said they weren't sure. I thought to myself, *This is the end of my life here.* I thought I would be deported. But I also had a small hope that some official would see that I had paid my debt to society by spending more than two years of my life in prison.

THEY SAW US AS ANIMALS

At first they took me to the federal processing center in downtown Manhattan, near City Hall. I asked if I could borrow a phone, and one of the officers lent me his mobile. I called my wife to tell her what had happened, because I knew she would be worried when I didn't come home after work. But she didn't pick up the phone, and I left her a short message letting her know that I had been detained. I told her that I didn't know what was happening next.

This was very different from what happened to me back in 1983, where the officers immediately explained the process I had ahead of me. But at the New York detention center, they told me nothing. All I understood from them was that I was leaving the country, and they didn't explain when or how.

Late that night, the officers dropped me off at the Passaic County Jail in New Jersey. I was confused because I thought they were going to put me on a plane back to Colombia. I just hoped that someone had realized that I had an American family and they would release me.

I arrived at a windowless building in the middle of a run down New Jersey neighborhood. The prison where I served time in St. Paul, Minnesota, and where I was later transferred to, Danbury, Connecticut, had been neat and quiet. But the New Jersey jail was nothing like that. Inside it looked old and extremely dirty. The walls were in need of repair and repainting. But the worst part was that there were too many people locked up.

I don't know how many of us were in there. I remember taking note that there were many old men, but most of the people were younger, in their twenties, thirties, and forties. As far as I could tell, most of the men were Latinos. There were rumors that the Arabs, the Pakistanis, and people from Muslim regions were being sent to separate jails, such as the Metropolitan Correctional Center in New York and the United States Penitentiary in Lewisburg, Pennsylvania.

But I do know that the jail kept us, the ones who were being deported, separated from the regular prisoners. In any case, the space wasn't big enough for us. The detainees slept wherever they could fit their bodies. In the larger rooms, people threw their beds on the floor; to get to the bathroom, you had to step on one another's mattresses.

I slept in a small room that had four bunk beds stacked two by two on top of each other. There was one person per bed. I slept on the bottom bunk, which I heard had belonged to a man who had broken his neck. He had fallen off the bed and died.

I realized quickly how lucky I had been in Minnesota and Danbury, where inmates were given a modicum of basic respect. At Danbury, every person had his own bed and a gray wool blanket. When it came to using the restroom, we had privacy. But at the New Jersey facility, you either waited to use the one-person restroom available during recreation, or you went in the toilet inside the room where you slept, while everyone was in there too. That was horrible because all of the inmates could see and smell everything you did. But sometimes you just had to go, because you were never really sure when the officers would take you to the recreation area.

That reminds me of another important difference about my earlier incarceration, mainly that the officers were very strict about sticking to a schedule. Every movement at the Minnesota and Danbury facilities was prompt. But at Passaic County, you didn't know when exactly you were going to eat or shower. And unlike the other prisons, where every day they gave you an hour to be outside and feel the sun on your head during recreation time, this place kept you indoors for the entire twenty-four hours.

The situation seemed like it could become dangerous at any moment. I had never seen this level of violence before. There were many fights. One day, one inmate stabbed another one in the eye and the guards rushed over and beat the first inmate with clubs. Jail officials used German shepherd dogs to intimidate the inmates. In the previous facilities, I eased the pain of being away from my family by reading magazines and books. But at Passaic County, it was difficult to relax in any way. One day, someone stole my flip-flops, and I had to walk barefoot for three or four days. I washed myself in the dirty shower rooms without my flip-flops. It was very uncomfortable because many people were bathing and urinating there, and it seemed that no one was cleaning it or other areas of the jail.

There were no activities to keep us preoccupied, so I became very sad in Passaic County. I missed my wife and my kids. Of our four children, my twelve-year-old daughter and my sixteen-year-old son lived with us at home, and they needed me. There was also the worry about suddenly having no income. My wife didn't earn enough money to pay for the rent, car insurance, food, and many household expenses. Luckily I had saved nearly $3,000, which my wife used to cover the expenses. Some family friends also lent us money.

My detention in 2004 was harder because I was treated like a nonhuman. Don't misunderstand me, Minnesota and Danbury weren't ideal, but there was a structure in place, there were standards, and I felt safe. The officers and administration officials were courteous. They spoke to me in a respectful way. They calmly woke us up in the morning, and there were civilized interactions between prison guards and inmates.

In Passaic County, we were treated like animals. I blame it on the many negative things elected officials around the country had said about immigrants and Arabs. Their comments made the public forget that we belonged here and that we were human. I thought, *If even the staff who are supposed to protect us see us as animals, I could definitely die here.*

THERE WAS SECRECY

At Minnesota and Danbury, what was happening with your case was clearly communicated, either verbally or with documents. But at Passaic County, getting clear information was incredibly difficult. We had no idea what was happening to us. We didn't know if we would have an audience with a judge, or simply be moved from one detention center to another until we boarded a plane to leave the country forever.

Some people had been in detention for over a year. Twice a week, lawyers would visit the jail and ask us questions. At first I thought they could help me get out and go home to Brooklyn, but when detainees would be deported or moved to other facilities, it became clear that they weren't capable of preventing anyone of us detainees from being deported.

The prison officials moved detainees to other detention centers around the country about once a week. They would come to our floor, round them up, and take them away. There was secrecy about where people were being sent. If someone were going to be moved, that person wouldn't find out until they were actually being relocated to a detention in another state. Often the detainees couldn't warn their families.

When my wife visited me, she was always afraid of finding out that I had been moved. She had seen it happen several times while in the waiting room, where families would be turned away because the inmate had been relocated. Moving detainees around without prior notification was new after September 11.

That's another thing: the officers who greeted the inmates' families in the waiting rooms were very aggressive and intimidating. My wife said they shouted at people if, for example, they asked why the wait was so long to see their relative, or if they dressed improperly or forgot the proper identification.

I was very lucky that my family visited me many times every week. Some of my family's friends visited me too. They reassured me that I would find my way back again if I were deported. Sometimes I too had a certain trust that I wouldn't be permanently separated from my family.

My wife told me to pray the rosary every day at 3:00 p.m. So I did it, even though I've never been a believer.

I FIT ALL THE CATEGORIES

All of the years that I lived in New York, few cared about who was here illegally. But from one moment to the next after September 11, there was a big rush to kick people out of the country. They didn't care that families were being separated, or that children were losing parents. They wanted certain people out; Muslims and Latinos. It didn't matter that you weren't a terrorist or that you had only committed a small infraction. You weren't welcome here anymore. And in some way I fit into all of those categories, because I looked like the people they wanted to deport, I had an Arabic name, I was Latino, and I had been convicted of a crime. In the eyes of certain Americans, I was less than human. To them, I was disposable. It didn't matter that I had American children or that I had helped, in my own way, to build the city and neighborhood where I lived.

I was at Passaic for exactly three months, and luckily I was never moved to another site. Mostly I had a lot of time to think about my life. I was afraid to leave the city I have loved most in my life, and to be far away from my family. I wondered why my name had come up for immigration officers to come looking for me. One reason I thought of was that it was easy to find me, because I have been living in the same apartment since 1978. But I also wondered if maybe they were looking for the kind of people who had Arab names like mine, and who also had an order to be removed from the United States.

Among the inmates, we suspected that the government was moving people around to prevent their families from working with a lawyer to reopen their deportation cases. So we lived in fear that one morning we'd wake up and be told to board a bus to another state. Many of the detained men were asking the lawyers and their families about reopening their deportation cases. Speaking to an immigration official was difficult because there were so many people waiting to meet with them. The inmates waited in a line, but it wasn't certain that you could actually reach him. When I finally spoke to one of the immigration officials who visited the prison, he told me there was nothing I could do to stay in the United States

The government seemed to be in a hurry to move people out. I was fairly sure the motivation behind the government's quick deportations was to be able to say to the American public that they were ridding the streets of terrorists and criminals. It was the best way to reassure a frightened public of their safety, since Osama bin Laden couldn't be found.

There was an immigration officer who could come every couple of weeks and interview people. He would call the detainees into his office and interview them. One of the questions he would ask was if the person wanted to be deported right away. If the detainee agreed, immigration officials would take the necessary steps, such as speaking with the inmate's consulate office to verify the person in question was from the country to which he claimed citizenship. That process took a few weeks, and then the detainee would be sent back to their home country. But most people, including me, did not want to be permanently separated from our families. I had never seen so many people afraid of being sent away.

During Farid's detention at Passaic County Jail, his family retained the legal services of Bryan Lonegan at the Legal Aid Society. Because the conviction was from 1985, there was still an opportunity to reopen Farid's case. At that time, the immigration authority was known as the INS, and allowed former non-citizen convicts to have a hearing. However, the window of time in which to reopen the case was rapidly decreasing due to the possibility that Immigration and Customs Enforcement would move Farid around the country from one district to another. Luckily, Farid had kept meticulous records, such as proof of tax, electricity, phone, rent, tuition, and car payments, dating as far back as the mid-1970s. Farid's papers made a strong argument that he had been a law-abiding citizen post-incarceration, and had been a contributing member to his community.

A climatic turn of events occurred when a judge agreed to reopen Farid's case. The next day, August 10, 2004, exactly three months after he had been detained, Farid was released pending disposition of his case.

Over the next year, Lonegan worked closely with the family to prepare Farid's case, free of charge. When Farid appeared in court on May 10, 2005—exactly one year after being detained—the judge restored him to full and permanent residency. Farid was also allowed to resume his custodial job.

LISTEN TO EACH OTHER'S STORIES

Days after we won the case, I went to my bank and applied for a $5,000 loan. Then I called Bryan and told him that I wanted to give him a small sum to thank him for all the help he gave me. He was very polite, thanked me, and explained that he wasn't allowed to take any money from me. He said that it had been his job, and that to accept anything would be unethical.

I think that word, "unethical," is one modest way to describe what has happened to immigrant communities since we, all of us, were attacked on September 11. People do unethical things when fear takes root in their minds.

I'm still moved by the idea that someone would help another without expecting any money in return. If Bryan had been a private lawyer, a man like me never could have afforded him. I buy a lotto ticket for him every week anyway. And if it wins, I will give it to him and let him donate the money wherever he wants.

Ten years after 9/11, this country is deporting more people than ever. As a nation, we are going through an ethical crisis if we don't see how separating families scars communities. It's important that we, especially those of us who come from "other" cultures, listen to each other's stories. It may inspire someone to ask for justice. Even though our immigration system is very confusing, I found a measure of justice. In the years I have left, I hope to see the system working fairly for the majority again. My prayer is that the detainees I spent time with find justice one day too.

SHAHEENA PARVEEN

AGE: *55*
OCCUPATION: *housewife, activist*
INTERVIEWED IN: *Queens, New York*

Shaheena came to the United States from Pakistan with her husband, son, and daughter to escape religious persecution. In 2004, Shaheena's son Matin was arrested and charged with plotting to commit a terrorist act. Drawing on conversations with Matin and court records, tapes, and transcripts, Shaheena spoke to us through an interpreter about her son's entrapment by a NYPD informant called Osama Eldawoody.

After 9/11, as part of the War on Terror, law enforcement sent informants into U.S. mosques to seek out and intercept terrorist plots. Like Matin, many of those who have been arrested and tried on resulting charges have pleaded in their defense that they were entrapped. Since her son's arrest, Shaheena has become part of the End Racial Profiling Campaign leadership team at DRUM (Desis Rising Up & Moving), a grassroots organization of South Asians fighting for immigrant and worker rights, educational justice, and against deportations, detentions, and policing in Muslim and immigrant communities. Through DRUM, Shaheena has become a leading voice against the use of informants and agents-provocateurs in Muslim communities, and also works with other families similarly affected by such policies. Over the course of two days, we interviewed Shaheena at her home in Jackson Heights, Queens, where she treated us to homemade snacks and a steady stream of chai tea.

We had a peaceful and healthy family. Now it's as if we don't have the ground beneath our feet or the sky above us.

To have your child snatched away, as my son has been, is to suffer both internally and externally.

Shahawar Matin is my one and only son. Shahawar means "worthy of a king" in Farsi. Matin is Arabic. I think it means "powerful" or "strong." But at home we called him Jojee.

Matin is a very good son with a pure heart. He looked after his parents and his sister Sanya. He was helpful, obedient, and naïve.

By punishing my son for a crime he did not commit, the government, the police, and the prosecutors have done a great injustice. I am suffering tremendously, and I cannot even describe it.

THE FIGHTING IS WHY WE CAME HERE

I was born in Karachi, April 5, 1956, the eldest of six sisters. My family was in Pakistan for a long time, since before Partition.[1] My husband Siraj and I are from the Ismaili community, who are a part of the Shia sect.[2] A good number of Ismailis are concentrated in Karachi. They generally tend to live in their own communities and are known for being very peaceful. Even when they are under attack, they generally don't retaliate.

Ever since our children were little, I would take them regularly to the Jamatkhana, the Ismaili place of worship, so that they could learn about their religion. However, my husband and I never forced anything upon them.

When I was younger, things used to be good and safe in Karachi, despite the fact that there were so many diverse communities, so many

---

[1] After India's independence from Great Britain in 1947, the Indian subcontinent was partitioned into India, with a secular government and a heavily Muslim population, and the newly created Muslim state of Pakistan. The division has been a source of much political violence.

[2] A denomination of Islam. Shia Islam comprises a community of ethnically and culturally diverse people living in over twenty-five countries around the world.

different sects. At that time, we didn't used to have any problems because we didn't think about identity in terms of sect. For example, I thought of myself as a Pakistani Muslim woman. At school, we had teachers and students who were Muslim, Hindu, Christian. We also had freedom, in terms of being able to go wherever we wanted.

It's not the same Karachi today. There's lots of in-fighting due to religious strife, and it's become more difficult for women to work. When Zia ul-Haq[3] came into power in 1977, slowly things started getting bad in Karachi. Then, as the strife picked up, people would target my family because we were a minority.

Early in 1999, my husband and I started facing incidents of religious persecution. We had a store in an all-Ismaili area, and we had several robberies. Once my husband was beaten up with the butt of a gun. At that point, we decided that we would go to America for the future of our children. Four of my sisters had already moved there, so we had a community there.

We decided we would stay there until things got better back home. Even now, just thinking about the religious strife is sometimes painful and disturbing.

We were given an entry visa to the United States for six months, and we arrived on June 7, 1999. We never came with an idea of permanency. When we left Pakistan, we put the store up for rent and we locked up our home. We thought it would be temporary, and that once things get better, we would go back. No one wants to leave their homeland.

REFUGE WHEN WE NEEDED IT

We think just as well of America as we think of our own homeland, because this is a place that offered us refuge when we needed it.

We were used to a very simple lifestyle back home, but because we

---

[3] Muhammed Zia-ul-Haq was the sixth president of Pakistan, in office from 1977 to 1988.

were starting from scratch here, it was still very difficult to establish something stable. We found a place to live in Jackson Heights, Queens, and my husband, Matin, and I had multiple jobs over time, whatever we could find. We worked at grocery stores, cellphone stores, and delis. My husband and Matin also worked at an Islamic bookstore owned by Matin's uncle.

At that time, Matin was sixteen and Sanya was twelve. Matin was taking computer classes at the same time as he was working, so it was a bunch of juggling, and it was difficult for him.

Slowly, we started becoming more integrated into the community. The children went to school, my husband and I were working, and we got to know our neighbors and develop relationships with people. Even though we missed our homeland and our country, we didn't feel excluded or marginalized here.

We've always mixed with all sorts of people. Matin and his dad worked in an Arab neighborhood in Bay Ridge, Brooklyn. Here, in Jackson Heights, there are other South Asians, Latinos, and African Americans. People have always liked us, and we've always liked other people.

Matin liked it here and didn't have problems transitioning. He was simple and easygoing. He didn't have a whole lot of spare time on his hands because mostly he was working, but the bit of spare time he did have, he'd spend it with the family or go visit relatives. I didn't let him go out too much. I raised him in the best of ways, taught him how to be respectful, how to be good. If he saw old people or young kids crossing the road, he would ask them, "Can I help you across?" He was the type of person who keeps others in mind and looks out for them.

YOU GUYS ARE ALL FUNDAMENTALISTS

When our visa was close to expiring, we got an extension. Later, when that extension was close to expiration, we applied for a second extension, but we did not get it. In March of 2003, the lawyer handling our immigration case sent us a letter telling us about the order for Special

Registration.[4] The requirement was that males had to register with the government if they were not a United States citizen, or if they came from a country that was on the Special Registration list. These countries were mostly Arab and Muslim. Pakistan was listed, so Matin and my husband had to register.

We had no apprehensions about the registration because this was the law, and we had always complied with it. We had come here legally, and our status was legal.

On March 19, 2003, Matin and my husband went to register. They left early in the morning to get to Federal Plaza because the lines had been huge every day. They didn't come home that day, and I got worried. I had no idea where they were or what was going on. I was thinking, *Federal Plaza is a government building that closes at a certain time. So where did they go? Why haven't they come home?*

The following evening, my husband and son finally came home. They had been held at Federal Plaza since the day before. They said that the immigration officials essentially stopped everyone who went in to register and held some of them there for questioning.

Matin said they had to fill out some forms, which asked if they had a lawyer, if they wanted to be sent back home, or if they needed to go in front of a judge. My husband had marked on the form that they wanted to go in front of a judge. Matin made a mistake on the form. When he realized this, he asked one of the officers there for a new form.

The officer told him, "Don't worry about it. Just write it down below, it's not a big deal."

But whatever that mistake was, I think that they seized upon it and harped on it. And that might be the cause of most of our problems now.

The immigration officials asked them about things like dates of birth, names, and spellings of grandparents' names. They questioned

---

[4] Through the program, United States immigration officials fingerprinted, photographed, and interviewed 85,000 Muslim and Arab non-citizens from November 2002 to May 2003. For more details, see Appendix III: United States Counterterrorism After 9/11.

them simultaneously, I think so that they could compare their answers and see whether they matched up.

It was like they had created a jail inside there, the way that they were holding some people. They would tie their feet together or lock them in a room. After a long time, my son had asked one of the officers, "How long are you going to keep us here? We haven't eaten all day. Can I go and get something to eat?"

And this officer said harshly, "Don't you know why you are here? First of all, you are Muslim. Second, you are Pakistani. You guys are all fundamentalists."

On the evening of March 20, Matin and his father were released, and Matin was given a date to appear in front of a judge. At his trial, the prosecutor really interrogated and pressed him about the mistake he'd made on his form, and he even questioned me about it.

At this point we applied for asylum. We felt hopeful about our asylum case, and expected things would work out in our favor. We thought that the U.S. government would see how bad the conditions were back in Pakistan. We thought they would allow us to stay here until things got better, and then we would go back.

After Special Registration, we had a hearing every few months. On August 27, 2004, a few days before our last hearing was scheduled, Matin got arrested on suspicion of terrorism.

SENT TO ENTRAP

Matin was entrapped by a man called Osama Eldawoody. He started approaching and targeting my son around late summer of 2003. He worked on him like a slow poison, putting things in his mind.

At that time, Matin was still working at the Islamic bookstore. It was in Bay Ridge, Brooklyn. Matin's uncle owned the store, and Matin helped him and my father manage it.

The bookstore was next to the masjid, the mosque. During prayers, this Eldawoody would be in the masjid, and he would cry immensely while he was praying. He claimed that he had liver cancer. People would see him crying and they'd have compassion and sympathy for him. Matin also worried for him and prayed for him.

Eldawoody talked to Matin in the bookstore. In the beginning, he didn't say anything suspicious or alarming to him. He would just read things from books, and say that he was a scholar, and that his father was a scholar. He sometimes gave Matin rides from the bookstore all the way back to Jackson Heights. All these things were done to gain his trust.

Initially, Matin wouldn't mention Eldawoody too much. He would just say he was a really nice guy, and that he was really sick. He said, "He has this condition with his liver. What's going to happen to his daughter when he dies?"

I didn't notice any sort of changes in Matin. He maintained his friendships, he interacted well with all sorts of people who came into the store, and he wasn't spending more time away from home. From a religious perspective, there was no change in his beliefs or his practice.

After six months of having developed a relationship with Matin and gaining his trust, Eldawoody began to show him pictures from Guantánamo, and he talked about the various ways that the U.S. government and military have oppressed Muslims in these places, and in other places. He would also show him news stories about young Muslim women who had been raped.

Then he would sort of taunt him and inflame him by saying things like, "You're a Muslim! You have a duty, you have to do something!" or "As a Muslim, what is your duty when you see all this stuff?"

Matin didn't know about or take an interest in these things until this guy came into the picture. My son never read the newspaper, and our family did not discuss or argue about whatever things were happening in Palestine or Iraq. But Eldawoody was showing him articles, horrible pictures, news stories, and more aggravating material, and talking to him about what was going on. He also started to interject religion into that conversation. Even at this point, Matin didn't realize that Eldawoody was trying to influence him through these conversations.

At other times, Eldawoody would tell Matin, "I don't want to die of sickness. I want to die fighting on the battlefield."

And in response, at least once, my son said, "Why? What's wrong with that? In Islam, you are considered a martyr if you die of a disease. It's considered the same as dying on the battlefield."

At various points, my son would disagree or argue with him over the ideas that he was putting out, and say, "That's not right, that's not appropriate, that's not Islamic." But because of the way that my son is, he would argue with him in almost a childlike manner.

There was one incident that struck me. One day Matin came home when the ten o'clock news was on, and they showed this picture of this guy from Abu Ghraib in a particular position. As soon as my son saw that, he got really upset and said, "Don't watch this. Turn this off."

I said, "What's wrong with you? I'm watching the news. It's just news."

He said, "No, no, no, don't watch this. Turn it off." He was really upset. You could say he was anxious, possibly fearful.

And it makes me wonder, what had Eldawoody done to him emotionally by that point? What had he put in his mind, that he became so excitable and so fearful of just this one picture?

My son didn't fully comprehend what was going on. At the time, he never mentioned the sort of conversations that he was having with Eldawoody. If he'd understood what was going on and told me, I would have made a complaint against Eldawoody, and warned Matin about him. Particularly after 9/11, I had heard about the targeting of young men throughout the country. I was always worried and thinking about these types of things.

*

First, Eldawoody worked on gaining Matin's trust. Then he started showing him all those things to put emotions into his mind and his heart. After that, he told Matin about a plot to bomb the subway station at 34th Street at Herald Square. Eldawoody said, "I've spoken to the Brotherhood. They've told me that everything is ready to go, and that we should move forward."

My son told him, "I'm not interested in doing anything that's going to hurt people."

But Eldawoody kept pursuing him and trying to get him involved. When he dropped Matin off at home after work, he would roll down his window and say, "Are you sure you're not going to do this? You have to do this."

But Matin would say, "I don't want to hurt innocent people. I will not pick up anything dangerous, anything that would cause damage."

And it just kept going around and around like this. This was the essence of the relationship that they had for the last few months.

If you read the case files, the only person that was actually engaging in actions and inciting actions was Osama Eldawoody. The rest of it was just conversations between the two of them.

I don't understand the full scope of the techniques Eldawoody used, but there were some conversations with Matin where he would say, "If you don't cooperate with me, if you don't join me in this, then anything could happen." This was said in a way that was threatening, and made Matin feel like something would happen to his family.

Eldawoody would also call here sometimes, and I would have to answer the phone. I didn't like him calling here. I don't know why, but there was just something about him I didn't like.

I remember that often times I would see that Matin wouldn't sleep at night, or that he would stay up late. At that time, I just thought that maybe he was just watching TV.

Eldawoody kept trying to push him. My son kept telling him no, to the extent that the last contact they had was on August 23, 2004. It the very last time that Eldawoody dropped Matin off here, and my son told him unequivocally, "I don't want to be involved. Leave me alone and don't bother me again."

Then Matin did not hear from him for four or five days.

ARE THEY TALKING ABOUT MY SON?

On August 27, 2004, Eldawoody called the house several times, but Matin didn't want to talk to him.

I kept saying to him, "Why does this guy keep calling? Just answer his call and deal with him." But Matin wouldn't answer.

That afternoon, there was a phone call from an officer from the NYPD. He wanted to talk to Matin. I told him that he was at the bookstore. I took his name and number and said Matin would call him back. Then I called my son and told him to give the officer a call, but Matin said that he had already called him multiple times, telling him to come down to the police station, that they needed him to do some paperwork or something along those lines. My son kept telling him that it was Friday prayers that day. He said, "I can't come right now, but maybe later on I will come."

After prayers, Matin called his uncle and told him, "I'm just going to go out for fifteen minutes, and then I'll be back." He didn't even shut down the store; he just locked the door and he went.

As Matin was walking toward the police station, there was a helicopter flying overhead. When he was about one block away from the station, some police officers jumped on him. There was no need for them to do that. They knew where he worked; they could have gone to the bookstore and arrested him there, or they could have waited till he got to the police station. There seems to be no reason for them to do this, except to shame my son in public, and to make an example or a news headline out of him.

They arrested him, put him in a car, and drove back along the same route that he had walked to the station. Then they parked the car in front of the bookstore. The whole time Matin was telling them, "I need to call my mother," but they wouldn't allow it.

As they parked the car, one of the officers reached into my son's pocket and took out the keys to the store. As the officer was about to open the door to the bookstore, Matin got really worried. He was thinking a thousand things, like, *Why do they want to go into the store? What do they want? What are they going to do?* He was thinking that this was his uncle's business, the family business. Any damage or loss to the store was a loss to the family.

As the officer opened the door, he heard a voice from inside. It was Matin's father; he had come to the store searching for him, because we hadn't heard from him for several hours and we hadn't been able to get in contact with him.

When the officer saw that somebody was in the store, he got back in the car and took Matin straight to Federal Plaza.

There, the officers interrogated him. They tried to take advantage of his ignorance and pressure him into talking. They took him from one interrogation room to another, asking him all sorts of questions, trying to confuse him so that they could get something out of him. It was so confusing that Matin himself doesn't know too much of what happened with him there.

He kept insisting, "I want to make a phone call."

But they just said, "We'll let you make the phone call after you tell us what we need to know."

The last I had spoken to Matin, he had called his uncle to let him know that he was closing the store and going out. So my husband, Matin's uncle, and I knew that he had gone to the police station, but when we didn't hear from him, they went from this precinct to that precinct looking for him. We couldn't get any information.

At around a quarter to nine that night, the officer on duty at Federal Plaza changed. The new officer allowed Matin to make his phone call.

I asked him, "Where are you?"

He told me, "They brought me to somewhere in Manhattan."

I asked, "Why are they holding you? What's going on?"

He said, "They think that I've said some horrible things, and they're holding me in relation to that."

Just as he had said this, someone snatched the phone away from him and hung up. I immediately called my husband and told him that the NYPD had arrested and taken Matin away.

At that point, I didn't know anything. We were just thinking, *What sort of horrible things would he have said? And what are they talking about? What is he referring to?*

We called our lawyer and left her a few messages, but she was leaving for London that day, and so we didn't hear from her.

*

Later that evening, Matin's father and his uncle were trying to get hold of a lawyer. Maybe because there were some holidays around that time, and the Republican National Convention was also coming up, a lot of people were either out of town or hard to get hold of. It made things very difficult for us.

While Matin's father and uncle were out, I was at home with Sanya, watching the news. There was a report that the NYPD had caught someone related to a terrorism plot. When they showed pictures, I thought I saw a sketch of my son!

I was completely lost. I could not comprehend what was happening. I never imagined in my whole life that I would see my son portrayed in this way, or see him on the news in relation to such a horrible thing.

I don't know what happened then. I don't know if I lost consciousness, but I was in a complete state of shock. Sanya got up and sprinkled water on my face.

The first time I saw the news item, I don't think I understood much of it. But a few minutes later, the same news item came on again. I got a better sense then of what they were saying, that there was some sort of plot to blow up a subway station.

That's when I saw Ray Kelly, the NYPD Police Commissioner, on TV. He was saying that there were no connections between the suspected terrorists and any terrorist groups or gangs. Kelly and the news station were using the term "homegrown."

This time there were photos of the suspected terrorists. When I recognized Matin in one of the photos, I was just in disbelief. I thought, *Are they talking about my son?*

*

We were so lost in our own worries that we didn't contact anyone from the family. But my sisters heard the news and they came over.

We don't even know how we passed that night. My husband had come home late, and then in the early morning, he went out again to look for a lawyer.

The following morning, the media came and swarmed our apartment building. They were all over the place, in the hallways, upstairs, down-stairs, talking to people in the building. That caused even more worry and confusion for me as to what was going on. One of them even got inside our apartment somehow!

That reporter asked me, "Do you know that your son's in the court-room today?"

I was shocked. I called my husband, and he and Matin's uncle rushed over to the Brooklyn Federal Court to see what was going on. When they got there, everything had already finished. Matin's government-appointed lawyer was just walking out of the courtroom, and they spoke with her. She then called me and gave me her number. She said, "If you have any questions, call me, and do not talk to anyone else at all."

I told her that there were all these media people swarming the place, and one of them was even inside my apartment and he wasn't leaving, even though I told him to. The lawyer told me to give the phone to him, and then she said to him, "Why are you there? Get out, or we'll have to come in and take you out." Then he left.

After Matin's arrest, whenever I left the house, someone from the press would accost me, grabbing me and trying to question me.

At first, my neighbors used to ask us how we were doing, but then they stopped doing that. Slowly, as people learned more and more about the case, they distanced themselves from us and started avoiding us. Even my family members became afraid of visiting us or talking to us. However, the people from the Bay Ridge masjid would still come to the store and ask how we were doing and offer work to us.

*

It must have been almost two months that they wouldn't allow me to see my son. He was in the high-security lockup at Metropolitan Detention Center in Brooklyn

When I finally saw Matin, he looked like a completely different person. His beard was long and matted, and he just looked in terrible condition.

I asked him, "Why do you look like this? Why haven't you shaved?"

He said, "They won't allow me to shave. They won't allow me to look the way that I want to look."

It seems to me that the prison officials were trying to make him look like a terrorist or a criminal, so that they could create the impression that he was.

Those first few times that I went to go see him, I asked him, "Be honest with me and tell me, what is your involvement? Did you really plan these things? Did you really do these things?"

And he told me, "No, I did not do these things. I didn't even know what happened. This guy, Eldawoody, this is what he did to me."

A 50/50 CHANCE

Matin's trial started in April of 2006. During the trial, Osama Eldawoody testified against Matin. Eldawoody told the jury that he became a paid informer for the NYPD in July 2003. He described how his police handlers dispatched him to mosques and cafés, telling him to "keep your eyes and ears open for any radical thing." Eldawoody testified that during his visits to the bookstore, Matin had showed him pictures of United States soldiers abusing inmates at Abu Ghraib prison. He also said that Matin had asked him about making bombs, and that he had told him of his plans to bomb the Herald Square subway station. He quoted Matin as saying, "I will teach these bastards a lesson."

The lawyer had given us a 50/50 chance of winning.

I saw Eldawoody for the first time in court. I didn't say anything to him. I was scared.

In court, people—whether they were from the government, the MTA, or the media—they would all look at me and make sounds, and say things like, "That looks like a Pakistani woman. She must be the mother." They thought I didn't understand, but I did. I just read and recited the Qur'an, and the name of God.

The trial was a very difficult time because I was worried about my son and also about my parents. They had come over from Pakistan. They were in old age, and fragile. During the trial, I would look at my son and then at my parents. I had never imagined that the U.S. government would seek to destroy my family in this way.

On one really cold day, they brought Matin into court wearing just an undershirt. They still weren't allowing him to shave. They wouldn't allow him to brush his teeth either, and they didn't give him breakfast. I brought clothes for him to wear in the courtroom, but they wouldn't allow me to give them to him. One particular day, my son protested to the judge.

The judge issued the order to them, saying, "Take him back. Fix him up the way that he wants to be fixed up. Let him shave, let him bathe, so that he comes back looking the way he wants to look."

After they'd fixed him up and brought him back, he looked like a shining prince, with a young baby face. Everybody in the courtroom was looking at him in wonder and amazement. This was the same guy that was here just a little while ago, and he didn't look like the terrorist that they claimed he was.

*

My son did not get a fair trial. The NYPD, the prosecutors, the judge—they all portrayed him as a liar, and said that he intended to carry out these acts of terrorism, even though he had expressly said to Eldawoody, "I don't want to be involved and I don't want to do this."

On May 24, 2006, the court found him guilty. When the verdict was announced, I was shocked. I didn't know what was going on; I just saw darkness before my eyes, and then I passed out. My husband held me, gave me something to drink.

On January 7, 2007, they sentenced my son to thirty years. I did not expect this anywhere in my wildest dreams. I couldn't believe that they would give him a sentence for just mere words—words that were incited!

As they were taking him out of the courtroom, he just kept turning around and looking back at me. I just tried expressing to him that I was praying for him and that I loved him.

Then I sat down and tried to gain control of myself, because I was completely lost. Then as I started to walk out with my family, the media people surrounded us and stuck microphones in my face, asking me, "What are you going to do now?"

I made my statement in Urdu, and a translator there translated it into English. I said, "My son did not receive true justice. He is innocent." I kept repeating, "I will fight this case, and I will fight it to the end. I will take it to appeal. I will fight it."

IN THE MIDDLE OF THE NIGHT, THEY TOOK US

That night, my husband, my daughter, and I were at home, sleeping. In the middle of the night, there was a knocking at the door. When I opened it, it seemed like there was an endless number of officers from ICE[5] and the police, and possibly from other agencies. There was at least one female officer with them. I don't remember whether they showed me some papers or not, but I do remember seeing a badge.

They had come to arrest us. I asked them why, but they didn't tell me.

I told them that our asylum case was still in process, and I showed them documentation of the fact. I had some of my medicine on the table, and one of the officers asked me if that was mine. When I said yes,

---

[5] Immigration and Customs Enforcement, a federal agency within the Department of Homeland Security, created through the 2003 merger of the INS and parts of the U.S. Customs Service.

he just took the medicine and shoved it into my mouth.

My husband was already stressed, and now he was in such a complete state of shock, he just couldn't say a word. He just sat down, looking around at what was going on.

We were all still wearing our sleeping clothes, and the officers were telling us, "Hurry up, hurry up, hurry up." They were pressuring us so much that it was hard for us to even change our clothes properly. They kept harassing Sanya, who was in her room trying to change. She was twenty at this time. She was crying, but they kept saying, "If you don't get ready quickly, we're just going to take you out into the cold in these clothes."

The NYPD officers were searching through our stuff. My worry was that my son had a sensitive case, and I didn't know what they were trying to do, if they were going to plant something or trying to create something else like another case against us.

When I told them to stop going through my stuff, a couple of the officers started laughing at me, and from what I perceived, they were saying something about us being afraid of them. I responded, "We're not afraid. It's just that my son has a sensitive case and I don't trust anyone, so stop touching my stuff."

Then we were handcuffed.

As we were leaving the apartment, I told them I had to lock the door. But they just slammed it and I heard something fall. I realized, as they were taking me away, that our door was open and our apartment was unlocked. I told them that my home had been robbed before, and to give me the key so I could lock the door, but they still wouldn't let me.

No one told us anything when they arrested us. They just put me and Sanya in the same car downstairs, and they put my husband in a separate car. They took us to Federal Plaza and then they took us to some other place, but I don't know where it was.

They kept me and Sanya in one room. They wanted us to sign a form that said we wanted to be deported, so that they could contact my embassy. I refused to sign the form. I told them that I wanted to talk to my lawyer, and that I wanted her present.

They kept trying to question me and get information from me, and when they saw that I wasn't going to budge, and that I wasn't going to give them any information, they finally allowed me to contact my lawyer.

While Sanya and I waited for my lawyer to come, they had processed us through all the paperwork, taken our fingerprints and photographs, and then late at night, they took us to some other unknown place. My lawyer finally came, but only for a few minutes, and I still didn't know what was going on. At around 1:00 a.m., they took the three of us to the Elizabeth Detention Center in New Jersey.

We were afraid, we were worried, we were in shock. We had an asylum case that was pending, and so we didn't understand why we were going through all of this. Furthermore, we were worried that if we got deported, who was going to be there for our son, to help him fight his case, to go visit him, to look after him? We didn't want him to be left alone in this country.

*

Sanya and I were at the detention center for about eleven days.

They were very calamitous days; we don't know how we passed them. There were almost a hundred other women there, and they were all really worried about their own situations. The first few days, Sanya and I were together, but then they separated her from me. That whole night, I didn't sleep. I stood at the door of the dorm and cried all night because I was really worried that they were going to do something to her.

Eventually Sanya and I came out on bail, but they hadn't allowed bail for my husband. Our bail was $35,000. $20,000 for me and $15,000 for Sanya. My brother-in-law and people from the community had collected this money and put up the bail.

My husband was at the detention center for just under six months. Our lawyer had said that they would most likely deport him because it was a very slim chance for his case.

After Sanya and I came home, we asked Matin's uncle for permission to work at the store, and he said yes. We needed a way to make ends meet. Our bank account had been frozen, so our rent didn't get paid that month and we were really worried about losing our shelter.

One day in June of 2007, my husband contacted me while I was working at the store. He said, "Please take care of my children and look after them."

I became worried and asked, "What are you saying? What are you talking about?"

He had stopped eating and drinking at the detention center. He had been getting more and more sick, and he was having some problems with his throat. He said, "Just whatever happens, take care of my children." Then the next day, immigration officials brought him home.

One of the conditions of his release was that he had to put on an ankle bracelet. He was also placed under house arrest from 11:00 p.m. to 8:00 a.m. They had initially wanted to place him under full house arrest, but we argued that we needed to support ourselves, and that my husband needed to go out for work.

There were many complications with the ankle bracelet. It was very uncomfortable for my husband, and it caused severe wounds and infections on his ankle. Even now, his skin there looks as if it's been burned off.

In November of 2010, they took off the ankle bracelet. Now they have some other system where he has to call and check in with them. An officer comes and visits the home once a month, and sometimes he has to go to their office.

They essentially tried to take away both the men of the house. First they took away my son, and now they have so severely restricted my husband that he can't go anywhere besides work. It's made it very difficult for me to even see my son. My son is currently incarcerated in Terre Haute, Indiana, but I cannot fly there because all my identification papers were taken by immigration officials, and my husband can't leave because he's on house arrest.

We've been suffering through this now for about seven years.

HOMEGROWN

One thing I want to really express is that I've raised my son very close to me. He has spent very minimal parts of his life away from me. He was always within my eyesight, always within my hearing, and I know the kind of character and personality that he has. He has never committed a crime in his life. He doesn't even like anything that would be considered a bad habit or bad behavior.

After Matin's case, I became an avid consumer of news. I took part in political education workshops within DRUM, and met and worked with other families similarly affected by such cases. Because of this, I have developed my own understanding of my son's case and the cases of others.

Since 9/11, officers, undercover agents, and informants have gone around and tried to entrap people, and they target innocent people like my son. Informants like Eldawoody are paid all this money. Obviously, they have to produce some results for that money. But despite all of Eldawoody's efforts, he was not successful in what he wanted to do because of who my son is and what his spirit is. Despite a full year of working on him, in the end, my son told him, "I will not participate in this crime. I will not hurt innocent people." They may have got what they wanted in court, but they were not able to change who he is, what he believes, and how he thinks.

They used this label of "homegrown" to describe him. If he is homegrown, then it is because police agents have inflamed and incited him for their own ends.

*

I am afraid, particularly when I see the faces of officers. I've seen how easily they can manufacture things and place any sort of blame, especially in regard to Muslims. They can say anything and people would be ready to believe it, and the media would be ready to broadcast it. They can say and do anything to me, but mostly I worry about whether they would do something to my daughter.

Things just seem to be getting worse. There was a glimmer of hope when President Obama was coming into office, but we've seen the same policies that allow the marginalization of Muslims, and the manufacturing of cases like my son's are continuing, and, in fact, have gotten worse in many ways.

If President Obama is as good and just as he seems, then he should further investigate this case and the similar cases of other families who are faultless and innocent. He claims to stand for justice; it would be better if he accorded justice to such families and sent their loved ones home.

*

Since all this happened to my family, one of the things that I've learned is that nothing is going to change by sitting quietly at home. And so we go out, we talk about what's going on.

My son's case is still pending, and we are fighting in the courts. But what we are also trying to do is raise awareness and fight it in the public opinion, whether through protests or public talks. I have tried to be outspoken, not only about my son's case, but also about the other families that have been affected by similar cases.

We've met with representatives in D.C. and spoken to them about these cases, about issues of immigration, and about other issues of justice that we are struggling for in this country. One of the things that we raise questions about is that, although there is a system of laws here, since 9/11, those laws have applied differently to Muslims, and that's something we have seen and experienced directly.

My husband and I always had faith in the system here. Even though a lot of the policies and laws are creating a lot of horrible situations, we still have hope that things can be rectified, and that things will get better.

I CAN ONLY WONDER

My son tells me that he's really tired and he just wants to come home. He repeatedly talks about what has happened to him, how it happened, and so I tell him, "Don't think about it too much; it's not good for you to worry about those things." I tell him that he should try to keep his mind occupied with more positive thoughts.

If this hadn't happened, he would have gotten a decent education. This was my fundamental aim, to come here and establish a future for Matin and Sanya by educating them. Matin's plan was to take the GED and then to go to college. He was also working to help pay for his sister's education. Once he finished his education and became established, I would have made preparations for his marriage. It would have brought joy and happiness to our home

Even now in prison, he is studying and trying his best.

Because of all the ways that I used to look after him, I can only wonder how he is eating, how he is sleeping, how he passes his nights on cold concrete.

Twenty-three years is a very long time to wait for my son's release. My life is passing away. When will he return, when shall I cast my eyes upon him? I wonder about the future: his future and ours. These are meant to be the prime years of his life, but so many have been wasted, and he will have grown up in prison. His life has been destroyed. Even when he comes out, will he be the same happy and carefree person?

This is what I think about, and I am in great pain. Only a mother can understand that pain, and I pray no mother has to suffer such things.

RAED JARRAR

AGE: *33*
OCCUPATION: *architect, blogger, and political advocate*
INTERVIEWED IN: *Washington, D.C.*

In March 2003, Raed's native Iraq was invaded by the United States. Raed was in Baghdad at the time with his parents and two brothers. In the eight years since the Iraq war, more than a million Iraqis have been killed, with millions more displaced. Raed and his family are currently living on three different continents. After the fall of Baghdad that year, Raed worked as the country director of CIVIC Worldwide, a door-to-door civilian casualties survey in Iraq. He also founded Emaar, a NGO that carried out humanitarian and reconstruction work in Baghdad and southern Iraq, and which drew on his training as an architect. In 2005, he came to the United States with his Iranian-American wife, after which he became increasingly politically active.

On August 12, 2006, Raed attempted to board a JetBlue flight from JFK to Oakland, California. JetBlue and Transportation Security Administration (TSA) staff denied him access to his flight until he covered his T-shirt, which read in English and Arabic, WE WILL NOT BE SILENT, claiming that passengers found it offensive. The incident led to Raed filing a federal lawsuit against JetBlue and the TSA that would go on to draw national media attention.

I always apologize to people when they ask me, "Where are you from?" because I have a long paragraph to answer that. I am half-Iraqi and half-Palestinian. My father is a Palestinian from Jenin, and my mother is an Iraqi from Hilla; they're both civil engineers. I was born in Baghdad, but I left when I was forty days old. After my birth, my parents moved us to Jordan for a few years. I grew up between Jordan, Iraq, and Saudi Arabia, and now I am also an American.

When I was thirteen years old, I went with my mother and my younger brothers Khalid and Majed to live permanently in Baghdad. It was after the 1991 war,[1] and everyone else was leaving at that time. They were fleeing a country that had been destroyed by excessive bombardment, but we were going back to my hometown. I was very excited about going back because I had felt so frustrated about being out of Iraq during the war. My dad, my uncles and aunts, and the rest of the family had been there throughout the bombardment. I wished I'd been with them all along rather than in a safer place like Amman, Jordan and worrying about them. We lost touch with my dad for weeks during the war, and I'd listen to the Iraqi radio news until five or six in the morning hoping to hear some details on what happened to our neighborhood. We didn't have satellite TVs at that time, nor did we have cell phones or internet. We just listened to radio stations from Europe, the United States, or from Iraq about the daily events of the war.

We arrived in Iraq in late June, three or four months after the end of military operations. Baghdad was completely destroyed. There was still shrapnel and the remains of collapsed buildings in the streets, and there was no electricity or water or phones.

WE ARE NOT AT WAR WITH THE MUSLIM WORLD

I never thought for a second that an al-Qaeda attack on the United States

---

[1] The Persian Gulf War (1990-1991). A coalition of forces led by the United States went to war against Iraq after its invasion of Kuwait.

would be seen as an attack by Muslims and Arabs. We, Muslims and Arabs, don't think of al-Qaeda as a representative of us, of our countries, or of Islam. It's a crazy marginal organization that no one except for a very small number of extremists identify with. Every single person who I know in the Arab and Muslim world never looked at al-Qaeda as a product of our countries, but of the CIA.[2]

On 9/11, I was living in Jordan. I'd finished my undergraduate studies in Iraq the year before and moved to Amman, where I was working full-time as an architect and studying for my master's degree in architectural engineering.

Everyone I knew in Jordan and Iraq was very sad and shocked about the 9/11 attack. There was a feeling of, *Why did this happen? All of these thousands of people were killed! This is unfair.* They also thought that Americans and the U.S. government would see themselves as victims of terrorism and attacks against civilians, and that they would then have a closer, easier identification with the suffering of Arabs and Muslims. So after they were attacked, the assumption was not, "Oh, we attacked them, that is very good." The assumption was, "Oh, now they will know how we've been suffering, and they will stop being indifferent to our suffering because they are suffering as well." I think that was the original take.

A few weeks after 9/11, an American online friend of mine, who I used to chat with all the time on Yahoo! Chat, said that she wanted to stop chatting with me because of the attack. I asked why, and she told me it was because I was a Muslim.

That was really shocking. I was thinking to myself, *What? Why would she stop talking to me?* It was the first instance where I was paying the price for what some crazy loony-toon did in New York. What made it even worse

---

[2] During the 1980s, the United States covertly supplied insurgents in Afghanistan with weapons and training in their fight against their government and the Soviet army. After the Soviet withdrawal, United States aid largely ended, but many believe that the weapons, lack of infrastructure, and power vacuum that resulted allowed for the influence of al-Qaeda in the area.

is that, although I do identify as a Muslim culturally, I am secular and I don't believe in any religion. So even if one wants to believe that Islam as a religion was to blame for the attacks, which is a thesis that I completely reject, blaming someone secular like me was even more ridiculous.

That night I went online and I found some extremely anti-Muslim videos, cartoons, and comments posted on a number of United States websites. The tone was just so racist, I was shocked. I'd never thought about that, never imagined this would happen, that the 9/11 attacks would become an anti-Muslim issue, or push Americans to have anti-Muslim feelings.

I also remember the comments that I read on those sites, and I was really terrified. I'd never experienced such racism in my life! The comments were about how dirty and lazy Muslims were, how they smell, how Muslim women are oppressed and beaten by their men. There were people calling Muslims animals and other names. I read the term "sand niggers" for the first time there. I was shocked that there was a consensus over these comments; there were no voices saying, "This is crazy," or, "Stop this nonsense." It was the first time in my life that I have seen such hatred toward all Muslims, rather than a political group or an armed group. I felt that it was about me personally, and I was thinking, *Why are Americans doing that? This will alienate the majority of people in the Muslim world.*

I remember talking to some of my friends about the hate and the backlash. They were saying that, despite what seems to be a wave of anti-Muslim sentiment among Americans, it wasn't in the U.S. government's interest to turn a conflict with a small, marginal organization into a conflict with the entire Muslim world. And I did not see the U.S. government adopting an anti-Muslim policy in the first weeks after the attack. The rhetoric was, at least from what we heard in the Middle East: "This was an attack by al-Qaeda, and we are not at war with the Muslim world." I thought that was smart, and so my assumption was that the U.S. government knew how to play this the right way, the smart way. I also thought that maybe those voices I'd heard and read online, and that friend of mine who stopped talking to me, were marginal voices that were not representative of how mainstream America thinks.

WE WERE SHOCKED AND AWED

In February of 2003, I was sure that the U.S. government would invade Iraq. I was sure that the Iraqi government would collapse, and that the United States would occupy the country. I was thinking to myself, *All my life I've lived with Palestine under a military occupation. Now my other country, Iraq, will fall under a military occupation as well.*

All of my family was in Iraq at that time; both my parents and both my brothers. I wanted to be with them, so almost four weeks before the invasion, I left my job, took a year leave of absence from school, and went back to Baghdad.

I wanted to be with my parents because I was still traumatized from the 1991 war. So once I arrived in Baghdad I felt so happy to be reunited with my family. We had things that we had to do to be prepared. We paid a contractor to dig a well in our backyard, and then we installed water filters and pipes. We already had an electricity generator, so we just cleaned it up and fixed it. We didn't need to buy so much food because the Iraqi government had given us six months' worth of food rations. We bought fuel for the cars and stored it underground, and made a safe room in the house. I taped over all the windows in case they broke.

I started getting into heated arguments with my dad about the invasion. What started as regular family chats ended up looking like loud political forums. My father was happy about the invasion; he thought that it would bring the much-needed change, and that it would be better than the Saddam Hussein dictatorship. But I had been developing a very strong opposition to the United States invasion in the months leading up to it. I started blogging in late 2002, and having to explain the situation to American and British readers helped me form my political position. I was opposed to the United States occupation, and I thought the crimes that had been committed by the Iraqi government did not justify a foreign invasion. I thought nothing justified a military occupation. That was my ideological line, and I was not ready to change it for my dad's sake. So there was some tension between me and my father during the invasion.

He was saying, "This government has no support. The Americans will just come and fix everything and leave in a few weeks." I remember he used this expression: "Americans will not come to Baghdad wearing bullet armor, they will come wearing their suits and ties." This was his imagination.

My mother and two brothers were more pragmatic in dealing with the situation. My mother wasn't a big supporter of a U.S. invasion, but she thought it might be better for us. My brothers were against it, but not as strongly as I was.

Even if the United States came and made Iraq heaven on earth, I was still against the United States invasion, period. Unfortunately, that wasn't the mainstream opinion in Iraq. I think most people fell in the same category as my mother, where they were not very happy with the government, they were not very happy with the invasion, but they thought, *Oh, it might be for our good.*

*

The real bombing started on March 21, 2003. This was the Shock and Awe.[3] We were shocked and awed indeed, even for a family like us that has gone through many campaigns of United States bombings. It was hell. Our house is located near Baghdad's airport and one of Saddam's palaces, and the bombs and missiles targeted these two sites intensively.

I remember the first night, my mother was very scared. She was hiding under a blanket and reading the Qur'an. Everyone was telling her the blankets would not save her if the ceiling fell on our heads, but she was really, really scared. My dad looked very frightened as well. My two brothers and I wanted to go to the roof to watch the bombs, like we usually did during United States attacks, but my parents didn't let us go.

---

[3] Post–Cold War United States military doctrine based on overwhelming military dominance. The term is associated with the early military campaign of the 2003 Iraq war.

RAED JARRAR

Within the first few hours, all of our windows were shattered. That night, our main door was ripped out of the wall and thrown inside the house. Just imagine the pressure. And every time a bomb falls, you see dust coming out of the walls. It's so crazy, the intensity.

These so-called bunker-buster bombs felt like earthquakes. Our house was shaking like a swing. It was going up and down and up and down, front and back. It was very intense. We all stayed in our safe room.

The bombing continued for days. It did not stop for a minute. It was just bombing and bombing and bombing and bombing. After the first three or four days, I remember one morning we woke up, and it was actually done. So we went outside to assess the damage. The destruction was huge. Nothing was working: we did not have electricity, we did not have water. And we could see some sites around our house that had been completely destroyed by United States missiles.

A few weeks later our neighborhood was attacked and we had to flee our house. We put some clothes and money in two large suitcases and ran to our cars. I still remember the sound of bullets flying around us, and huge explosions. People running around in the streets, ambulances with a bunch of injured people in each of them. I drove one car with one of my brothers, and my parents took the other car with my other brother. Someone was running away, pushing his TV on his bike, with his wife and children were running behind him. People were driving away very fast. We left everything—our house, the well, the food, the fuel, the safe room—and stayed at my uncle's place until Baghdad fell on April 9.

We heard it on the radio. They described the statue being pulled down. Then I saw the first United States tank rolling down the street. We thought it was an Iraqi tank, but then we saw a United States flag. Some people were cheering for the tank from their roof tops. That broke my heart. I cried.

After the fall of Baghdad, Raed worked for an organization called the Campaign for Innocent Civilians in Conflict (CIVIC Worldwide), which aimed to create a civilian casualty archive and an architectural archive for buildings that had been destroyed during the war. He also founded Emaar, an organization that carried out humanitarian and reconstruction work in Baghdad and southern Iraq. After six months, the organization's work became more difficult after coming under scrutiny from militia groups. At one point, Raed was kidnapped and interrogated by a small militia group. He says of the experience, "I'd heard many stories of people who were taken and found the next day in the garbage, or without their head. I thought I was very lucky, and that I shouldn't test my luck again."

IRAQ WAS UNLIVABLE

A year after the invasion, in March of 2004, I went back to Jordan to finish my master's degree. By the time I finished in February 2005, the rest of my family had all got out of Iraq.

By that time, Iraq had become unlivable. I wanted to go back, but there was nothing to go back to.

While I was away, my youngest brother, Majed, had gone to study in Canada. Then my mom was attacked by a gang with machine guns who stole her car and purse. She was really traumatized, and left the country. A couple of months after her incident, my brother Khalid disappeared. He went to school that morning, but did not come back. It's like one of the hundreds of stories that ends with, "We found him dead on that street or this street." My father was the only one left in Iraq by this time. He spent two weeks searching among dead bodies for Khalid. They all looked the same—the same age, the same skin color, the same facial hair. Just imagine him, going through dozens of dead young Iraqi bodies with bullet holes in their heads and chests.[4] A couple of times he thought some of them were Khalid. A couple of times he called us and he said, "I can't do this anymore." When I saw my dad after that, he'd aged ten years.

---

[4] According to iraqibodycount.org, an estimated 99,901 to 109,143 civilian deaths due to violence have been documented since the beginning of the war, while many Western sources cite figures as exceeding 1.2 million. More information and survey results are published on civilians.info.

After two weeks, Khalid called us. He said, "I'm safe, I'm alive, and I'm in the prison of the Ministry of Interior." He'd been arrested by one of the Iraqi governmental militias, or as they call themselves, the Ministry of Interior Forces. They're nothing more than a sectarian militia loyal to one of the ruling parties. Khalid was caught reading my blog in his school's internet café, and he had facial hair that looked like he was from the "wrong" sect for that militia.

My dad spent thousands of dollars in bribes, not to get him out, but to get him to a judge, because we didn't want him to be tortured with others in the Minister of Interior Forces' dungeons. So we got Khalid out after a few weeks and we got him out to Jordan the day of his release. My parents had a party for him, and I remember the irony of how low the bar was set. We were partying and all of our neighbors were congratulating us as if we had this great news. My brother had been kidnapped and beaten, so the good news was that he was alive. Being alive was a reason to celebrate.

I remember him sitting there, in the middle of the couch. He was staring into nothing. His silence was so painful. I felt like I should be feeling sad, but we still celebrated.

So by the time I finished my master's degree in 2005, every single person I knew had left Iraq—my parents, my brothers, my cousins, my uncles and aunts, my neighbors, my co-workers, my colleagues at the university, my friends. Each and every one of the millions of Iraqis who were displaced because of this war have a long painful story.

COMING TO AMERICA

I met Niki around the end of 2003. She was one of the readers of my blog, and then we met in person in Jordan. Niki's Iranian-American. She was born in Iran and moved with her parents to California in the eighties during the Iraq-Iran War. We got engaged in 2004 and lived in Amman.

When I finished my studies in 2005, she was still a PhD student at the University of California. So we were thinking, *Should we stay in Jordan or go back to Iraq? Should we go to the Emirates or to Iran? Should we move to the*

United States? We had many choices, but we ended up deciding to come to the United States, mostly because Niki had to finish her PhD.

I had mixed feelings about this; I was running to the United States from a conflict that was created by that country's government. I was making the United States my new home after it destroyed my previous one. So it was a complicated situation.

I didn't have very high expectations, unlike many of my friends who come to the United States and think the streets are made out of gold. I did not have any of those illusions. I knew there were good things and bad things about the United States. I knew I had rights that I could fight for.

I came to the United States in September 2005. Moving here was extremely easy. From the moment we applied for a fiancé visa until the moment I became a United States citizen, I had the most incredible, positive experience with immigration. I did not have a single thing with the immigration process that was unpleasant. Everyone was extremely nice. I don't know, when I tell people about that they're surprised because I have many "buzz words" on my paperwork, like *Iraq* and *Iran* and *Palestine* and *Muslim*. I just tell them that I followed the instructions and everything went smoothly.

EVERYONE IS A STRANGER HERE

Just a few days after I arrived in the Bay Area, I started finding my new political voice: as an Arab in the United States; as someone from Iraq in the United States and as someone from Palestine in the United States, I'd never thought of myself in that context before, but it was the only thing that people wanted to talk to me about. When I opened my mouth, they'd hear that I had a foreign accent, and they'd ask me where I was from. I'd say, "I just came from Iraq." That's the only thing they'd want to talk about. They didn't want to talk about the weather or our neighborhood. They'd just say, "Oh, you were there during the invasion. How was it?" And then I'd end up telling the story of how it was, what my perspective is.

Then, slowly, I became this voice of what the Iraqis think, because no one is talking about that. You never see that on the news. The few Iraqis who are on CNN and Fox News are horrible. They don't represent what even one percent of the Iraqi public thinks or says. So I started finding this new corner, a new niche where I felt, *Oh, actually my voice is needed here. Maybe I should do some political work.* That was the first time in my life that I actually thought about doing something completely outside the scope of an architectural career.

So I started getting more involved in politics. The Bay Area is a very welcoming place for immigrants. Everyone is a stranger, so I didn't feel like an outsider. In a few months, I started actually feeling this was home. I liked how my America looked like, and I liked my new American friends.

BROWN PEOPLE LIKE US

A couple of weeks after arriving in the United States, a friend of Niki's said something like, "You know, brown people, like us"—it didn't even make any sense for me. What does "brown people" mean? I thought to myself, *I am Arab, I am an Iraqi, I am a Palestinian, I'm a Muslim, I'm an architect and a blogger.* Skin color has nothing to do with identity and self-recognition where I grew up. Instead, we have class divisions in Iraq, Jordan, Iran, Palestine and other places around the region. It's not like everyone hangs out together, but the divisions are more about your level of education, your profession, or how rich you are, or sometimes it is along the rural vs. urban fault-lines. But there is no such thing as people with fair skin or dark skin all hanging out together because of their skin color. What a crazy idea!

I wasn't very aware of identity politics in general. I wasn't interested in searching for who I am or how people view me. All of these things came to me later.

I don't mind becoming a member of this community, the Bay Area community. I don't mind becoming an American. Actually, I like it. But I don't like this crap about, *Oh, this is white and this is black.* Our identities should go beyond this. I believe that I shouldn't be hanging out only with Arabs because I'm Arab, or only with Muslims because

I'm Muslim. I shouldn't be given less or more authority or chances because of my skin color either.

An organization that I was working with at the time offered me a People of Color leadership position. I was offended, and people didn't really get why. I thought it was just as offensive to offer me a position because of my foreign accent and skin color as it would be offensive to deny me the position. Why don't you just chill out and see if I'm appropriate for the position or not? The entire thing didn't make any sense to me. I didn't get identity politics. I refused to play by those roles.

WE WILL NOT BE SILENT

Once I got my green card I became the Iraq project director with Global Exchange, an international human rights organization based in San Francisco. My work was to reach out to Iraqi parliamentarians and put them in touch with American congressmen. In the fall of 2006, Niki and I decided to move to D.C. because my job was focusing more on working with Congress. Before the move, I had a trip with Global Exchange to Jordan and Syria, then I had a speaking event in New York city. Our plan was to drive across the country with our furniture once I got back home from New York.

My flight back to the Bay Area was on August 12, 2006. I went in the morning to JFK. It was an early flight. I checked in everything and I went through the security checkpoint. It did not beep, but the officers still took me to the secondary checkpoint. It was the first time I'd gotten a secondary check. They asked me to sit down, they tested my shoes for explosives, and they asked me for my driver's license and boarding pass. They went away with my documents for a few minutes, and then they came back. I took my driver's license and boarding pass back and went inside the terminal.

I walked around, I bought my breakfast, and then I searched for the best place to sit. I saw a nice place in the sun. So I was just having a good morning, eating some grapes and cheese, when this TSA officer approached me. He said, "Excuse me." I didn't see his face; I just saw this badge flashed in my face. So I looked up and it was a young guy. He said, "Can I talk to you for a minute?"

I left my breakfast there on the seat and I walked with him toward the boarding counter. Another two people were waiting for us there: a woman from JetBlue and a guy in a suit. It was now a bigger operation, so I was getting more worried about it. They were just staring at me. They didn't say anything, so I said, "Hi." The JetBlue woman was nice. She said, "Hi," but she looked worried, on alert.

The first man who took me, I came to learn his name was Inspector H. He asked me, "Where are you going?"

I said, "California."

"What do you do for a living?"

I opened my wallet to give him my business card, and then he peeked in my wallet and asked me, "Is that a green card?"

I said, "Yeah."

He asked, "Can I have it?"

"Sure." I gave it to him, and he wrote down all of my information.

Then he said something to the effect of, "People are offended because of your T-shirt. People complained."

I looked down at my T-shirt to see which one I was wearing. I'd just woken up that morning, put on a clean T-shirt and whatever, jeans, sneakers. The T-shirt was black, and it said in both Arabic and English, WE WILL NOT BE SILENT. An artist group in New York had made the shirt and given it to me as a gift. For me, the message meant, "We will not be silent about the murders that are happening in Palestine or Iraq." They had other T-shirts in Spanish. At the time I'd said, "Whoa, it's such a smart idea, because the Spanish one makes it seem like it's about immigration, and the Arabic one makes it seem like it's about wars."

So I looked down at the T-shirt and I was so puzzled. It wasn't in the realm possibilities of why they would stop me. I said, "Who complained?"

They were being ambiguous about it. Inspector H. just asked me, "What does it say?"

I said, "It's the same thing that it says in English. WE WILL NOT BE SILENT."

He said, "Oh, but we can't be sure that's the translation."

I was so confused that I didn't know how to answer. Then he said, "We want you to take the T-shirt off, or put it on inside out."

I said, "I think it's my constitutional right to wear this T-shirt. If you have any regulations against Arabic T-shirts, show them to me and I will take it off or cover it."

I was more surprised than afraid. I thought, *Is this a joke or something? Are they for real? They want me to take off my T-shirt?* So anyway, the conversation became more tense because all three of them were saying, "No, you have to take it off," and I was saying, "No." It just went back and forth.

The guy in the suit, I think he felt bad for me. He thought I was this naïve new immigrant who believes in some ideals. So he came closer and he said, "You know, people here in the United States, they don't really know about the constitutional rights stuff that you're talking about."

I replied, "I'm in the United States and I know about it, and I think it is my right to wear the T-shirt."

All of them were probably thinking, *Is this guy crazy? Why is he taking all of this stuff seriously?* And I *was* taking it seriously. My First Amendment is my First Amendment. I wasn't shouting or fighting, I was very polite, but it was becoming a scene and people were looking at us.

I said, "I am more than happy to take off my T-shirt, but I will not take it off unless you either show me a regulation or let me speak to your supervisor."

They refused to let me speak to a supervisor or to show me the regulation. Then I started feeling afraid because this fourth guy came—very hostile, didn't say hi to me. I saw his ID, and I think he worked security with JetBlue. He talked to me without looking at me. First he asked the other officers, "Did you take his information?"

They said, "Yes."

Then he wrote down my green card information and stuff. So I was thinking, *Oh, I'm getting into bigger trouble.* And then, laughing, he said,

"You've got the nicer guys here, so you should just do whatever they've told you."

I was like, *Whoa, whoa, whoa—where is this going?* It was escalating. I was thinking that I'd end up missing my airplane or getting arrested or deported. The woman from JetBlue saw the escalation, and she said, "Why don't we just reach a compromise? We will buy you a T-shirt and put it on top of this one."

I said, "That's not a compromise. I will cover this T-shirt with the other T-shirt that you will buy, just because you are not letting me board. But I will pursue the case with a constitutional rights organization as soon as I arrive in California."

The four of them had a conversation about the T-shirt. They said, "What type of T-shirt should we buy him? Should we buy him the I HEART NEW YORK T-shirt?"

The hostile one said, "No, we don't want to take him from one extreme to another."

I interrupted them. I said, "Why do you assume that I don't like New York? Because I have a T-shirt in Arabic?"

The hostile guy didn't look at me, didn't recognize me. The JetBlue woman left and returned a few minutes later with a grey T-shirt that said NEW YORK. It was way too large. I put it on top of my T-shirt, and I said, "This is not over. I'm going to pursue this through a constitutional rights organization."

And the hostile guy said, "Do whatever."

They just left. They didn't say anything, they weren't apologetic. I felt so humiliated. It was like the entire freakin' airport was looking at me. Everyone was staring, but I walked back to my grapes and cheese and sat there, feeling self-conscious. I felt like my cheeks were red, I could see them red. And I was thinking, *Is this for real? Is this happening to me in the United States?* It's not like I thought everything here was perfect and rosy. I didn't have illusions. But I thought, *This is the same country that invades Iraq, destroys my nation, and makes me leave my home in the first place. And now, this is what they do to me in New York. They take away my freedoms here as well*. It was such an irony. It was so painful.

Anyway, after I'd sat there for five minutes, they called me again. Someone from the boarding counter, he called my name in an Americanized way, *Rye-eed Jur-are* or something. So I looked up and this guy beckoned me with his finger. It was very disrespectful. So I just looked at him without moving, until he finally said, "Sir, can you please come here?"

So then I went over to him. It was very tense. He said, "Can I have your boarding pass?"

I said, "Sure."

He took my boarding pass and tore it up. He said, "We need your seat."

My seat was in the front of the airplane. It was the third seat, 3A. He issued me another boarding pass in the back of the airplane.

I asked him, "Why did you change my seat? Is there a reason?" I'd booked my seat in the front of the airplane way in advance because I don't like sitting in the back of the airplanes near the bathroom.

He said, "Yeah, we need the seat for a toddler." He didn't look at me. He just said, "Bring your things and board the airplane now."

So I was the first to board the airplane. I was alone. All of the flight attendants were whispering and looking at me for ten minutes. Of course it's not the same historic equivalent of putting African Americans on the back of the bus, but I had just been reading about it. I didn't want to sit at the back of the airplane. I didn't want to cover my T-shirt because it was in Arabic and I looked like an Arab.

I just sat down for the rest of the flight. I didn't do anything, I didn't say anything. I went to the restroom once. I didn't look at anyone. I just looked at my TV. I was feeling so uncomfortable. I was feeling watched.

I later learned, during the lawsuit, that a flight attendant had been put behind me to watch my movements, and she was writing down the channels that I watched. She had noted that I watched Fox News and some sports channel or whatever.

When I landed in Oakland, I tried to call Niki, but the call wasn't going through. I got a message that the service had been disconnected. So I was like, *Ohhhhh, that's it. They're going to deport me, that's it. They cut my phone and now there will be an officer waiting at the door there, and they'll take me to jail.* Then I was just thinking, *Okay let me remember what I have to finalize in the United States before being kicked out.* I was thinking, *Do we owe people money?* this type of stuff, I swear to God, thinking about the final arrangements. Later I discovered that it was just a very bad coincidence, and that we'd forgotten to pay our phone bill that month.

Anyway, I landed and I got out. I was expecting to see an officer, but no one stopped me. I went to the baggage claim area and Niki was waiting for me there. She was wearing the same T-shirt, in Persian! What complete coincidence. I thought to myself, *Oh my God, now they will deport both of us.*

*

Until that moment, I was all invested in becoming an American. I'd told everyone, "I'm a new American. I don't want to be put in a corner and be called an Arab-American or a Muslim-American or a brown-American or whatever, I just want to be an American." But after this happened to me in the airport, I thought to myself, *This wouldn't happen to some white guy with blue eyes and blond hair.* I came to realize it was not an option for me to be just an American, even if I wanted to. The moment they put that T-shirt on me, that was the end of it, seriously. I came to understand my identity the hard way.

ALL FOR MY FREAKIN' T-SHIRT

In August 2007, Niki and I filed a lawsuit with the American Civil Liberties Union (ACLU).[5] It was both a First Amendment freedom of expression

---

[5] A civil rights group that often provides legal assistance in civil rights cases. For more details, see the glossary.

and a Fourth Amendment due process under law[6] lawsuit against JetBlue and the TSA.

The case took forever. It was such a painful process. First I had to meet with my lawyers and the defendants' lawyers, give them information. The defendants' lawyers seriously tried to dissect my life. They wanted information about everything in my life, from the moment I was born until now. All of it for my freakin' T-shirt.

They had crazy theories that they wanted to prove, to scare me or intimidate me with. They subpoenaed information about our taxes, my immigration files, everything, just to find something wrong to point out. And then we had two days of face-to-face interviews where they asked me questions about my entire life, about my childhood, if I was traumatized because of the war. Some crazy questions.

At a court hearing, the JetBlue and TSA legal defense argued that it was okay to humiliate me because I'd grown up in Iraq and I was used to being humiliated. In his written ruling, the judge said, in a much more judgely and legal way than I'm saying, something to the effect of, "Are you serious? This is your argument?!"

The defense had crazy theories about me planning this thing all along. They said I planned it to take money from them, to make a political point. They interrogated me for weeks or months to prove that I went to the airport wearing that T-shirt "on purpose," as if it's a crime to wear a T-shirt. They harassed me, Niki, and my friends for years.

Toward the end of 2008, a year and a half after we filed the lawsuit, I got a call one day from my lawyers at ACLU. They said JetBlue and the TSA wanted to settle out of court, and that the judge wanted us to settle too. They said, "They are giving you $240,000, and $240,000 will give a clear message that what happened to you was wrong and it should not happen to anyone else."

---

[6] Amendments guard against unreasonable searches and seizures, and require probable cause and warrants. For more information on the protections these amendments provide, see Appendix III: United States Counterterrorism After 9/11.

I have to admit that I was very skeptical about the settlement because I was afraid that it would be read the wrong way. But my lawyers were right; it did actually have a huge impact. JetBlue and the TSA at first tried to make the settlement secret or put some other conditions on it. I thought that would be the most pathetic thing that I could do. How ironic that would be: I go to an airport wearing a T-shirt saying I will not be silent, then they give me $240,000 and I become silent. I wasn't going to do that. So they ended up giving me the $240,000 settlement,[7] which got a lot of media attention.

I think it does prove that what happened was wrong; it should not have happened to me, and it should not happen to other people in the future. That is something that I'm very interested in—fighting racial profiling and working against any policies that would justify treating people differently because they look Arab or Muslim.

I will not fly with JetBlue again because they never apologized to me. Although JetBlue and the TSA ended up paying hundreds of thousands of dollars, they have not admitted wrongdoing to this day.

The legal process is so depoliticized, and it just ends up being these very abstract fights between lawyers where I don't really know what they're talking about. I didn't want that to be the case, and I actually proposed twice that I meet with the people who met me in the airport and talk about what happened, because I don't think it was an individual act. The thing that I wanted to get out of my case was to prove that these people acted because they felt this was how their institution wanted them to act. It's a TSA issue, it's a U.S. government issue, it's the way that the system functions more than how individuals take positions. But unfortunately I never got to meet with them. My lawyers didn't let me meet with them. Their lawyers didn't let us meet either.

The fact that the case had a positive ending affected me a lot back then. Before, I was thinking that if I lost this case I would actually move

---

[7] For more information about this and other legal settlements that have resulted from the War on Terror, see Appendix IV: Payouts and Settlements.

out of the United States and not become a United States citizen. I didn't think I would appreciate staying in a place where I was seen as a criminal just because of the way I look. But after the outcome, I felt more comfortable with staying here and investing more years of my life in this country, and more of my money and expertise. I felt more comfortable living here and becoming a United States citizen. It helped me to integrate in the United States and feel that this is my country.

IT'S A PLACE WHERE WE CAN FIGHT BACK

I did not witness the pre-9/11 America. I came to the post-9/11 America, and this is the only America that I know. Now what I see is not very optimistic. During the first four years that I lived here under Bush, the rhetoric against Muslims in the United States wasn't as bad as it is now. The last year and a half I think have been the worst since I came to the United States—all of the new rhetoric about homegrown terrorism, the fight over the Islamic center in lower Manhattan,[8] and the attacks against Muslims around the United States that are on the rise. It seems like every year it's worse than the year before.

I used to reject identity politics, but I've realized that I don't have the privilege of saying, "I'm just an American", because I am viewed as an American-Muslim or American-Arab anyway. In addition, I started to realize that it's not responsible to try to dismiss identity politics in the United States. It's irresponsible of me as a new immigrant to say, "Let's all live in a place that has no identity politics, let's say we're all equal and not look back at your history," because that will be harmful to some other Americans' struggle, to their calls for reparations and search for roots. Unless we have reached a place where we can compensate other people who were harmed and discriminated against in this

---

[8] Controversy around the construction of an Islamic community center, known as Park51 or Cordoba House, to be located two blocks from the site of the World Trade Center. For more details, see the glossary.

country because of their minority status—Native Americans, African Americans, Asian Americans, Muslim Americans, and Jews—I don't think it makes sense to move on and just forget about the past. That past is still affecting our present.

*

I was naturalized in D.C. in the spring of 2009. The morning I went to the ceremony, I was feeling a little bit defensive because I thought it would be filled with fake patriotism, with some flags shoved in our faces and stuff, but it was so down-to-earth. It was an amazing ceremony. We were sworn in by a judge who is an immigrant himself. He's an Afro-Caribbean. He gave an excellent speech about how the United States is not a place where it's all good or all bad, and that he grew up being discriminated against himself because of his national origin and skin color. And there are many of us who will be discriminated against, and who will have hard lives. But the bright side is that this is still a country where many of us can fight back.

NICK GEORGE

AGE: *23*
OCCUPATION: *programmer for legal consulting company*
INTERVIEWED IN: *New York City, New York*

In August 2009, Nick attempted to board a flight from Philadelphia to Cali-
fornia, where he was to start his senior year at Ponoma College. At an airport
security screening point, he was prompted by Transportation Security Authority
(TSA) agents to empty his pockets. After producing a set of English–Arabic flash-
cards he was using for a college course, Nick was detained by the TSA agents in the
screening area for thirty minutes. A TSA supervisor then arrived and interrogated
him about his feelings about 9/11. He was subsequently handcuffed and held in
a locked cell for several hours. During his detention, he was never informed of his
rights, or of why he was handcuffed, detained, or arrested.

I certainly didn't think this would be the kind of thing I'd be a spokesperson for. Having your civil rights violated is not the kind of thing you
can anticipate.

*

I was born in Philadelphia, and I now live just north of the city. I went to Pomona College, where I majored in physics with a minor in math. I had a language requirement for my course, and I'd already studied French in high school and it bored me. I thought it would be fun to try and take Arabic and travel in the Middle East.

I've always been very interested in the history of the Middle East. I guess if I'm to be perfectly honest, I have to admit that some of it might have started when my dad showed me *Lawrence of Arabia* years ago.

I spent my first semester junior year studying Arabic abroad in Amman, Jordan. I chose Jordan because it's someplace very friendly to foreigners, especially in Amman. When I was going to Jordan, my father mentioned that my great-grandfather was Lebanese. I was completely surprised. I think it's cool to know that I'm part-Lebanese.

I came to love Ammam, and I really started to love Arabic. It became more than just a side hobby, it became something I was focusing on more. The summer after I graduated, I did intensive Arabic study through the State Department's Critical Language Scholarship Program[1] in Alexandria, Egypt.

YOU KNOW WHAT LANGUAGE
BIN LADEN SPOKE, RIGHT?

In August 2009, I was traveling from Philadelphia to California, going back to school in the fall semester of my senior year. At the airport I checked in, perfectly normal. Then I went to the security line and was pulled aside for the secondary screening.

I guess I'm a pretty average-looking Caucasian male with blonde hair, green eyes. I think I had a beard at that point. It's worth noting beforehand that when I put my bag through the conveyor belt, two TSA officers asked what was in it, and I said that I had some speakers in there. I was bringing a speaker system to college for a stereo.

---

[1] Through this program, the United States State Department offers students intensive summer language study overseas in "critical need" foreign languages.

He said, "You have to take that out and put it through separately."

I did that. Then they took me aside for the secondary screening. I don't know if they did it because of my speakers, but at any rate, they later claimed it was because I was acting suspiciously. But I fly ten times a year or something, so the idea that I'd be acting suspiciously is nonsense.

They said, "Empty your pockets of anything else that's non-metal."

I had in my pockets a set of Arabic flashcards that I had made, and my wallet and passport.

I had my passport because I use it as ID. Sometimes things get funny because my full name is Nicholas Joseph Putter George. On my driver's license, I have my last name as Putter George, and on my passport it's a hyphenated last name, so sometimes I carry both, just in case they give me trouble about it.

The officers went through my wallet, which had my Jordanian school ID. I told them, "I studied abroad in Jordan, this is my student ID."

I gave them my flashcards and they patted me down. They didn't find anything. The flashcards were index cards that had a word in Arabic on one side and English on the other. There were like two-hundred of them or so, and almost all of them were innocuous words, like the verb "to smile." Maybe seven were words that I had written down from al-Jazeera to study, words like "bomb," "terrorist," "explosion." Obviously these were the ones that scared them the most. So they called me over to the table where they were looking through all of my stuff.

They asked, "What are these cards?"

I told them. One of them would talk to me and the other would go off and talk on his cell phone for a little bit and come back and so on. The two of them were like Tweedledee and Tweedledum, trying to figure out what they were going to do with me. They talked to me for a half hour, and at this point, I noticed that my plane was leaving really soon, and they didn't seem too concerned. They bomb-swabbed every one of the two-hundred flashcards and they were bomb-swabbing my phone repeatedly.

Originally I thought how silly this was. I was thinking, *This will be done in a minute*, and then, *They're going to make me miss my flight because of this nonsense*.

Eventually a woman came over. She was the TSA supervisor. She started asking me questions and being really aggressive. She gestured to a couple of books I had, one of which was called *Rogue Nation*.[2]

She asked me, "Okay, you obviously read. You know who did 9/11?"

I didn't really say anything because I assumed it was a rhetorical question.

But she asked it again, so I said, "Osama bin Laden."

She asked, "Yeah, you know what language he spoke, right?"

And I said, "Arabic."

I was talking to her for maybe fifteen minutes, and by that time, I had already missed the flight Then all of sudden there was a police officer behind me. He really just popped out of nowhere. He told me to put my hands behind my back, cuffed me, and just started leading me out through the terminal.

Up until then, I just assumed it was going to be a passing thing and pretty soon they'd realize this was ridiculous and let me go. But when they finally cuffed me, that's when I realized this wasn't going to end soon.

ARE YOU AN ISLAMIC?

I asked the police officer, "What's going on?"

He said, "We're taking you for additional questioning."

Eventually we got to the police station, and as he put me in the cell, he asked me if I'd ever been arrested.

I said, "No, am I being arrested now?"

---

[2] Clyde Prestowitz's *Rogue Nation: American Unilateralism and the Failure of Good Intentions* (2003) analyzes American foreign policy and unilateralism during the early Bush administration. Prestowitz was Secretary of Commerce under President Reagan.

He said, "No, you're being detained."

The airport has its own little police department. It's a big room with a bunch of desks, where all the police are working, and at the one end they have the cell: this one glass wall, and then it's all tile floors and ceiling and wall, with a little bench.

I was put behind bars with my hands cuffed behind my back.

Then the lieutenant came in with the original arresting officer and had him come in and uncuff me. They led me to the bathroom and I asked, "Hey, do you know what's going on here?"

The officer said, "I don't know. What did you do?"

To me, that's a sign that something's really wrong, when you get arrested and you ask the police officer why and they don't have an answer for you.

I said, "I don't know. I'm trying to learn Arabic."

Then they put me back in the cell and left me there for another two and a half hours.

I didn't ask if I could call anyone. I guess I was just figuring this was all going to work itself out soon enough. I kept telling myself, *Just do whatever they say.*

It was about one in the afternoon when the FBI showed up. They did their own personal check through of all my belongings, taking apart my speakers and putting them back together and photocopying my flashcards.

I'd checked in my luggage, and that's the funniest thing—the luggage that got checked still flew. So if there had been a bomb in there, I would have been the luckiest terrorist of all.

Then the FBI agents took me to a room with a big, long table and they asked me questions for a half hour. They were all just really dumb questions. They thought it was really strange that I was going to a liberal arts school if I was studying physics, and they asked me why I wasn't going to a technical university.

I said, "Because I also want to study other things. For instance, Arabic."

Then they asked me, "So you understand why you're here, right?"

At this point I had been there long enough to get angry but I still wasn't taking any kind of tone with them. I said, "Honestly, I really don't."

And they said, "Well then, you're a fucking idiot. Do you need me to go get the flashcards?"

I said, "No, I don't need you to get the flashcards. I've seen them."

They asked me about all the countries I'd been to, what I was doing there, if I'd ever met someone that wanted to overthrow the U.S. government, if I was a member of any communist groups on campus. I just answered no.

They asked me if I was "an Islamic," which took me aback a little bit. Presumably, they meant to ask if I was Muslim, and I said no.

At that point they said, "Our job is really more of an art than a science."

They explained that when there's a problem like this, they get called in to talk to the person and decide whether or not they're a real threat. They determined that I wasn't a threat and they took me back to the terminal. They talked to the airlines and got me a flight for the next day, so I didn't have to pay.

By then I was feeling angry. When I first got arrested, it was just shock. But then you're sitting in the cell for four hours, which gives you the time to realize this is totally wrong.

NO APOLOGY AT ALL

When I got back to the terminal I called my parents. I told them briefly what happened and they said okay. They didn't really say much at that point, but my whole family drove out. I think they all got pretty angry on the car ride over.

My father used to be a public defender. I think both of my parents are extremely perceptive people. They're very good at taking an issue and seeing to the heart of it, like in the case of an injustice. It's very simple to them when something's wrong. I think that's a value they've instilled in us.

When they arrived, I told my dad that they had found my flash-cards, arrested me, held me in the cell for four hours, and that I'd only now been released.

We went to talk to the TSA agent. It was a different agent who said, "I don't know who was on at that point. It's not my shift. I didn't do it."

We got absolutely nowhere. Then my dad went to the police department and he yelled at the lieutenant for a while. The lieutenant said, "I'm sorry you don't like it, but this is the way we do things." Absolutely no apology at all.

My dad was just trying to figure out why it happened. Everything about it was crazy. It was wrong and illegal.

My brother was taking a lot of details. He wanted to write a letter, like an op-ed for the local paper. Actually, they didn't take his piece, but they did send one of their top editors to interview me, and he ended up writing a piece himself.

That was the first reporting of it, and then the ACLU saw that piece and they got in touch with me from there.

Once the ACLU got in touch, their attorney explained to me why he thought we had a case, that constitutionally what they did counts as an arrest, and there's no way you can argue that they had probable cause for anything. So to him, it was a pretty clear Fourth Amendment violation. He told me to think about it and talk it over with my family and decide what I wanted to do.

Filing a lawsuit made a lot of sense to me, so I went forward. The suit against the TSA, the FBI, and the Philadelphia police was filed in February 2010. The ACLU sued for Fourth Amendment violations, and I think they have a First Amendment claim as well.[3] Illegal search and seizure, illegal arrest. I was not Mirandized.[4]

---

[3] For details on the protections these amendments provide, see Appendix III: United States Counterterrorism After 9/11.

[4] Prior to arrest and interrogation, police are required to inform suspects of their constitutional rights through a statement known as the Miranda warning.

Fox News published some piece that included all this nonsense about how I was acting suspiciously and that the TSA behavior specialist picked me out. That's the current claim the government is making. But I fly all the time. There's no reason I'd be even vaguely suspicious. It's just like the Occam's Razor principle: the simplest solution is the right one. Which is more likely? They picked me out because of my behavior, and then I just happened to also have these flashcards, or they picked me out because of the flashcards?

I think the lawsuit's really important, because there's a culture of immunity in the TSA. You have to make the point that it's not okay, that the rules still apply in the airport, and they can't just do whatever they want.

It would make a lot more sense to be encouraging Arabic speakers,[5] rather than treating them like criminals, you know? The Foreign Service and the military are desperately short of Arabic speakers, so it's crazy to have this incredibly paranoid and suspicious attitude toward someone learning Arabic. Especially someone like me, who'd really like to do something like join the Foreign Service.

I am probably even more determined now to study Arabic. Especially after the State Department program, my Arabic is in much better shape than it's ever been.

I haven't had any trouble flying since then, though the first couple of times I was flying, I was really scared when I'd go in through the metal detectors, thinking, *What are they going to do this time?*

But I still travel, and with flashcards.

---

[5] The increased United States military and intelligence presence in Arabic-speaking countries since 9/11 has revealed a shortage of Arabic speakers in government positions. A 2006 report by the Government Accountablity Office (GAO), for example, found an acute shortage of Arabic speakers at United States embassies in the Muslim world, and that more than one-third of public policy diplomacy positions at Arabic-language posts were filled by people below the designated language-proficiency level.

APPENDICES

I. GLOSSARY

ORGANIZATIONS

American-Arab Anti-Discrimination Committee (ADC)—A civil-rights organization founded by former senator James Abourezk in 1980. Since its founding, the ADC has contributed to influential reports on anti-Arab discrimination in the United States, assisted in litigation, and provided counseling to victims of discrimination or defamation.

American Civil Liberties Union (ACLU)—An organization founded in 1920 that works to protect civil rights and individual liberties across a number of issues, including immigrant rights and national security. The ACLU works through courts, legislatures, and publicity campaigns.

Anti-Defamation League (ADL)—An advocacy organization founded in 1913 to promote civil rights and combat anti-Semitism. The ADL has been an outspoken critic of Islamic extremism.

Arab American Institute (AAI)—Founded in 1985, the AAI is an advocacy organization dedicated to the civil and political empowerment of Americans of Arab descent.

Association of Arab-American University Graduates (AAUG)—Founded in 1967, AAUG is one of the first organizations to focus on the relationship between Arab and American people, and to promote the idea of an Arab-American identity in the wake of the Arab-Israeli war.

Center for Constitutional Rights (CCR)—An organization founded in 1966 by attorneys working in the civil-rights movement in the southern United States. The CCR provides legal and educational assistance on issues involving civil liberties and human rights.

Council on American Islamic Relations (CAIR)—The largest Islamic civil liberties group in the United States, founded in 1994. Much of CAIR's work focuses on enhancing understanding of Islam in the United States, protecting civil liberties, and empowering American Muslims.

Department of Homeland Security (DHS)—A United States cabinet-level agency formed in 2003 as part of a post-9/11 reorganization of the United States federal government. After its formation, DHS was given the authority to oversee a number of government functions, such as immigration, customs, and transportation, which had previously existed in separate, decentralized agencies.

Desis Rising Up & Moving (DRUM)—A membership-led organization, DRUM was founded in early 2000 to assist South Asian low wage immigrant workers, families fighting deportation and profiling as Muslims, and youth in New York City.

Hamas—A major Palestinian political party and advocacy group with a history of using militant violence as well as public outreach to achieve pro-Palestinian political goals.

Hamas was founded in 1987, and was placed on the first United States list of Specially Designated Terrorist Organizations in 1995.

Holy Land Foundation for Development and Relief (HLF)—The HLF was originially founded as the Occupied Land Fund (OLF) in 1989. Once the largest Islamic charity in the United States, it was shut down after it became the target of a controversial federal material support investigation and prosecution. In 2008, five HLF leaders were convicted of charges related to material support.

Muslim Student Association/Muslim Student Union (MSA)—A student group comprised of a collection of chapters on college and university campuses in the United States and Canada that work to empower and create a supportive on-campus community for Muslim students and Islamic life. The MSA was first founded at the University of Illinois at Urbana-Champaign in 1963.

Office of Foreign Assets Control (OFAC)—The office within the United States Department of the Treasury responsible for enforcing United States economic and trade sanctions, including material support of terrorism.

Office of the Director of National Intelligence (ODNI)—Founded in 2004 on the recommendation of the 9/11 Commission, the ODNI is the lead office of the sixteen agencies that make up the United States intelligence community. The relationships between these agencies, which include the Central Intelligence Agency (CIA) and the National Security Agency (NSA), were reorganized after the Commission's report found that intelligence shortcomings and lack of information sharing contributed to the failure to prevent the 9/11 attacks.

Park51/Cordoba House—A Muslim-American community center planned for construction in lower Manhattan, near the site of the World Trade Center. Although plans for its construction had been known since December 2009, the project's first public presentation occurred soon after an unsuccessful, unrelated attempt to detonate a car bomb in Manhattan's Times Square the following May. This was followed by a national controversy in which the center was often labeled the Ground Zero Mosque.

Sikh Coalition—The Sikh Coalition is a community-based civil and human rights organization that provides direct legal services and does advocacy and education work. The Sikh Coalition was founded in the immediate aftermath of 9/11 in response to attacks on one elderly Sikh and two teenagers in Queens, NY.

South Asian American Leaders of Tomorrow (SAALT)—A national advocacy organization that works with South Asian communities in the United States, and the issues affecting them. Founded in 2000.

Transportation Security Administration (TSA)—An agency within the Department of Homeland Security, responsible for the security of United States transportation infrastructure. The TSA was created in response to the 9/11 attacks, and is perhaps most well known for overseeing airport screenings.

People, Themes, and Concepts

Black sites—A network of covert prisons and compounds outside of the United States used by the CIA for the interrogation of suspected terrorists. Their creation and use in the War on Terror were reportedly conceived in the months immediately after 9/11. The operation of black sites has been reported in Afghanistan, Bosnia, within Guantánamo Bay, Iraq, Kosovo, Lithuania, Morocco, Pakistan, Poland, Romania, Thailand, and the British territory Diego Garcia. Black sites became public knowledge after a report was published in *The Washington Post* in 2005. The black site program was reportedly suspended in late 2006.

Extraordinary rendition—A covert CIA program to locate, abduct, and transport suspected terrorists outside of the normal legal processes of extradition. President Bush authorized secret CIA rendition teams on September 17, 2001, but the practice that has become known as "extraordinary rendition" has reportedly been in use against terrorists since 1995. (Before 9/11, each individual rendition had required presidential approval.) Suspects were often transferred through the CIA network of black sites, and/or deposited for interrogation in countries known to use methods of torture. Experts, including the ACLU, have noted that the extraordinary rendition program is a clear violation of international law, and the European Parliament and Council of Europe have investigated the involvement of EU member states. The exact number of individuals who have been subject to extraordinary rendition is extremely difficult to determine, but investigative reporter Stephen Grey estimated in 2007 that "150 [people] or so...have been through the CIA's own black sites or been rendered into foreign hands or both."

Five Pillars of Islam—The fundamental tenets of Islamic faith. They are: (1) shahada—belief or profession of faith, (2) salat—five daily prayers done while facing Mecca, (3) sawm—fasting during the daylight hours of the month of Ramadan, (4) zakat—giving alms/donating charity to the poor, and (5) hajj—undertaking a pilgrimage to Mecca at least once, if one is physically and financially able.

Gurdwara—A Sikh house of worship.

Material support—A term usually associated with the crime of aiding terrorism or supporting a terrorist organization. What constitutes material support, and how laws prohibiting it have been utilized in United States counterterrorism initiatives, have undergone a number of changes since the first United States responses to the 9/11 attacks, and have been a point of heated debate.

PATRIOT Act—The common name of the USA PATRIOT Act, an acronym for Uniting and Strengthening America by Providing Appropriate Tools Required to Intercept and Obstruct Terrorism. Signed into law in October 2001, the act significantly changed a number of rules regarding law enforcement, immigration, individual privacy and civil liberties, surveillance, and government authority. (For more details, see Appendix III: United States Counterterrorism After 9/11.)

Sharia—Islamic law based on the teachings of the Koran and the traditions of the Prophet Muhammad.

Shia Islam—One of the two main branches of Islam. Shia Islam is especially prevalent in Iran. This branch of Islam rejects the first three Sunni caliphs and sees the fourth caliph, Ali, as Muhammad's first successor.

Sikhism—A monotheistic religion founded by Guru Nanak, Sikhism first appeared in Punjab during the 15th century.

Sunni Islam—One of the two main branches of Islam. Sunni Islam is often described as orthodox, and differs from Shia Islam in its understanding of the Sunna (a portion of Muslim law/practice based on the teachings of Muhammad) and in its acceptance of the first three caliphs.

Veiling—Islamic religious attire for women, traditionally believed to promote virtue and modesty. As certain Islamic practices have gained the attention of secular and Western countries, veiling in particular has become a political flashpoint for debates between religion and secularism. Arguments for banning the practice in certain settings have occurred in the U.K., Quebec, and Turkey. In 2011, France became the first European country to formally ban the wearing of full-face veils in public. Recently, Islamic authorities have begun debating whether veiling is a requirement of the religion today.

Although specific garments may vary by region and by specific Islamic traditions, some that are commonly used include:

> **Abaya**—A loose robe covering the body that starts at the shoulders or at the top of the head.

> **Burqa**—A head-to-toe cloak with mesh over the eyes, often associated today with Afghan Islam.

> **Chador**—A single garment covering the head and body, most frequently worn in Iran.

> **Hijab** (also **Khimar**)—A head scarf that covers the hair. The term "hijab" also refers to the Muslim code of dress in general for both men and women.

> **Niqab**—A veil covering most of the face.

II. TIMELINE

1790—The Naturalization Act of 1790 creates the first naturalization law for the United States, benefiting "free white persons" of "good moral character" who had lived in the country for two years. Its terms will be significantly amended in 1870, extending naturalization to "aliens of African nativity and persons of African descent."

1880s—Arabic-speaking immigrants begin arriving in the United States in large groups, largely originating from Greater Syria. In 1899, United States immigration services begins the use of the term "Syrian" as a standard classification for these immigrants.

1906—Creation of the United States Bureau of Immigration and Naturalization, a national body with the power to naturalize aliens. The bureau will eventually evolve into the Immigration and Naturalization Service (INS), and later will become a part of the Department of Homeland Security (DHS).

1917—Congress passes an immigration act that bars immigration from within a set zone of latitude and longitude (the Asiatic Barred Zone), including much of the Middle East, Asia, and the Pacific islands.

1919–1923—With the end of World War I and the Turkish War of Independence, the Ottoman Empire falls. A number of postwar treaties partition former Ottoman lands, creating new countries and European colonies.

1921—Congress passes the Emergency Quota Act, initiating a quota system for United States immigration. The act sets an annual immigration limit based on numbers found in the 1910 United States Census, mandating that only 3 percent of the number of an existing immigrant population are permitted to come to the United States each year. These limits result in a significant drop in new immigrants.

1965—With the passage of the Immigration Act of 1965, Congress ends the immigration quota system that had been in place in various forms since 1921. A second wave of large-scale immigration to the United States begins, comprising many immigrants from non-European nations.

1967—The Arab–Israeli War, or Six-Day War, is fought between Israel and Egypt, Jordan, and Syria. With United States support, success in the war brings Israel control of new territories. Pro-Israeli and anti-Arab coverage of the war by United States sources catalyzes political involvement within Arab-American communities. This leads to the formation of national organizations and advocacy groups, as well as broad changes in Arab-American identity. This leads to the formation of national organizations and advocacy groups, as well as broad changes in Arab-American identity and immigration to the United States.

1972—Israeli Olympic participants are held hostage at the Munich Olympic Games by Black September, a group demanding the release of Palestinians from Israeli jails. Nine

Israelis die. News and images of the event are circulated around the world.

—In the United States, the Nixon Administration initiates Operation Boulder, an anti-terrorism surveillance program targeting Arabs and Arab-Americans. The program ends end in 1975.

1973–1974—Members of the Organization of Arab Petroleum Exporting Countries (OPEC) declare an oil embargo. Appearances of racial caricatures of Arabs and sheikhs increase in the United States press.

1977—Congress passes the International Emergency Economic Powers Act (IEEPA), giving the president certain regulatory powers during a national emergency over financial and commercial transactions involving foreign parties. This law later finds expanded use in post-9/11 counterterrorism programs.

1978—Congress passes the Foreign Intelligence Surveillance Act (FISA), establishing different rules for domestic surveillance and foreign intelligence.

1979–1981—More than sixty United States citizens are taken hostage when Islamic revolutionaries take control of the United States Embassy in Tehran, Iran. The event receives extensive coverage by the United States news media, effectively reorienting American representation and understanding of the region.

1989—The Occupied Land Fund charity organization is founded in Los Angeles. In 1993, it will change its name to the Holy Land Foundation for Relief and Development.

1991—The United States launches Operation Desert Storm, aiming to expel Iraqi troops from Kuwait. Full operations end with Iraqi acceptance of UN resolutions within two months. The American-Arab Anti-Discrimination Committee reports an increase in hate crimes targeting Arabs within the United States during this period.

1993—The Anti-Defamation League publishes the report "Hamas, Islamic Jihad, and the Muslim Brotherhood: Islamic Extremists and the Terrorist Threat to America." The report groups the Holy Land Foundation with Islamic extremists and terrorist organizations.

—A group of conspirators led by Ramzi Yousef, a self-proclaimed Muslim fundamentalist, detonate a van packed with explosives in the basement garage of the World Trade Center. The explosion kills six people and injures one-thousand.

1995—Timothy McVeigh and Terry Nichols detonate a truck bomb at the Alfred P. Murrah Federal Building in Oklahoma City, killing 168 people.

—President Clinton issues an executive order extending IEEPA for use beyond nation-states, outlawing knowing engagement with Specially Designated Terrorists. The order introduces this new category into American law.

1996—Congress passes the Antiterrorism and Effective Death Penalty Act, criminalizing material support to designated terrorist organizations.

—Congress passes the Illegal Immigration Reform and Immigrant Responsibility Act (IIRAIRA), which sets a two-year deadline for the development of an electronic entry and exit data system. This will eventually evolve into the post-9/11 Special Registration Program.

1998—Al-Qaeda detonates truck bombs at United States embassies in Nairobi, Kenya, and Dar Es Salaam, Tanzania. Thousands are wounded, and 224 (including twelve Americans) are killed.

2000—Congress passes the Data Management Improvement Act, amending IIRAIRA. This designates a task force to oversee the implementation of the integrated entry and exit data system.

—An al-Qaeda group drives a motorboat packed with explosives into the side of the U.S.S. *Cole*, a destroyer stationed in Yemen. Seventeen American sailors are killed.

2001

Sept 11—Four commercial aircraft in the United States are hijacked, two of which crash into the towers of New York's World Trade Center. One crashes into the Pentagon, and the other in a field in Pennsylvania. The attacks cause more than 2,600 deaths at the World Trade Center, 125 deaths at the Pentagon, and 256 deaths onboard the planes.

Sept 13—The White House makes an announcement that it has found "overwhelming evidence" that Osama bin Laden coordinated the September 11 attacks.

Sept 14—Congress issues a joint resolution authorizing the president "to use all necessary and appropriate force against those nations, organizations, or persons he determines planned, authorized, committed, or aided the terrorist attacks that occurred on September 11, 2001, or harbored such organizations or persons."

Sept 17—President Bush secretly authorizes the CIA use of extraordinary rendition to black sites, an international network of classified detention facilities set up for the imprisonment and interrogation of suspected members of al-Qaeda.

Sept 18—The Department of Justice issues an interim expansion of some of its powers, allowing it to detain non-citizens (including legal immigrants) indefinitely, in the event of an "emergency or other extraordinary circumstance." Previously, detained immigrants had to be either released or charged with a crime or visa violation after twenty-four hours. In the five weeks until Congress passes the USA PATRIOT Act, this expanded rule is used to detain hundreds of people.

Sept 20—President George W. Bush announces the formation of the Office of Homeland Security. The office begins operations on October 8.

Sept 23—President Bush issues an executive order naming twenty-seven Specially

Designated Global Terrorists, and authorizing the Secretary of State and the Secretary of the Treasury to add other groups or individuals to the designated list. Under IEEPA, the order makes transactions with these groups criminal.

Oct 2—The USA PATRIOT Act is introduced in Congress.

Oct 7—The United States begins bomb strikes in Afghanistan, targeting training and military facilities of al-Qaeda and the Taliban.

Oct 11—The Department of Justice and Attorney General Ashcroft assume full control of terrorism-related prosecutions previously overseen by the New York office of the United States Attorney.

Oct 26—The USA PATRIOT Act is signed into law, reportedly before many members of Congress had read the legislation in its entirety.

Dec 4–14—The Treasury's Office of Foreign Asset Control (OFAC) lists three large Muslim charities among other groups named as Specially Designated Terrorist Organizations. The assets of all three—the Holy Land Foundation, the Global Relief Foundation, and the Benevolence International Foundation—are frozen, and their offices are subject to a series of raids.

Dec 11—Zacarias Moussaoui, a French citizen of Moroccan descent, is charged in the first criminal indictment to come out of the 9/11 attacks.

Dec 17—The last major grouping of Taliban resistance is defeated in the battle of Tora Bora.

Dec 22—Richard Reid, a British citizen and Muslim convert, is arrested for attempting to detonate a bomb hidden in his shoe while onboard a commercial airplane destined for Miami.

2002

Jan 11—The first prisoners from Afghanistan arrive at the United States detention center at Guantánamo Bay

Jan 23—*Wall Street Journal* reporter Daniel Pearl is kidnapped by al-Quaeda operatives in Karachi, Pakistan. A video recording of his murder will surface the following month.

Jan 29—President Bush uses the State of the Union address to name the so-called Axis of Evil, governments he accuses of aiding terrorism and seeking weapons of mass destruction—Iraq, Iran, and North Korea.

March 19—CIA Director George Tenet claims links between al-Qaeda and Iraq in a testimony before the Senate Intelligence Committee.

June 1—In a speech delivered during the graduation ceremonies at West Point, President Bush makes the first public proclamation of what will later become known as the Bush

Doctrine of pre-emptive military action: "If we wait for threats to fully materialize, we will have waited too long. We must take the battle to the enemy, disrupt his plans, and confront the worst threats before they emerge."

July 16—The Department of Justice announces a proposal for the civilian surveillance program Operation TIPS (Terrorism Information and Prevention System) For more details, see Appendix III: United States Counterterrorism After 9/11.

Aug 1—The Justice Department's Office of Legal Counsel presents the White House with a memo forwarding the argument that the interrogation of suspected terrorists would not violate prohibitions against torture unless it creates physical pain equivalent in intensity "to organ failure, impairment of bodily function, or even death." Knowledge of this memo does not become public until June 2004.

Sept 11—The Department of Justice begins implementation of the National Security Entry-Exit Registration System (NSEERS). For more details, see Appendix III: United States Counterterrorism After 9/11.

Sept 17—The United States military publishes an updated National Security Strategy that codifies preemptive military action as official United States policy.

Sept 18—The joint congressional committee formed to investigate the events of 9/11 holds its first public hearing.

Oct 11—Congress passes a joint resolution authorizing the president to use military force "against the continuing threat posed by Iraq."

Nov 25—President Bush signs legislation creating the Department of Homeland Security, officially reorganizing twenty-two federal government agencies.

Nov 27—President Bush signs legislation creating the 9/11 Commission.

Dec 6—After months of debate and conflicting reports about Iraq's ability to acquire weapons of mass destruction (WMDs), UN chief weapons inspector Hans Blix calls on the U.S. government to assist the international investigation of weapons in Iraq by releasing the secret intelligence that the United States has claimed offers proof of the Iraq–WMD link.

Dec 20—Blix publicly criticizes the United States and British governments for their failure to provide intelligence to weapons inspectors.

2003

Feb 5—After various statements from UN officials declining the need for the use of military force against Iraq and noting that investigations have yet to find strong evidence of a large-scale weapons program there, United States Secretary of State Colin Powell presents the Bush administration's case against Iraq to the UN Security Council. Experts later find that key evidence was misrepresented in the presentation.

Feb 7—The details of a new anti-terrorism bill that becomes known as the USA PATRIOT Act II are leaked to the public. The bill, which had been prepared in secret, slowly becomes a target of popular criticism.

Feb 28—UN weapons inspector Hans Blix submits an inspection report to the UN Security Council finding that there's no evidence to support the existence or development of WMDs in Iraq.

March 18—The Department of Homeland Security announces Operation Liberty Shield, requiring the detention of asylum seekers who originate from any of thirty-four listed countries with active terrorist groups.

March 20—President Bush announces that military operations against targets in Iraq have begun.

April 19—United States forces gain control of Baghdad. Images of the fall of a large statue of Saddam Hussein circulate internationally.

May 1—President Bush, speaking from the aircraft carrier U.S.S. *Lincoln*, declares an end to "major combat operations" in Iraq.

June 15—The United States begins a series of military raids across Iraq called Operation Desert Scorpion.

July 7—The White House releases a statement acknowledging that a claim President Bush made in his 2003 State of the Union address—that Saddam Hussein had sought uranium from Africa with the intent to use it to manufacture weapons—was based on documents that had been forged.

July 24—The 9/11 Commission releases the report of its investigation into the 9/11 attacks, which commission members complain was delayed by the White House until major operations in Iraq had been completed.

Sept 24—Congress eliminates funding for the Total Information Awareness (TIA), a proposed intelligence operation. Elements developed for TIA are reportedly later used in other intelligence operations.

Dec 13—Saddam Hussein is captured by American forces in Iraq.

2004

Jan 26—A federal judge declares the part of the USA PATRIOT Act related to material support to be in violation of the Constitution.

April 4—The United States begins a military offensive on Fallujah, Iraq.

April 30—Journalist Seymour Hersh publishes photographs and a report of prisoner abuse at Iraqi's Abu Ghraib prison.

June 2—The United States military expands its Stop-Loss Program with an announcement that thousands of soldiers will be forced to remain in Iraq and Afghanistan past the scheduled end of their service.

June 3—CIA Director George Tenet announces his resignation, effective July 11.

June 8—*The Washington Post* publicizes the existence of a Department of Justice memo that discusses the torture of suspected members of al-Qaeda. (See entry: August 1, 2002).

June 28—The United States transfers political authority in Iraq to an interim government. In an attempt to avoid insurgent attacks aimed at disrupting the event, the transfer occurs two days ahead of schedule.

July 19—Halliburton receives a grand jury subpoena from the United States Attorney's office regarding its business transactions with Iran.

Sept 23—The House of Representatives introduces an intelligence reform bill that includes provisions for extraordinary rendition.

Dec 17—Congress passes the Intelligence Reform and Terrorism Prevention Act, reforming United States foreign-intelligence operations and creating the centralized Office of the Director of National Intelligence (ODNI).

2005

Nov—The CIA destroys videotapes of its 2002 interrogations of two detainees, Abu Zubaida and Abd al-Rahim al-Nashiri. Members of Congress are not informed of this for at least a year, and it does not become public knowledge until December 2007.

Dec 4—*The Washington Post* publishes an article revealing the existence of covert CIA prisons known as "black sites," and the practice of extraordinary rendition.

Dec 6—Khalid el-Masri and the ACLU file a lawsuit against the CIA for el-Masri's abduction and rendition to Afghanistan.

Dec 15—The *New York Times* reveals the existence of the NSA's unwarranted wiretapping program, a confidential domestic eavesdropping and surveillance program that had been secretly authorized in 2002. The *Times* faces criticism for its admission that it had held back the story for more than a year, a period that included the 2004 elections.

2006

Feb 7—Law professor Mark Denbeaux releases a report finding that only 5 percent of the detainees at Guantánamo Bay had been captured by the United States, and that many of them had been handed over to the United States in Afghanistan by either the

Northern Alliance or Pakistani soldiers for monetary reward. The report also finds that there is no evidence for ties to radical or terrorist groups for over 60 percent of the Guantánamo detainees.

March 9—President Bush signs a reauthorization of the USA PATRIOT Act into law.

Aug 10—British authorities thwart a plot to detonate explosives onboard commercial airplanes headed from Heathrow airport to the United States. The following month, the United States Senate Subcommittee on Homeland Security holds a hearing in order to learn from the British approach to counterterrorism.

Sept 6—In a speech, President Bush publicly acknowledges the existence of CIA black sites for the first time.

2007

Aug—Congress passes a number of amendments to FISA, one of which removes the requirement of a warrant to conduct surveillance on communication when one party is "reasonably believed" to be outside the United States.

Oct—The federal terrorism-financing case against the Holy Land Foundation and five of its leaders ends in a mistrial. The government states its intention to retry the case.

Dec—The CIA's 2005 destruction of the videotapes of its interrogation of two detainees becomes public knowledge. Inquiries into a potential criminal investigation begin.

2008

Nov 16—President-elect Barack Obama states that he plans to shut down the Guantánamo Bay detention center.

Nov 24—On retrial, five leaders of the Holy Land Foundation are convicted of money laundering, tax fraud, and material support for terrorism.

2009

Jan 20—During his inaugural ceremonies, President Obama orders the suspension of all military prosecutions of terrorist suspects held in detention at Guantánamo Bay. That week, he signs a number of executive orders mandating the closure of the detention center at Guantánamo Bay within one year, as well as the closure of the CIA's black sites.

Feb 5—Leon Panetta, President Obama's nominee for Director of the CIA, states that the CIA will not conduct extraordinary renditions under his tenure.

March 28—A Spanish court begins work toward opening an investigation of the Bush Six—Bush administration officials suspected of war crimes related to torturing prisoners at Guantánamo Bay.

Nov 5—Major Nidal Malik Hasan, an Army psychiatrist, opens fire at the Fort Hood military base in Texas, killing thirteen people and wounding approximately thirty.

Dec 25—Abdul Farouk Abdulmutallab is subdued after attempting to detonate an explosive device on a transatlantic flight destined for Detroit.

2010

May 1—Faisal Shahzad, an American citizen originally from Pakistan, unsuccessfully attempts to detonate a car bomb in New York's Times Square.

May 25—A local community board in downtown Manhattan reviews the proposal for a Muslim community center to be built near the site of the World Trade Center, attracting national controversy.

2011

March—Congressman Peter T. King convenes a series of hearings titled "The Extent of Radicalization in the American Muslim Community and That Community's Response." The hearings are largely received as controversial, and reveal a partisan split in opinions on terror investigations and the role of mosques in American communities. Unrelated Senate hearings led by Senator Richard Durbin later in the month, focusing on discrimination and the civil rights of American Muslims, attract far less media attention.

April—Pastor Terry Jones sets fire to a Qur'an after holding it to a mock trial at his church in Gainesville, Florida. In a response to the burning, thousands of protestors assail a United Nations compound in Mazar-I-Sharif, Afghanistan, killing at least twelve people.

May 1—President Barack Obama announces that Osama bin Laden has been killed by United States forces in Pakistan.

III. U.S. COUNTERTERRORISM AFTER 9/11

The attacks of September 11, 2001, and the legislative changes implemented since then, sparked a number of debates that continue to this day. These debates have focused on issues that include the level of accountability that a democracy demands of its law enforcement, the violation of civil rights in the name of national security, and concerns about racial and religious discrimination. But as the initial sense of crisis has receded, they appear, more profoundly, to build a dialogue about the role of the state and how it should respond to 9/11 and to terrorism.

How heavily, and through what instruments, should government shape domestic life? Even the most effective legal arguments and counter-arguments that responded to anti-terrorism initiatives were not designed to fully answer this question. Although many reports, lawsuits, and investigations succeeded in bringing anti-terrorism laws and programs into debate, almost all were molded to take on a specific point of law or public policy. As this exchange—which continues today, through the courts, the newspapers, and the other media of public discussion—sorts the details of a what post-9/11 government will be, some of the ways the early and still-influential arguments misrecognized the larger changes underfoot have slowly become clear.

LIBERTY VERSUS SECURITY

In *Less Safe, Less Free*, lawyers David Cole and Jules Lobel write that the INS Special Registration Program, an anti-terrorism measure that began processing predominantly Arab or Muslim non-immigrant aliens in 2002, had called in 80,000 people in its first five years. Other initiatives "sought out another 8,000 young men from these same countries for FBI interviews, and placed more than 5,000 foreign nationals [in the United States] in preventive detention. Yet as of January 2007, not one of these individuals stands convicted of a crime." Sociologist Louise Cainkar has argued that "at least 100,000 Arabs and Muslims living in the United States experienced" some manner of post-9/11 domestic security measures, while other experts have surmised twice as many; a former FBI section chief has estimated "about half a million" FBI interviews alone.

A 2005 report by New York University's Center on Law and Security further emphasized a premise underlying Cole and Lobel's research, announcing that because "there have been relatively few indictments, fewer trials, and almost no convictions on charges of dangerous crimes, the legal War on Terror has yielded few visible results." A follow-up report in 2006 reiterated, as a statement of fact, that "conviction...is the primary goal," and the center found only 998 defendants indicted through Department of Justice terrorism prosecutions from 2001 to 2010. Only 315 of these indictments contained a charge "under one of the core terrorism statutes." "The vast majority of cases," the center found, "turn out to include no link to terrorism once they go to court."

Almost all discussions about the USA PATRIOT Act or post-9/11 governance have followed Cole, Lobel, and Cainkar to argue that convictions in open court should be the sole indicator of the success of domestic security programs. But to assume that conviction is the objective of these programs is to neglect a set of facts about which their designers and administrators have been quite vocal. According to journalist Bob Woodward, Attorney General John Ashcroft addressed early FBI concerns about how certain investigation tactics might hamper convictions with a pointed explanation that "the chief mission of United States law enforcement…is to stop another attack and apprehend any accomplices to terrorists… If we can't bring them to trial, so be it." Michael Chertoff, who served as Secretary of the Department of Homeland Security after overseeing the investigation of the 9/11 terrorist attacks at the Justice Department, was equally forthright in public, telling *The New Yorker* in November 2001 that "we thought that we were getting information to prevent more attacks, which was even more important than trying any case that came out of the attacks." Domestic programs like Special Registration, prolonged detention, and visa holds—frequent targets for analysts and civil-rights advocates—weren't, in fact, devised to obtain criminal convictions.

As Chertoff and Ashcroft make clear, there was no need to search for ulterior motives or hidden justifications—the explanations for post-9/11 law had always been in plain sight. More thoroughly hidden, at least initially, were the details of how these programs were carried out. And this is probably the most significant reason why evaluating post-9/11 laws and regulations based only on convictions, or lack thereof, can be so misleading. Although the research and investigations whose conclusions focused on convictions have introduced new knowledge into the public record and uncovered genuine abuse, they do not challenge certain rules about what this information means and how it should be used. This research accepts specific parameters to the debate about the role of government and what its goals in fighting terrorism should be. In general, this is a debate that proceeds by finding some measure of how effectively a given program contributes to safety—the number of terrorist convictions is one favored measurement of this type—and assessing that against some other measurement of a program's cost to personal freedoms and civil rights.

David Cole has called this type of comparison "the tension between liberty and security." But "liberty" versus "security" rarely measures the two terms using the same scale: "When a democratic society strikes the balance between liberty and security in ways that impose the costs of security measures equally on all," Cole explains, "one might be relatively confident that the political process will achieve a proper balance. Since September 11," he continues, "we have repeatedly done precisely the opposite, sacrificing the rights of a minority group—noncitizens, especially Arab and Muslim noncitizens," as well as the rights of those often mistaken for them, "in the name of the majority's security interests." It is rarely stated explicitly, as philosopher and constitutional scholar Ronald Dworkin adds, that "with hardly any exceptions, no American who is not a Muslim and has no Muslim connections actually runs any risk of being labeled an enemy combatant and locked up in a military jail." For most Americans, "the only balance in question is between the majority's security and other people's rights."

As security proposals were debated and legislated in the days and weeks after 9/11, there were a number of plans that supported dispersing the costs more "equally on all." One of these, the creation of a national security card, as Cole noted in 2003, had been "on the table since September 12," but had "gone nowhere." Another, a 2002 Justice Department proposal for Operation TIPS (Terrorism Information and Prevention System), which would have formalized a way for millions of Americans to report suspicious activity as they came across it throughout their day, failed in the face of overwhelming public criticism. (This was partly due to the department's suggestion that this role could be held by mail carriers, utility workers, transportation employees, and other people who had access to private homes but were not law enforcement agents.) These rejections were swift and forceful: the legislation that created the Department of Homeland Security (DHS) the next year included language—reportedly at the insistence of House Majority Leader Richard Armey—to prevent DHS from forming a national identity card program, and explicitly prohibited the federal government from forming TIPS in the future.

Another post-9/11 initiative, Total Information Awareness (TIA), also faced broad opposition to the idea of spreading the costs of security widely. TIA was a Pentagon data-mining program that proposed creating a central database to collect transaction data, financial and medical records, communication records, and travel data, as well as the development of biometric identification and tracking technology. Strong opposition arose even though most of this information was already available in different places, and legal scholars speculated that the program may have been able to withstand a constitutional challenge. Congress voted to withdraw funding from TIA's research proposal in 2003, though David Cole noted that the language used to do so blocked the program's implementation only "as applied to United States persons," a specific legal term that does not include sub-populations of foreigners who are in the United States "in any status as other than permanent residents." At the time TIA's funding was withdrawn, a number of reporters and security experts speculated that parts of the program would end up in other federal agencies or as a classified operation. A state-level pilot program with similar capabilities, called MATRIX, was intermittently accepted by some states, but only for use on limited populations, such as felons and sex offenders. When, in 2005, a classified and unwarranted NSA wiretapping program that appeared to have the potential for indiscriminate surveillance was discovered, it was received as a national scandal. The longest-lasting program to spread the costs of security relatively evenly across the population as a whole has been TSA airport screening. This too, however, has been implemented in a number of unbalanced and discriminatory ways, and has generated civil-rights complaints and lawsuits against the TSA.

"What the metaphor of balance between freedom and security conceals," political scientist Corey Robin wrote in the *London Review of Books* in 2006, "is the fundamental imbalance of power between groups in society; unequal costs are paid in return for unequal gains." Robin employs a parallel example to illustrate that the same kind of unbalanced social forces, not statistics or any rational calculation of probability, create the environment that allows profiling and discriminatory practices against Arabs and Muslims to be passively accepted in the name of national security. When presented with research showing that 2 percent of American males aged eighteen to twenty-one are arrested for drunk driving, the United States Supreme Court rejected as unconstitutionally discriminatory a law keeping young men in this age group from buying alcohol (*Craig v. Boren*). Far less than 2 percent of Arabs and Muslims in the United States engage in terrorist activities, Robin continues, yet targeted enforcement is common. DUI numbers alone, in complete ignorance of the social forces at work, would suggest age profiling against young male drivers to be a sound road-safety enforcement strategy. One of the reasons why a program like this seems so absurd is that these social forces—and the imbalances they create—are inescapable. In part, they explain why the USA PATRIOT Act defined international terrorist activity much more expansively than domestic terrorism. Even in the immediate aftermath of 9/11, at a time when immediate safety was a universal national concern, the Justice Department explained its Special Registration of non-immigrant aliens by claiming to target people from countries where al-Qaeda had established a presence, but neglected to interview any foreign nationals from Britain, France, Germany, or Spain, all countries in which there was previous knowledge of an al-Qaeda presence.

A single-minded focus on criminal convictions, and the way such a tight focus restricts determinations of successful post-9/11 law to comparisons of liberty versus security, neglect the other effects legal initiatives have on life in the United States. Criminal convictions are a failed measuring device of the successful implementation of such laws because much of the cost—as well as the actual implementation of post-9/11 security law and governance—is borne outside of the courts, or through social instruments that rarely advance there. To understand how these laws work, how they are implemented and enforced in practice, one needs to look not at the courts, or even to averages of the nation as a whole, but to the specific, concentrated populations affected. This is part of the reason why so much of the more recent analysis of security law and scholarship on the role of government in post-9/11 domestic life has relied heavily on interviews and ethnographies. Still, a bulk of the analysis of the government's reaction to 9/11 and to the threat of terrorism can read like two different conversations. These conversations range from interviews and ethnographies that gravitate toward themes of social inclusion, immigration, and community, to legal or security analyses that critique specific initiatives, or try to revamp calculations and variables of particular security strategies that failed to prevent a growing threat.

IMMIGRATION LAW AS A COUNTERTERRORISM TOOL

"The missed opportunities to thwart the 9/11 plot," the 9/11 Commission concluded, "were also symptoms of a broader inability to adapt the way government manages problems to the new challenges of the twenty-first century." These are the challenges of computer technology, cellular and fiber-optic communication, and increasingly fluid borders, where the Cold War distinctions between a criminal investigation and an intelligence operation, and between law enforcement and a military threat, no longer hold as steadily. Since around 2003, when the climate of national crisis receded, shifting these distinctions to effectively confront the threat of terrorism and protect not only the safety but the civil rights of the United States has been conducted less through the creation of new laws and regulations than by the creative reworking of laws already in place, mostly in two broad fields: immigration and intelligence.

"The War on Terrorism has been waged largely through anti-immigrant measures," David Cole wrote in 2003.

In part, this is because the immigration law is such a useful pretext; it imposes a wide range of technical obligations on all foreign nationals. Because our economy literally depends on illegal immigration, we have long tolerated the presence of... millions of noncitizens who have violated some immigration rule. This means that the attorney general has extremely broad discretion in how and when to enforce immigration obligations; any immigrant community he targets will inevitably include many persons here in violation of their visas.

One of the most explicit uses of immigration law as a counterterrorism tool was the so-called Absconders Initiative, launched in January 2002. The Immigration and Naturalization Service (INS) announced a plan to track down and deport noncitizen males from "Middle Eastern" countries—no specific list was made public—who had been ordered deported by an immigration judge but had yet to leave the United States. At the time, the majority of the estimated 314,000 "absconders" in the country originated from Latin America, and fewer than 2 percent were Middle Eastern. By the middle of 2003, the Justice Department reported that 1,100 people had been detained. INS entered the detainment data and immigration status of known absconders into the federal crimes database, which made it available to state and local officials, such as police officers making traffic stops. In 2004, Louise Cainkar reported attending a meeting of a United States attorney and INS leadership with Chicago's Arab-American community, in which the federal officials explained that the Absconders Initiative was not racial profiling because other communities would be approached next; in 2009, Cainkar wrote that this had yet to happen.

In September 2002, INS implemented its Special Registration Program (also operated under the name NSEERS), requiring "certain non-immigrant aliens" to report to INS within thirty days of their arrival, and annually thereafter, to be registered, photographed, fingerprinted, and questioned, with the answers given under oath and recorded by an immigration officer. Later that year, a more controversial domestic "call-in" component was added, soliciting 80,000 males aged sixteen and older who were in the United States through temporary visas from certain Muslim-majority countries, North Korea, and heavily Muslim Eritrea. Notices were published in the Federal Register and also advertised via flyers posted in certain ethnic communities with the heading THIS NOTICE IS FOR YOU. The flyers were reminiscent to some scholars of the publicity materials for Japanese internment.

In general, though, the program's public outreach has been judged as insufficient. Some of the non-immigrant aliens who fell under the Special Registration qualifications did not become aware of the program until they later applied for a green card, and were then found in "willful" violation of the program and denied employment authorization. A number of the families who included someone with irregular immigration status chose to leave the United States rather than submit to registration. When the numbers taking flight for asylum in Canada became too overwhelming, the INS implemented rigid outbound checks and police roadblocks to stop traffic at New York's Lacolle–Champlain port of entry.

The legal foundation for Special Registration originates in 1996, when Congress passed a law introducing a plan for a computerized system to maintain immigration arrival and departure data. This plan was modified slightly by another law passed in 2000. After 9/11, Congress revisited this idea through the USA PATRIOT Act, and called for the implementation of the database. A 2009 report by the American-Arab Anti-Discrimination Committee (ADC) and Penn State University's Dickinson School of Law Center for Immigrants' Rights, however, noted that "the NSEERS program as initiated by the Department of Justice [which oversaw INS] is quite different from the program initially proposed by Congress via statute, because the NSEERS program targeted visitors from Muslim-majority countries and went beyond tracking the arrivals and departures of noncitizens."

In 2003, the Department of Homeland Security, which had taken over the duties of the INS during a government reorganization that year, announced a suspension to parts of the program, but continued most of it on a case-by-case basis. Non-immigrant aliens who had failed to comply with any of the previous requirements found themselves still subject to penalties from the earlier period, which could include criminal charges. At the time of the suspension, DHS made statements indicating that NSEERS would be integrated into a more comprehensive system called United States-VISIT, but the 2009 ADC/Penn State report found NSEERS "alive and well," despite a number of legal challenges and although public notice about its requirements have remained lackluster. The study also found that

> most of the individuals who legally challenged the NSEERS program entered the United States lawfully, diligently complied with the NSEERS program, were predominantly male and Muslim, and had an immigration violation such as overstaying a visa that came to the attention of the immigration agency after complying with NSEERS... Many individuals impacted by the NSEERS program do not appear to have terrorism charges or criminal histories...many... had meaningful family, business, and cultural ties to the United States.

James Ziglar, a former INS commissioner, has doubted that terrorists would voluntarily submit to the program's scrutiny—rather than attempt to stay in hiding somewhere in the United States—and stated, "to my knowledge, not one actual terrorist was identified." Citing this lack of a tangible contribution to public safety, David Cole has written of the Special Registration program as "the most aggressive national campaign of ethnic profiling since World War II." But perhaps Edward Alden, a senior fellow and terrorism expert at the Council on Foreign Relations, has most clearly explained why profiling fails as a counterterrorism tool, adding in 2008, "The notion that simply by aggressively reinforcing immigration laws you would catch terrorists—I think—is wrong. I think you will catch immigration violators."

Material support

Another anti-terrorism initiative with its origin in immigration law—though it has expanded from there since—is the prohibition on providing material support to any of the groups deemed by the Justice Department to be terrorist organizations. As an attempt to cut off terrorist funding, material support prosecutions have found little success and have become extremely controversial for the damage they have inflicted upon charitable organizations later found to have no terrorist ties. As of 2008, seven United States nonprofits had been shut down, but only three faced criminal prosecution. Some experts speculate that government agencies have avoided prosecutions so that they could avoid making the evidence against the organization public, which would be a requirement of a trial. None of the three attempted prosecutions resulted in a conviction. Other charities have since recast the focus of their work to avoid politically sensitive regions of the world. A series of reports by government watchdog OMB Watch found that

> since 2001, the Treasury's Office of Foreign Assets Control (OFAC) and the Justice Department have incrementally expanded their interpretation of prohibited "material support" beyond direct transfers of funds or goods to include legitimate charitable aid that may "otherwise cultivate support" for a designated organization…[making] it increasingly difficult for charities and foundations to predict what constitutes illegal behavior.

At times, charities or individuals have been prosecuted for providing human-rights training or certain legal aid, or spending money in support of an organization that does not appear on any federal government watch list. Additionally, the ACLU's Spy Files project has uncovered domestic spying targeting the financial records of charitable groups that vocally dissent from post-9/11 policies. David Cole, a practicing lawyer and a professor at Georgetown University's law school, has written in detail about his involvement representing "material support" defendants:

> Virtually all of the cases in which the government has actually charged individuals with a crime relating to terrorism allege not acts of terrorism per se, but only "material support" to a group the government has labeled terrorist… In one case in which I am representing a human rights group, for example, the government has argued that the law prohibits the group from offering "training" in human rights advocacy to a Turkish organization, even though the government does not dispute that the intent of the training is precisely to discourage terrorism and encourage peaceful resolution of disputes.

Another case Cole documented described the prosecution of New York criminal-defense attorney Lynne Stewart for inappropriately providing legal counsel:

In June 2000, while representing Sheik Omar Abdel Rahman, who is serving multiple life sentences for conspiring to bomb the bridges and tunnels around Manhattan, Stewart issued a statement from the sheik to the press, and thereby violated an administrative restriction that barred him from contact with the outside world. Before September 11, the government responded, appropriately, by revoking Stewart's visiting privileges and insisting that she sign a more restrictive agreement before visiting the sheik again. But after September 11, the government charged Stewart with the crime of providing "material support for terrorism." She was convicted in February 2005 after the trial in which the government presented highly prejudicial and largely irrelevant evidence—including a tape from Osama bin Laden, played for the New York jury around the anniversary of the September 11 attacks, even though neither Stewart nor her codefendants were alleged to have had any ties to al-Qaeda.

Stewart's conviction led to her automatic disbarment. One of her codefendants, Mohammed Yousry, is an American citizen who was working as a translator while pursuing a doctorate in history at NYU. He is of Egyptian origin, but not a practicing Muslim, and married to an evangelical Christian. Stewart and another of Rahman's lawyers hired Yousry to translate documents for Rahman's defense, which Yousry thought could potentially become useful material for his doctoral dissertation. Though the prosecution admitted that Yousry has no ties to, or sympathy with, any terrorist organizations, his translation of Rahman's statement was enough to convict him of providing material support for terrorism—even though, unlike Stewart, he had not signed an agreement to follow the prison regulations that restricted Rahman's communications. After the FBI had impounded Yousry's computer and taped thousands of hours of phone conversations spanning three years, they produced no additional evidence at his trial. "Some of the convictions for 'material support' that the administration has obtained," Cole noted, "seem to have to do more with inflating the numbers shown on its website than with any actual threat to national security."

Like Special Registration, the statutory—and philosophical—origins of material-support prosecution predates 2001. "When Congress repealed the Cold War–era immigration law provisions that authorized deportation for mere membership in groups advocating Communism and other proscribed ideas," Cole explains, noting that these laws had been found to be in violation of the First Amendment for penalizing individuals who support only a group's lawful ends, "it substituted provisions making foreign nationals deportable for engaging in terrorist activities. The INS immediately interpreted this new law, however, to make noncitizens deportable not merely for engaging in or supporting terrorist activity, but for providing any material support to a terrorist organization, without regard to the purpose or effect of the support." In 1996, Congress brought this immigration statute into criminal law, making material support of any foreign organization designated as terrorist by the United States Secretary of State a crime. The USA PATRIOT Act extended this further, prohibiting any associational support regardless of whether any link could be made between an individual's support and an organization's terrorism, or even between an individual's support and an organization's violence. After court challenges, the law was amended again in 2004, and subsequent challenges to the vagueness of what exactly constitutes terms such as "expert advice and assistance"—one of the law's definitions of material support—have been litigated as recently as 2007.

A previously unrelated law, the 1977 International Emergency Economic Powers Act (IEEPA), has also found new life in criminal prosecutions of material support. The law was initially passed to clarify presidential powers during a national emergency, and came into use when the Treasury Department's Office of Foreign Assets Control needed to issue an embargo against a foreign nation. In 1995, IEEPA was extended beyond use against other nation-states, and began forbidding knowing engagement in transactions with Specially Designated Terrorists. This provided a way of freezing a supporting organization's funds while bypassing the criminal-law process. IEEPA was designed for emergency economic sanctions and targets assets, not preparation for a criminal prosecution. As such, an organization could be effectively shut down without a charge or a hearing. On September 23, 2001, President George W. Bush issued an executive order naming twenty-seven Specially Designated Global Terrorists—such as al-Qaeda, Osama bin Laden, and jihad groups—immediately blocking their assets and making economic transactions with them criminal. He additionally authorized the Secretary of State and the Secretary of the Treasury to add others to the list.

Part of the USA PATRIOT Act amended IEEPA to allow the Treasury Department to freeze an individual's or organization's assets on a "reasonable suspicion, pending an investigation," and to defend freeze orders with evidence held secret and presented in a confidential court hearing—not disclosed to the party whose funds were targeted by the order. As OMB Watch reported, "In fact, due to the government's state secrets privilege and its liberal definition of classified evidence, the organization typically never sees much of the evidence that led to OFAC's action." Additionally, IEEPA today "carries no knowledge requirement, so even accidental transactions can result in severe OFAC actions." In December 2001, OFAC froze assets of three of the largest Muslim charities in the United States—the Holy Land Foundation (HLF), the Global Relief Foundation, and the Benevolence International Foundation.

David Cole noted that "in all three cases, [OFAC] did so without a hearing, based not on allegations of criminal conduct, but on alleged associations with other groups blacklisted by the president." In an analysis of what he calls the "financial War on Terror," international-business scholar Ibrahim Warde commented, "Reforming the Islamic charities system was long overdue, yet post–September 11 policies proved mostly counterproductive; they weakened mainstream, 'controllable' charities, while building up informal, unchecked, and potentially dangerous charitable and donor networks." OMB Watch has added that, as the definition of activities qualifying as material support have expanded, "the United States nonprofit community operates in fear of what may spark OFAC to use its power to shut them down."

Cole suggests that the reason the wide use of material-support initiatives has "sparked relatively little protest" "likely rests on a perception that the tactics have been and will be targeted principally, if not exclusively, at Arab and Muslim foreign nationals"—despite the potential threat the laws hold for all Americans. There has been some compelling evidence for the truth of this perception. In one well-documented example: From 1997 to 2004, Chiquita Brands International purchased protection in Colombia for $1.7 million from the United Self-Defense Forces of Colombia (AUC) and the Revolutionary Armed Forces of Colombia (FARC)—two groups designated as terrorist organizations by the United States Although attorneys notified the company in 2003 that the payments violated United States counterterrorism laws, Chiquita continued payments until June 2004, when it sold Banadex, a Colombia subsidiary. A Chiquita board member disclosed this violation to Attorney General Michael Chertoff in 2003, who allegedly confirmed its illegality but told the company to wait for more feedback, and eventually placed three Chiquita officers under a Justice Department investigation. In 2007, the investigation ended without criminal charges, and Chiquita Brands International paid a $25 million fine.

Likewise, in 2005, news began to surface that Halliburton, the oilfield services corporation, had been under investigation by OFAC and the Department of Justice since 2001 for its business involvement with Iran, a designated state sponsor of terrorism. OFAC proceeded by sending an inquiry to the company requesting "information with regard to compliance," to which Halliburton responded in writing, making an argument that it was acting in compliance with the law since it conducted business with Iran through a subsidiary registered in the Cayman Islands and headquartered in Dubai. (Business with Iran was this subsidiary's sole source of revenue.) More than two years later, OFAC sent a follow-up letter requesting additional information, to which Halliburton again responded in writing, and in July 2004, Halliburton received a grand jury subpoena from the United States Attorney's office, requesting documents. The case was referred to the Department of Justice, and in 2005, Halliburton formally agreed to "take appropriate corporate action to cause its subsidiaries to not bid for any new work in Iran," but its business commitments there didn't conclude until 2007. Around the same time, statements agreeing to stop accepting business in Iran were also made by G.E., CooperCameron, and ConocoPhillips. A 2010 *New York Times* investigation found nearly 10,000 OFAC licenses granted since 2000 that allowed companies to do business with "countries blacklisted as state sponsors of terrorism," administered through a loophole originally written to provide humanitarian aid.

FOREIGN AND DOMESTIC INTELLIGENCE LAW

The modifications to foreign-intelligence law demonstrate even more clearly how antiterrorism initiatives resisted the pre-9/11 distinctions between domestic law enforcement and a military conflict. For decades, military engagements and law enforcement operations have used surveillance and reconnaissance in notably different ways. But the treatment of terrorism after 9/11 began to define these distinctions in new ways, for the purpose of engaging in surveillance more widely. "To begin with," travel writer Jonathan Raban noted in *The New York Review of Books* in 2005, "it wasn't a war. In the immediate aftermath of September 11, the attacks were spoken of, like the 1993 bombing of the World Trade Center, or the bombing of the Alfred P. Murrah Federal Building in Oklahoma City in 1995, as acts of criminal atrocity, for which those who were responsible could, the President said, 'be brought to justice.' But within nine days the war was under way."

Since the 1970s, as a result of the fallout from Watergate and a Supreme Court decision declaring that the Fourth Amendment, guarding against unreasonable searches and seizures, applied to wiretaps, different sets of rules for domestic and foreign intelligence have been in place. Before these rules were established and codified through the Foreign Intelligence Surveillance Act (FISA), in 1978, "every President used either law enforcement or intel to conduct activities in the interest of national security by tapping telephones of Americans," according to former United States Director of National Intelligence Mike McConnell.

Morton Halperin, a former official in the Johnson, Nixon, and Clinton administrations, and former director of the ACLU's Washington office, explained the reasons for the FISA rules to *The New Yorker*: "In the discussions leading up to the passage of FISA, the government said when we tap the Russian Embassy we're not looking for crimes; we're looking for what they're saying back to Moscow. The purpose is not to indict anybody but just to gather information." The laws regulating standard law-enforcement surveillance, for use in catching criminals, require probable cause that a crime has been or is being committed before a warrant for surveillance can be granted. FISA, oriented toward foreign-intelligence gathering, allows surveillance warrants to be granted in confidential FISA-court proceedings, which are overseen by seven federal judges, and instead require intelligence agencies to establish that their surveillance targets are agents of a "foreign power," regardless of probable cause or criminal activity. During the Cold War, when most United States intelligence work was aimed at Moscow, the distinction between domestic crime and foreign intelligence was generally clear. When the "criminal atrocities" of September 11 became the War on Terror, the implication was that the case could be made for FISA warrants approving surveillance of "agents" of terrorism, wherever its "embassies" may be.

But FISA's passage into law also preceded the prevalence of cell phones, email, and the outsized growth of globalized communication networks. Today, as journalist James Risen has described, "it is now difficult to tell where the domestic telephone system ends and the international network begins." The NSA has justified post-9/11 domestic wiretapping, classified and done outside of FISA, by explaining that "the switches carrying calls from Cleveland to Chicago...may also be carrying calls from Islamabad to Jakarta." Mike McConnell explained FISA's failure to keep up with the times by explaining that when the law was passed, almost all international communication worked by passing signals through satellites, while today's system is dominated by fiber-optic cables woven across borders throughout the globe. "Terrorist on a cell phone, right here, talking to a tower, happens all the time, no warrant," he once explained to the journalist Lawrence Wright, pointing to a map of Iraq. "Goes up to a satellite, back to the ground station, no warrant. Now, let us suppose that it goes up to a satellite, and in the process, [passes through the United States]. Gotta have a warrant!" Playing by FISA rules, McConnell argues, hampers legitimate international intelligence-gathering.

When the USA PATRIOT Act was presented in Congress shortly after 9/11, the only vote in the Senate against passing it into law came from Wisconsin Democrat Russ Feingold. Part of Senator Feingold's reason for voting against it was due to his opposition of the lowered standards for FISA warrants that the USA PATRIOT Act proposed. "The law allows regular criminal investigations to be taken into this secret court, which frankly isn't much of a court at all," Feingold told *The New Yorker* in late 2001. Newer technology presented communication that could avoid FISA, because its older regulations had failed to adapt but simply lowering the barriers to what could be decided in the FISA court created the opposite problem: "It's the Attorney General's private playground."

The surveillance standards that Senator Feingold opposed became law when the USA PATRIOT Act passed. Before 2001, foreign intelligence had to be the sole or "primary purpose" of an investigation; when the USA PATRIOT Act became law, the requirement was amended to investigations where foreign intelligence was a "significant" purpose, and failed to define this term. FISA was also amended to allow previously barred surveillance techniques such as "roving wiretaps," which intercept communications from a targeted person regardless of the communication device used, and can monitor devices—such as public computers—that the target may use in the future. Previously, in order to do this, the law had required assistance from third-party telephone or communications carriers for each device under surveillance. After the changes, it could monitor these devices without this step, and so no longer had to notify third-party companies that surveillance was taking place. In 2007, intelligence law was amended again to allow the U.S. government to sidestep the FISA court when wiretapping communications that begin or end in a foreign country, and legal experts disagree widely on how broadly the new regulations can be interpreted. Congress has debated various FISA-related amendments in the years since, sometimes in closed-door sessions, and Mike McConnell has publicly called for a wholesale update of the law.

Clearly, details about domestic intelligence kept confidential by a FISA court, or classified and conducted entirely outside this system—like the warrantless wiretapping by the NSA revealed by the *New York Times* in 2005—will rarely become public knowledge. But a nearly decade-long campaign of litigation and requests filed under the Freedom of Information Act has brought some facts to light. David Cole has reported that the number of FISA searches "has dramatically increased" since the USA PATRIOT Act was passed, and FISA-warranted wiretaps first outnumbered conventional criminal-investigation, probable-cause wiretaps in 2004. Journalist Pete Yost reported that the FBI had issued 192,499 "national security letters" to United States businesses from 2003 to 2006; reports of other government agencies also using this intelligence tool began to surface toward the end of the decade. These letters require organizations like financial institutions, telecommunications companies, libraries, or medical facilities to disclose data and records about customers or clients of federal interest, and prevent the institutions from publicizing these demands. They are issued without judicial review.

Changing definitions of terrorism

Overall, 9/11 allowed for a number of legislative changes that had been in the works for decades, even if circumstances had previously prevented their wider acceptance and implementation. "Over the past sixty years, frustrated Presidents and lawmakers have commissioned more than forty studies of the nation's intelligence operations, to determine how to rearrange, reform, or even, in some cases, abolish them," Lawrence Wright noted in 2008, reporting on the consolidation of the nation's intelligence capabilities into a single office. "Most of these studies have concluded that the rivalries and conflicting missions of the warring agencies could be resolved only by placing a single figure in charge. Yet, until September 11th, there was no political will to do so." The creation of this single position was recommended again by the 9/11 Commission; Congress created the Office of the Director of National Intelligence in 2004, and named the first director the following year.

Ronald Dworkin, responding in 2003 to the passage of the USA PATRIOT Act and the ways that some of the earliest post-9/11 legislation had found questionable use even then, commented that

conservatives have for many years wanted government to have the powers that administration officials now claim are legitimate; September 11 may have served them as only an excuse. John Ashcroft's Justice Department has been using its new powers under the USA PATRIOT Act, which were defended as emergency provisions against terrorists, to investigate and prosecute a wide variety of more ordinary crimes, including theft and swindling.

Once laws are put in place, investigators and prosecutors use them to do their jobs, regardless of how those laws may have been presented to the public. The *New York Times* reported in 2003 that the USA PATRIOT Act had become particularly powerful in pursuit of financial crimes and cash smuggling unrelated to terrorism. "The government is using its expanded authority under the far-reaching law to investigate suspected drug traffickers, white-collar criminals, blackmailers, child pornographers, money launderers, spies, and even corrupt foreign leaders," the newspaper reported. "Justice Department officials say they are simply using all the tools now available to them to pursue criminals— terrorists or otherwise." One internal Justice Department employee guide for prosecuting financial crimes asked, "We all know that the USA PATRIOT Act provided weapons for the War on Terrorism. But do you know how it affects the war on crime as well?"

But some of the deepest changes of the last decade have been to the exact definition of terrorism—both as a statutory matter and, in the description of the Transactional Records Access Clearinghouse (TRAC), a government-research organization based at Syracuse University, as a cultural one: "the shift in the way almost all Americans think about the problem." Not only did the USA PATRIOT Act define "domestic terrorism" differently from "terrorist activity," but since the latter category is defined much more broadly and oriented toward foreign activity and immigration, some acts qualify as terrorism when done by a foreign national but not when done by a United States citizen. Additionally, different federal agencies charged with combating terrorism have utilized their own definitions for terrorism, whose implementation can require subtle judgments made by federal officials. A 2003 report by the Government Accountability Office (GAO), compelled by a *Philadelphia Inquirer* article tracking inconsistencies and alleging inflated government stats, found "there is no single, uniform definition of terrorism." The GAO report confirmed many of the newspaper article's allegations, and a 2007 Department of Justice internal audit found statistics inaccurately reported in twenty-four out of twenty-six DOJ categories.

A 2003 report by Syracuse's TRAC found that even when government agencies began to consolidate—early in the decade, terrorism had been pursued by more than twenty, "many of them previously unheard from"—"the new rules have not been consistently applied. Thus," TRAC found, "INS cases that appear very similar are sometimes classified as international terrorism, sometimes as domestic terrorism, sometimes as anti-terrorism (immigrants), and sometimes not under a terrorism category, but simply as an immigration case." The organization cites one example from March 2002:

> when sixty-six mostly Hispanic workers at the Charlotte/Douglas Airport in western North Carolina were indicted under multiple laws involving the misuse of visas, permits, and social security numbers as well as one charge of entering an aircraft or airport area in violation of government security requirements. Most of the workers—whose immigration status was in question—eventually pleaded guilty to the airport security law and got time served (about a month) and a small fine. At that point they were released to the custody of the INS. Assistant United States Attorney David Brown said the investigation leading to the indictments was "necessary and successful" because it made Charlotte's airport less vulnerable to terrorists. In previous years, these sixty-six cases almost certainly would have been classified as simple immigration matters. But in the post-9/11 world...each one was officially placed in the "domestic terrorism" category.

After reviewing case files related to a number of terrorism convictions, TRAC concluded that "several examples of 'terrorism' cases that resulted in significant sentences...may not match the public's idea of terrorism arising out of the attacks of 9/11." In addition to cases involving material support, addressed above, the organization also cited "domestic terrorist" cases, such as a Georgia man who detonated a pipe bomb in an empty car belonging to his girlfriend.

As late as mid-2009, TRAC's near-annual analyses had not seen meaningful changes: not only had a federal judge complained that the vague and inconsistent definitions "sweeps in not only the big guy, but also the little guy who poses no risk," but "witnesses in Congressional hearings, various legal groups, and even some Justice Department officials have expressed...how the lack of a clear understanding of what constitutes terrorism has resulted in numerous civil liberties violations at the same time as it was undermining effective enforcement. Eight years after 9/11," TRAC wrote, "federal agencies can't seem to agree on who is a terrorist and who is not."

Approaches to Counterterrorism in the
United Kingdom and the United States

A month after the United Kingdom successfully prevented a 2006 plot to bomb transatlantic flights traveling from Heathrow to the United States and Canada, the United States Senate Subcommittee on Homeland Security held a hearing to see what could be learned from the British approach to counterterrorism, and which elements of this approach, if any, could be replicated within the United States. Senator Judd Gregg, chairman of the subcommittee, opened the hearing by commending the "strides" taken by the intelligence capabilities of the English system, which he attributed to the absence of an English Bill of Rights, and the nation's "capability to pursue a potential threat more aggressively than we appear to be able to pursue it [in the United States] prior to the event occurring." When a former British intelligence officer and counterterrorism expert named Tom Parker spoke at the hearing, he thanked the committee for their commendation of British intelligence, but clearly, and very diplomatically, testified that Senator Gregg's reasoning was wrong.

"In the early 1970s a series of missteps in Northern Ireland—notably the introduction of internment, the deployment of troops armed with live ammunition in public order situations, and the use of coercive interrogation," Parker testified, resulted from the government's decision to address the Irish "acts of terror" as a military threat. "The legacy of this policy was a major escalation in the level of violence across the Province and the extension of the national terror campaign.

A change in government in 1974 ushered in a new approach in Northern Ireland, one that aimed to delegitimize PIRA [Provisional Irish Republican Army] violence by treating terrorism as just another criminal activity to be dealt with at a local level. This strategy...has become a benchmark for British governmental responses to terrorism...Since 1974 successive British governments from the two major parties have pursued a policy of treating terrorism—both foreign and domestic—as a law enforcement problem. Having tried brute force and found it wanting, the British government has come to appreciate the importance of legitimacy in counterterrorism operations. Criminalizing terrorism adds greatly to the appearance of legitimacy. It also creates a framework which significantly mitigates the sort of abuses that can discredit a government internationally.

David Cole was living in London at the time of the hearing to compare the two nations' counterterrorism approaches. He began with some of the same assumptions as Senator Gregg, and admits to being "surprised" at what he found: the ability of a nation to learn from its recent mistakes. "While it is customary to worry about what will happen in the United States after 'the next attack,'" he wrote in an essay recounting his time overseas in *The New York Review of Books*, "the U.K. has already been the victim of a long, bloody, and quite relentless series of 'next attacks' in the course of its thirty-year struggle with the IRA. It has not suffered any single attack on the scale of September 11. But in a country with only one-fifth the United States's population, the IRA killed 1,800 persons and injured 20,000."

Recent "homegrown" U.K. attacks, and the 2006 foiled Heathrow plot, indicate a "serious problem" with the U.K.'s domestic Arab and Muslim communities, Cole wrote, who are generally "poorer, less educated, more alienated, and more vulnerable to radicalization than in the United States, where Arabs and Muslims, on average, have higher education levels and income than the average American." The lesson Cole took from his research, in London and elsewhere, is that successful protection from terrorism is not only a matter of smart policy, but of discretion and smart implementation as well. "Most liberal democracies have preventive detention laws," he wrote elsewhere, addressing a post-9/11 policy that, in the United States, has been a near-constant target for civil-liberties advocates. "A carefully formulated preventive detention law, preserving prompt judicial review, and restricting resort to other laws that might have been abused for preventive detention purposes in the past, might lead to fewer innocents wrongly detained while preserving the authority to hold the truly dangerous." Additionally:

"There are plenty of preventative counterterrorism measures that conform to the rule of law—such as increased protections at borders and around vulnerable targets; institutional reforms designed to encourage better analysis of data and information sharing among the many governmental agencies responsible for our safety; prosecutions for conspiracies to engage in terrorist acts; even military force and military detention when employed in self-defense. The real problems emerge when the state seeks to inflict highly coercive measures—depriving life, liberty, or property or going to war—on the basis of speculation about the future, without adhering to the processes long seen as critical to regulating and legitimating such force."

A number of these policies, as well as the foundations of American law, are written to protect all people within the borders of the United States—those who were born here as well as those who immigrated or who are not residents, citizens and noncitizens alike. In some ways, "the Constitution does distinguish...between the rights of citizens and noncitizens," Cole noted in 2003:

The right not to have one's vote discriminatorily denied and the right to run for federal elective office are expressly restricted to citizens. All other rights, however, are written without such a limitation. The Fifth and Fourteenth Amendment due process and equal protection guarantees extend to all "persons." The rights attached to criminal trials—including the right to a public trial, a trial by jury, the assistance of a lawyer, and the right to confront adverse witnesses—all apply to "the accused."

And, he reminds readers, "both the First Amendment's protections of political and religious freedoms and the Fourth Amendment's protection of privacy and liberty, apply" not to residents or to American citizens, but "to 'the people.'"

IV. PAYOUTS AND SETTLEMENTS

In the ten years since the start of the War on Terror, some of the most discriminatory or extrajudicial tactics that it employed—mass arrests, unlawful detainment, prisoner abuse, and collusion with a government that took part in any of the above—have resulted in lawsuits brought against government agencies and law-enforcement officials across the world. Although many of the suits are filed with the hope of a criminal conviction or official investigation, at the very least they have been responsible for bringing often-secret counterterrorism policies and procedures into public view, by requiring them to be presented to the court and entered into evidence. Even a successful suit, however, can be settled without any party having to admit fault or liability, and the appeals process often takes years. While settlements have begun to appear in the past five years, a number of cases remain ongoing. Below, the reader will find a listing of the most publicly known payouts and settlements to date.

2006

The U.S. government paid $300,000 to settle a lawsuit brought by Ehab Elmaghraby, an Egyptian who was one of hundreds of noncitizens arrested in the weeks after 9/11, held for months in the Metropolitan Detention Center in Brooklyn, New York, and deported after having been cleared of any ties to terrorism.

The U.S. government paid $1.9 million to settle a lawsuit brought by Oregon lawyer Brandon Mayfield (with $25,000 to his wife and each of his three daughters) after the FBI misidentified fingerprint evidence connecting Mayfield to a 2004 train bombing in Madrid, Spain. Mayfield, an American Muslim, also received a formal apology from the FBI.

2007

The prime minister of Canada offered a formal apology to Canadian citizen Maher Arar after ordering an inquiry into his detainment. He was compensated with approximately $9.8 million. Arar was arrested in 2002 when changing planes at New York's JFK International Airport. He was detained, then sent to Syria as part of the United States' "extraordinary rendition" program. Arar's attorneys were also awarded approximately $870,000 in legal fees. In 2010, the United States Supreme Court declined to hear a case Arar had brought in the United States.

2009

TSA and JetBlue paid $250,000 to settle a lawsuit brought by Raed Jarrar, who was told to cover a T-shirt printed with Arabic writing when attempting to board a plane at New York's JFK International Airport in 2006. In the settlement, JetBlue and the TSA screeners denied any wrongdoing. For more details, see Raed's narrative in this book.

London's Metropolitan Police paid £60,000 damages to Babar Ahmad, a man arrested during a raid on his home in 2003. Ahmad was never charged with a crime. In 2010, the Director of Public Prosecutions of England and Wales announced that four of the five officers involved in Ahmad's arrest would face criminal charges.

The European Court of Human Rights in Strausbourg, France awarded a group of nine claimants led by Abu Qatada £2,500 each, plus £53,000 for costs, after ruling that their detention without trial in the "public emergency" immediately after September 11, 2001 violated the European Convention on Human Rights.

The U.S. government paid $250,000 to settle a lawsuit brought by Abdallah Higazy, an Egyptian man who was jailed for more than a month after he was wrongly suspected of assisting the 9/11 hijackers with a two-way radio. The radio found in his hotel room was determined to belong to the hotel security guard, who had said he found it in Higazy's room. Higazy claimed his confession was coerced after the FBI threatened his family members in Egypt.

Five men claiming they were detained arbitrarily and mistreated by immigration officials in 2001 were awarded a class-action settlement of $1.26 million from the U.S. government. The government did not admit wrongdoing as part of the settlement. The Center for Constitutional Rights, which helped the men bring the case, also filed an additional class-action suit with new plaintiffs.

2010

Rahinah Ibrahim, a Stanford doctoral student, accepted a $225,000 settlement from the San Francisco police and United States Investigations Services, a private contractor hired by the TSA. Ibrahaim was handcuffed and briefly jailed in 2005 when her name was found on the No-Fly List at the San Francisco airport. She was released and allowed to fly home to Malaysia the following day, but discovered that her visa had been revoked when she attempted to return to San Francisco. She continues to pursue a claim against the federal government.

The U.S. government was ordered by a federal court to pay $2.5 million in damages and attorneys fees to the leaders of the Al-Haramain Islamic Foundation, a now-defunct Islamic charity put under unlawful NSA surveillance. Members of the Al-Haramain had first learned that their telephone calls were being monitored after copies of conversations with their attorneys regarding a material-support prosecution were given to them by United States officials, apparently by accident.

The British government awarded compensation reportedly totaling £10 million to a group of fifteen British residents and citizens formerly detained at Guantánamo Bay, and one resident still detained there at the time. Prime Minister David Cameron appointed an independent panel to investigate British collusion in rendition, torture, and mistreatment of detainees in foreign prisons. The settlement included "no concession of liability" involving the torture allegations, and "no withdrawal of the allegations" made by the former detainees. In December 2010, the ACLU filed a petition asking the United States Supreme Court to hear a case involving some members of this group.

The Australian government awarded a confidential but "substantial" settlement to Indian doctor Mohamed Haneef, who was detained and wrongfully accused of ties to terrorism when working in Queensland in 2007. A judicial inquiry in 2008 cleared Haneef of any wrongdoing.

SOURCES

National Commission on Terrorist Attacks. "The 9/11 Commission Report." 2004.

————"The 9/11 Commission Report: Final Report of the National Commission on Terrorist Attacks Upon the United States – Executive Summary." 2004.

Abdulrahim, Sawsan. "'Whiteness' and the Arab Immigrant Experience." In *Race and Arab Americans Before and After 9/11*, edited by Amaney Jamal and Nadine Naber, 131–146. Syracuse: Syracuse University Press, 2008.

Abraham, Sameer Y. and Nabeel Abraham, eds. *Arabs in the New World: Studies on Arab-American Communities*. Detroit: Wayne State University Center for Urban Studies, 1983.

Abu-Laban, Baha and Michael W. Suleiman, eds. *Arab Americans: Continuity and Change*. Belmont, Massachusetts: Association of Arab-American University Graduates, Inc.: 1989.

Ahmad, Muneer. "Homeland Insecurities: Racial Violence the Day After September 11." *Social Text 72*, Vol. 20, No. 3 (Fall 2002): 101–115.

Ahmed, Gutbi Mahdi. "Muslim Organizations in the United States." In *The Muslims of America*, edited by Yvonne Yazbeck Haddad, 11–24. New York: Oxford University Press, 1991.

Aidi, Hisham. "Let Us Be Moors: Islam, Race and 'Connected Histories.'" *Middle East Report* 229 (Winter 2003). Accessed March 3, 2011. www.merip.org/mer/mer229/mer229.html.

Alsultany, Evelyn. "The Changing Profile of Race in the United States: Representing and Racializing Arab- and Muslim-Americans Post-9/11." PhD diss., Stanford University, 2005.

American-Arab Anti-Discrimination Committee. "Report on Hate Crimes and Discrimination Against Arab Americans: The Post-September 11 Backlash, September 11, 2001 – October 11, 2002." Edited by Hussein Ibish. 2003.

American-Arab Anti-Discrimination Committee and the Center for Immigrants' Rights at Penn State's Dickinson School of Law. "NSEERS: The Consequences of America's Efforts to Secure Its Borders." March 31, 2009.

American-Arab Anti-Discrimination Committee Research Institute. "Report on Hate Crimes and Discrimination Against Arab Americans, 2003–2007." 2008.

American Civil Liberties Union (ACLU). "Policing Free Speech: Police Surveillance and Obstruction of First Amendment-Protected Activity." September 29, 2010.

Asian American Legal Defense and Education Fund, New York Civil Liberties Union and the Sikh Coalition. "Bullying in New York City Schools: Educators Speak Out." Dec 2011.

Bakalian, Anny and Mehdi Bozorgmehr. *Backlash 9/11: Middle Eastern and Muslim Americans Respond*. Berkeley: University of California Press, 2009.

Becker, Jo. "U.S. Approved Businesses With Blacklisted Nations." The *New York Times*. Dec 23, 2010. Accessed March 27, 2011. www.nytimes.com/2010/12/24/world/24sanctions. html?pagewanted=all

Bobbitt, Philip. *Terror and Consent: The Wars for the Twenty-First Century*. New York: Knopf, 2008.

Boyd, Roderick. "Halliburton Agrees to Leave Iran, Thompson Says." *New York Sun*. March 25, 2005. Accessed March 25, 2011. www.nysun.com/business/halliburton-agrees-to-leave-iran-thompson-says/11150.

Butterfield, Jeanne A. "Do Immigrants Have First Amendment Rights?: Revisiting the Los Angeles Eight Case." *Middle East Report* 212 (Fall 1999). Accessed March 3, 2011. www.merip.org/mer/mer212/212_butterfield.html.

————"The Prime-Time Plight of the Arab Muslim American After 9/11." In *Race and Arab Americans Before 9/11*, edited by Amaney Jamal and Nadine Naber, 204–228. Syracuse: Syracuse University Press, 2008.

Cainkar, Louise A. *Homeland Insecurity: The Arab American and Muslim American Experience After 9/11*. New York: Russell Sage Foundation, 2009.

————"The Impact of the September 11 Attacks on Arab and Muslim Communities in the United States." In *The Maze of Fear: Security and Migration After 9/11*, edited by John Tirman, 215-239. New York: The New Press, 2004.

————"No Longer Invisible: Arab and Muslim Exclusion After September 11." *Middle East Report* 224 (Fall 2002). Accessed March 3, 2011. www.merip.org/mer/mer224/224_cainkar.html.

————" Post-9/11 Domestic Policies Affecting U.S. Arabs and Muslims: A Brief Review." *Comparative Studies of South Asia, Africa, and the Middle East*. Vol. 24, No. 1 (2004): 245–248.

————"Thinking Outside the Box: Arabs and Race in the United States." In *Race and Arab Americans Before 9/11*, edited by Amaney Jamal and Nadine Naber, 46–80. Syracuse: Syracuse University Press, 2008.

The Center on Law and Security at NYU School of Law. "Findings of the Terrorist Trial Report Card Update, Sept. 11 2006 – Jan. 1 2008." 2008.

————"Terrorist Trials, 2001-2007: Lessons Learned." 2007.

————"Terrorist Trials: A Report Card." 2005.

————"Terrorist Trial Report Card: September 11 2001 – September 11, 2009." 2010.

————"Terrorist Trial Report Card: September 11 2001 – September 11, 2010." 2010.

————"Terrorist Trial Report Card: September, 11, 2008." 2008.

————"Terrorist Trial Report Card: Terror Financing Through Charities." 2008.

————"Terrorist Trial Report Card: Update January 1, 2008." 2008.

————"Terrorist Trial Report Card, United States Edition." 2006.

————"Terrorist Trials, September 11, 2001 – April 1, 2008." 2008.

Chermak, Steven. "Marketing Fear: Representing Terrorism After September 11." *Journal for Crime, Conflict and the Media* 1 (1): 5–22.

Cole, David. "Are We Safer?" *The New York Review of Books*. March 9, 2006.

————"The Brits Do It Better." *The New York Review of Books*. June 12, 2008.

————"Chewing Gum For Terrorists." The *New York Times*. January 2, 2011. Accessed March 27, 2011. www.nytimes.com/2011/01/03/opinion/03cole.html.

————*Enemy Aliens: Double Standards and Constitutional Freedoms in the War on Terrorism.* New York: The New Press, 2003.

————"The Grand Inquisitors." *The New York Review of Books*. July 19, 2007.

————"In Case of Emergency." *The New York Review of Books*. July 13, 2006.

————*No Equal Justice: Race and Class in the American Criminal Justice System.* New York: New Press, 1999.

————"Uncle Sam Is Watching You." *The New York Review of Books*. November 18, 2004.

Cole, David and James X. Dempsey. *Terrorism and the Constitution: Sacrificing Civil Liberties in the Name of National Security.* New York: New Press, 2002.

Cole, David and Jules Lobel. *Less Safe, Less Free: Why America is Losing the War on Terror.* New York: The New Press, 2007.

The Constitution Project. "The Use and Abuse of Immigration Authority as a Counterterrorism Tool: Constitutional and Policy Considerations." 2008.

Denbeaux, Mark and Jonathan Hafetz, eds. *The Guantánamo Lawyers: Inside a Prison Outside the Law.* New York: NYU Press, 2009.

Dudziak, Mary L., ed. *September 11 in History: A Watershed Moment?* Durham: Duke University Press, 2003.

Dworkin, Ronald. "Terror & the Attack on Civil Liberties." *The New York Review of Books*. Nov 6, 2003.

Eisgruber, Christopher L. and Lawrence G. Sager. "Civil Liberties in the Dragons'

Domain: Negotiating the Blurred Boundary Between Domestic Law and Foreign Affairs After 9/11." In *September 11 in History: A Watershed Moment?*, edited by Mary L. Dudziak, 163-179. Durham: Duke University Press, 2003.

Electronic Privacy Information Center (EPIC). "Foreign Intelligence Surveillance Act (FISA)." Accessed March 25, 2011. epic.org/privacy/terrorism/fisa.

Ghanea Bassiri, Kambiz. *A History of Islam in America: From the New World to the New World Order*. New York: Cambridge University Press, 2010.

Gualtieri, Sarah. "Becoming 'White': Race, Religion, and the Foundations of Syrian/Lebanese Ethnicity in the United States." *Journal of American Ethnic History* Vol. 20, No. 4 (Summer 2001): 29–58.

———*Between Arab and White: Race and Ethnicity in the Early Syrian American Diaspora*. Berkeley: University of California Press, 2009.

Haddad, Yvonne Yazbeck. "American Foreign Policy in the Middle East and Its Impact on the Identity of Arab Muslims in the United States." In *The Muslims of America*, edited by Yvonne Yazbeck Haddad, 217–235. New York: Oxford University Press, 1991.

Haddad, Yvonne Yazbeck, ed. *The Muslims of America*. New York: Oxford University Press, 1991.

Hagopian, Elaine C., ed. *Civil Rights in Peril: The Targeting of Arabs and Muslims*. Ann Arbor: Pluto Press, 2004.

Haney-López, Ian. *White By Law: The Legal Construction of Race*. New York: New York University Press, 1996.

Hassan, Salah D. "Arabs, Race and the Post-September 11 National Security State." *Middle East Report* 224 (Fall 2002). Accessed March 3, 2011. www.merip.org/mer/mer224/224_hassan.html.

Hooglund, Eric J., ed. *Crossing the Waters: Arabic-Speaking Immigrants to the United States Before 1940*. Washington, D.C.: Smithsonian Institution Press, 1987.

Human Rights Watch. "'We Are Not the Enemy': Hate Crimes Against Arabs, Muslims, and Those Perceived to be Arab or Muslim after September 11." Vol. 14, No. 6 (G). Nov 2002.

———"Witness to Abuse: Human Rights Abuses Under the Material Witness Law Since September 11." Vol. 17, No. 2 (G). June 2005.

Jabara, Abdeen M. "A Strategy for Political Effectiveness." In *Arab Americans: Continuity and Change*, edited by Baha Abu-Laban and Michael W. Suleiman, 201–205. Belmont, Mass.: Association of Arab-American University Graduates, Inc.: 1989.

Jamal, Amaney and Nadine Naber, eds. *Race and Arab Americans Before and After 9/11: From Invisible Citizens to Visible Subjects*. Syracuse: Syracuse University Press, 2008.

Kaplan, Amy. "Homeland Insecurities: Transformations of Language and Space." In *September 11 in History: A Watershed Moment?*, edited by Mary L. Dudziak, 55-69. Durham: Duke University Press, 2003.

Khalaf, Samir. "The Background and Causes of Lebanese/Syrian Immigration to the United States Before World War I." In *Crossing the Waters: Arabic-Speaking Immigrants to the United States Before 1940*, edited by Eric J. Hooglund, 17–35. Washington, D.C.: Smithsonian Institution Press, 1987.

Lautenberg, Frank R. "Dick Cheney, Iran and Halliburton: A Grand Jury Investigates Sanctions Violations." The Office of Senator Frank R. Lautenberg. [n.d.]

Lee, Sharon M. "Racial Classifications in the United States Census: 1890–1990." *Ethnic and Racial Studies* Vol. 16, No. 1 (Jan 1993): 75–94.

Lichtblau, Eric. "U.S. Uses Terror Law to Pursue Crimes From Drugs to Swindling." The *New York Times*. Sept 28, 2003. Accessed March 26, 2011. www.nytimes.com/2003/09/28/us/us-uses-terror-law-to-pursue-crimes-from-drugs-to-swindling.html.

Luo, Michael. "Senators Question Halliburton Executive About Dealings in Iran." The *New York Times*. May 1, 2007. Accessed March 25, 2011. www.nytimes.com/2007/05/01/washington/01halliburton.html.

Majaj, Lisa Suhair. "Arab-American Ethnicity: Location, Coalitions, and Cultural Negotiations." In *Arabs in America: Building a New Future*, edited by Michael W. Suleiman, 320–336. Philadelphia: Temple University Press, 1999.

———"Arab-Americans and the Meaning of Race." In *Postcolonial Theory and the United States: Race, Ethnicity, and Literature*, edited by Amritjit Singh and Peter Schmidt, 320–337. Jackson: University Press of Mississippi, 2000.

McAlister, Melani. *Epic Encounters: Culture, Media, and U.S. Interests in the Middle East Since 1945*. Berkeley: University of California Press, 2005.

McCarus, Ernest, ed. *The Development of Arab-American Identity*. Ann Arbor: University of Michigan Press, 1994.

Meissner, Doris and Donald Kerwin. "DHS and Immigration: Taking Stock and Correcting Course." Migration Policy Institute, Feb 2009.

Naber, Nadine. "Ambiguous Insiders: An Investigation of Arab American Invisibility." *Ethnic and Racial Studies* Vol. 23, No. 1 (2000): 37–61.

———"Arab Americans and U.S. Racial Formations." In *Race and Arab Americans Before and After 9/11*, edited by Amaney Jamal and Nadine Naber, 1–45. Syracuse: Syracuse University Press, 2008.

———"The Rules of Forced Engagement: Race, Gender, and the Culture of Fear Among Arab Immigrants in San Francisco Post-9/11." *Cultural Dynamics* Vol. 18, No. 3 (2006): 235–267.

Naff, Alixa. "Arabs in America: A Historical Overview." In *Arabs in the New World: Studies on Arab-American Communities*, edited by Sameer Y. Abraham and Nabeel Abraham, 8–29. Detroit: Wayne State University Center for Urban Studies, 1983.

————*Becoming American: The Early Arab Immigrant Experience*. Carbondale and Edwardsville: Southern Illinois University Press, 1985.

Omi, Michael and Howard Winant. *Racial Formation in the United States: From the 1960s to the 1980s*. New York: Routledge & Kegan Paul, 1986.

Pierce, Gareth. "Was It Like This for the Irish?" *The London Review of Books* Vol. 30, No. 7 (April 10, 2008): 3–8.

Pew Forum on Religion & Public Life. "Mapping the Global Muslim Population: A Report on the Size and Distribution of the World's Muslim Population." Oct 2009.

Raban, Jonathan. "The Truth About Terrorism." *The New York Review of Books*. Jan 13, 2005.

Rana, Junaid. "The Story of Islamophobia." *Souls* Vol. 9, No. 2 (2007): 148-161.

Robin, Corey. "Was he? Had he?" *The London Review of Books* Vol. 28, No. 20 (Oct 19 2006): 10–12.

Saïd, Edward. *Orientalism*. New York: Vintage, 1979.

Salaita, Steven. *Anti-Arab Racism in the USA: Where It Comes From and What It Means for Politics Today*. London: Pluto Press, 2006.

Saliba, Therese. "Resisting Invisibility: Arab Americans in Academia and Activism." In *Arabs in America: Building a New Future*, edited by Michael W. Suleiman, 304–319. Philadelphia: Temple University Press, 1999.

Samhan, Helen Hatab. "Not Quite White: Race Classification and the Arab American Experience." In *Arabs in America: Building a New Future*, edited by Michael W. Suleiman, 209–226. Philadelphia: Temple University Press, 1999.

————"Politic and Exclusion: The Arab American Experience." *Journal of Palestine Studies* Vol. 16, No. 2 (Winter 1987): 11–28.

Shryock, Andrew. "The Moral Analogies of Race: Arab American Identity, Color Politics, and the Limits of Racialized Citizenship." In *Race and Arab Americans Before and After 9/11*, edited by Amaney Jamal and Nadine Naber, 81–113. Syracuse: Syracuse University Press, 2008.

The Sikh Coalition. "Hatred in the Hallways." June 2007

————"Making our Voices Heard… A Civil Rights Agenda For New York City's Sikhs." Dec 2006.

————"Sikh Coalition Bay Area Civil Rights Report 2010."

Singh, Amritjit and Peter Schmidt, eds. *Postcolonial Theory and the United States: Race, Ethnicity, and Literature.* Jackson: University Press of Mississippi, 2000.

————"On the Borders Between U.S. Studies and Postcolonial Theory." In *Postcolonial Theory and the United States: Race, Ethnicity, and Literature,* edited by Amritjit Singh and Peter Schmidt, 3–69. Jackson: University Press of Mississippi, 2000.

Sorokin, Ellen. "Security Bill Loses ID Card, TIPS." *Washington Times,* July 19, 2002. A1.

Suleiman, Michael W., ed. *Arabs in America: Building a New Future.* Philadelphia: Temple University Press, 1999.

Tehranian, John. *Whitewashed: America's Invisible Middle Eastern Minority.* New York: New York University Press, 2008.

Toobin, Jeffrey. "Crackdown: Should We Be Worried About the New Antiterrorism Legislation?" *The New Yorker.* Nov 5, 2001.

Transactional Records Access Clearinghouse (TRAC). "A Special TRAC Report: Criminal Enforcement Against Terrorists." Dec 3, 2001. Accessed March 27, 2011. trac.syr.edu/tracreports/terrorism/report011203.html.

————"As Terrorism Prosecutions Decline, Extent of Threat Remains Unclear." May 18, 2010. Accessed March 27, 2010. trac.syr.edu/tracreports/terrorism/231.

————"Criminal Enforcement Against Terrorists and Spies in the Year After the 9/11 Attacks: A TRAC Special Report." Feb 13, 2003. Accessed March 27, 2011. trac.syr.edu/tracreports/terrorism/fy2002.html.

————"Criminal Enforcement Against Terrorists: A TRAC Special Report Supplement, June 17, 2002." 2002. Accessed March 27, 2011. trac.syr.edu/tracreports/terrorism/supp.html.

————"Criminal Enforcement Against Terrorists: A TRAC Special Report Supplement, September 5, 2002." 2002. Accessed March 27, 2011. trac.syr.edu/tracreports/terrorism/supp_apr.html.

————"Criminal Terrorism Enforcement in the United States During the Five Years Since the 9/11/01 Attacks." Sept 4, 2006. Accessed March 27, 2011. trac.syr.edu/tracreports/terrorism/169.

————"Criminal Terrorism Enforcement Since the 9/11/01 Attacks: A TRAC Special Report." Dec 8, 2003. Accessed March 27, 2011.trac.syr.edu/tracreports/terrorism/report031208.html.

————"Terrorism Enforcement: International, Domestic and Financial." March 19, 2007. Accessed March 27, 2011. trac.syr.edu/tracreports/terrorism/177.

————"What Do These Counts Mean? Criminal Enforcement Against Terrorists." 2002. Accessed March 27 2011. trac.syr.edu/tracreports/terrorism/countsmean.html.

————"Who Is A Terrorist? Government Failure to Define Terrorism Undermines Enforcement, Puts Civil Liberties at Risk." Sept 28, 2009. Accessed March 27, 2011. trac.syr.edu/tracreports/terrorism/215.

Tsao, Fred. "Losing Ground: The Loss of Freedom, Equality, and Opportunity for America's Immigrants Since September 11." Illinois Coalition for Immigrant and Refugee Rights. September 2002.

United States Census Bureau. "2010 Census Constituent FAQs." July 2009. Accessed March 3, 2011. http://2010.census.gov/partners/pdf/ConstituentFAQ.pdf.

————"American Community Survey and the United States Census." Last Revised Feb 22, 2011. Accessed March 3, 2011. www.census.gov/acs/www/about_the_survey/american_community_survey_and_2010_census.

————"The American Community Survey." [n.d.] Accessed March 3, 2011. http://www.census.gov/acs/www/Downloads/questionnaires/2011/Quest11.pdf.

United States. Congressional Senate. Committee on Appropriations. *Catching Terrorists: The British System Versus the U.S. System. Hearing before a Subcommittee of the Committee on Appropriations.* Sept 14, 2006. 109th Cong., 2nd sess. Washington: Government Printing Office, 2006. Accessed March 26, 2011. www.fas.org/irp/congress/2006_hr/british.html.

United States Department of Justice (DOJ). "Counterterrorism White Paper." United States Department of Justice, Counterterrorism Section. June 22, 2006.

————"The Department of Justice's Internal Controls Over Terrorism Reporting." United States Department of Justice Office of the Inspector General, Audit Division. Audit Report. 07-20. Feb 2007.

United States General Accounting Office (GAO). "Justice Department: Better Management Oversight and Internal Controls Needed to Ensure Accuracy of Terrorism-Related Statistics (Report to the Honorable Dan Burton, House of Representatives)." GAO-03-266. Jan 2003.

Volpp, Leti. "The Citizen and the Terrorist." In *September 11 in History: A Watershed Moment?*, edited by Mary L. Dudziak, 147–162. Durham: Duke University Press, 2003.

Warde, Ibrahim. *The Price of Fear: The Truth Behind the Financial War on Terror.* Berkeley: University of California Press, 2007.

Wittes, Benjamin. *Law and the Long War: The Future of Justice in an Age of Terror.* New York: Penguin, 2009.

Wright, Lawrence. "The Spymaster: Can Mike McConnell Fix America's Intelligence Community?" *The New Yorker.* Jan 21, 2008.

ACKNOWLEDGEMENTS

We would like to acknowledge the generous support of the Security and Rights Collaborative, a Proteus Fund Initiative, and the San Francisco Arts Commission's Cultural Equity Grant Program.

Special thanks to Dimple Abichandani, Fairuz Abdullah, Monty Agarwal, Wajahat Ali, Noor Elashi, Kiran Jain, Shilen Patel, and Sree Sreenivasan. We would additionally like to thank the following people for their expert consultation and assistance in completing this book:

DALIA HASHAD
Public Interest Attorney and Consultant

ALEXIS AGATHOCLEOUS
Center for Constitutional Rights

ATEQAH KHAKI
American Civil Liberties Union

MARIA LAHOOD
Center for Constitutional Rights

NUSRAT JAHAN CHOUDHURY
American Civil Liberties Union

RACHEL MEEROPOL
Center for Constitutional Rights

BEN WIZNER
American Civil Liberties Union

SHARMEEN OBAID-CHINOY
Citizens Archive of Pakistan

ABED A. AYOUB, ESQ
American-Arab Anti-Discrimination Committee

ALIYA HASHIM
Citizens Archive of Pakistan

TITI LIU
Asian Law Caucus

ZAHRA BILLOO
Council on American Islamic Relations

VEENA DUBAL
Asian Law Caucus

FAHD AHMED
Desis Rising Up & Moving

KIRAN JAIN
Asian Law Caucus Board of Directors

MONAMI MAULIK
Desis Rising Up & Moving

WAJAHAT ALI
Center for American Progress

LING WOO LIU
Korematsu Institute

MEG SATTERTHWAITE
NYU Center for Human Rights and Global Justice, NYU School of Law

LAMA FAKIH
NYU Center for Human Rights and Global Justice, NYU School of Law

EDINA LEKOVIC
Muslim Public Affairs Council

TEJPREET KAUR
Sikh Coalition

PAUL RUSSELL
Sikh Coalition

RAJDEEP SINGH
Sikh Coalition

SONNY SINGH
Sikh Coalition

NEHA SINGH
Sikh Coalition

AMARDEEP SINGH
Sikh Coalition

VALARIE KAUR
Filmmaker, writer, advocate

LINDA MORENO
Attorney

MOHAMMAD MERTABAN
University of California Los Angeles

MARYA BANGEE
Muslim Students Association West

About THE EDITOR

ALIA MALEK is an author (*A Country Called Amreeka*, Free Press, 2009) and a civil rights lawyer. Born in Baltimore to Syrian immigrant parents, she began her legal career as a trial attorney at the U.S. Department of Justice's Civil Rights Division. After 9/11, in addition to her regular duties at the Department of Justice, which focused on Americans' civil rights in educational contexts, Alia's responsibilities came to also include reaching out to and serving the needs of vulnerable groups targeted by backlash discrimination and hate crimes.

After working in the legal field in the U.S., Lebanon, and the West Bank, Malek, who has degrees from Johns Hopkins and Georgetown Universities, earned her master's degree in journalism from Columbia University. Her reportage has appeared in *Salon*, *The Columbia Journalism Review*, the *New York Times*, the *Nation*, *Christian Science Monitor* and *WashingtonPost.com*

The VOICE OF WITNESS SERIES

Voice of Witness is a nonprofit book series, published by McSweeney's, that empowers those most closely affected by contemporary social injustice. Using oral history as a foundation, the series depicts human rights crises in the United States and around the world. This is the eighth book in the series. The other titles are:

SURVIVING JUSTICE
America's Wrongfully Convicted and Exonerated
Edited by Lola Vollen and Dave Eggers   Foreword by Scott Turow

These oral histories prove that the problem of wrongful conviction is far-reaching and very real. Through a series of all-too-common circumstances—eyewitness misidentification, inept defense lawyers, coercive interrogation—the lives of these men and women of all different backgrounds were irreversibly disrupted. In *Surviving Justice*, thirteen exonerees describe their experiences—the events that led to their convictions, their years in prison, and the process of adjusting to their new lives outside.

ISBN: 978-1-934781-25-8   469 pages   Paperback

VOICES FROM THE STORM
The People of New Orleans on Hurricane Katrina and Its Aftermath
Edited by Chris Ying and Lola Vollen

The second book in the McSweeney's Voice of Witness series, *Voices from the Storm* is a chronological account of the worst natural disaster in modern American history. Thirteen New Orleanians describe the days leading up to Hurricane Katrina, the storm itself, and the harrowing confusion of the days and months afterward. Their stories weave and intersect, ultimately creating an eye-opening portrait of courage in the face of terror, and of hope amid nearly complete devastation.

ISBN: 978-1-932416-68-8   320 pages   Paperback

UNDERGROUND AMERICA
Narratives of Undocumented Lives
Edited by Peter Orner   Foreword by Luis Alberto Urrea

They arrive from around the world for countless reasons. Many come simply to make a living. Others are fleeing persecution in their native countries. But by living and working in the U.S. without legal status, millions of immigrants risk deportation and imprisonment. They live underground, with little protection from exploitation at the hands of human smugglers, employers, or law enforcement. *Underground America* presents the remarkable oral histories of men and women struggling to carve a life for themselves in the United States. In 2010, *Underground America* was translated into Spanish and released as *En las Sombras de Estados Unidos*.

ISBN: 978-1-934781-15-9   379 pages   Hardcover and paperback

OUT OF EXILE
The Abducted and Displaced People of Sudan
Edited by Craig Walzer
Additional interviews and an introduction by Dave Eggers
and Valentino Achak Deng

Millions of people have fled from conflicts and persecution in all parts of Sudan, and many thousands more have been enslaved as human spoils of war. In *Out of Exile*, refugees and abductees recount their escapes from the wars in Darfur and South Sudan, from political and religious persecution, and from abduction by militias. They tell of life before the war, and of the hope that they might someday find peace again.

ISBN: 978-1-934781-13-5   465 pages   Hardcover and paperback

HOPE DEFERRED
Narratives of Zimbabwean Lives
Edited by Peter Orner and Annie Holmes   Foreword by Brian Chikwava

The sixth volume in the Voice of Witness series presents the narratives of Zimbabweans whose lives have been affected by the country's political, economic, and human rights crises. This book asks the question: How did a country with so much promise—a stellar education system, a growing middle class of professionals, a sophisticated economic infrastructure, a liberal constitution, and an independent judiciary—go so wrong?

ISBN: 978-1-934781-94-4   304 pages   Hardcover and Paperback

NOWHERE TO BE HOME
Narratives from Survivors of Burma's Military Regime
Edited by Maggie Lemere and Zoë West   Foreword by Mary Robinson

Decades of military oppression in Burma have led to the systematic destruction of thousands of ethnic minority villages, a standing army with one of the world's highest number of child soldiers, and the displacement of millions of people. *Nowhere to Be Home* is an eye-opening collection of oral histories exposing the realities of life under military rule. In their own words, men and women from Burma describe their lives in the country that Human Rights Watch has called "the textbook example of a police state."

ISBN: 978-1-934781-95-1 496 pages   Hardcover and Paperback

Thanks to the generosity and assistance of many donors and volunteers, Voice of Witness is currently at work collecting oral histories for a variety of new projects around the world. For more information about the series, or to find out how you can help or donate to the cause, visit the Voice of Witness website:

VOICEOFWITNESS.ORG